about

musicals

TEACH YOURSELF BOOKS

. about

musicals

Susan Sutherland

TEACH YOURSELF BOOKS

For UK order queries: please contact Bookpoint Ltd, 39 Milton Park, Abingdon, Oxon OX14 4TD. Telephone: (44) 01235 400414, Fax: (44) 01235 400454. Lines are open from 9.00–6.00, Monday to Saturday, with a 24 hour message answering service. Email address: orders@bookpoint.co.uk

For U.S.A. & Canada order queries: please contact NTC/Contemporary Publishing, 4255 West Touhy Avenue, Lincolnwood, Illinois 60646–1975, U.S.A. Telephone: (847) 679 5500, Fax: (847) 679 2494.

Long renowned as the authoritative source for self-guided learning – with more than 30 million copies sold worldwide – the *Teach Yourself* series includes over 200 titles in the fields of languages, crafts, hobbies, sports, and other leisure activities.

A catalogue entry for this title is available from The British Library.

Library of Congress Catalog Card Number: 98-65856

First published in UK 1998 by Hodder Headline Plc, 338 Euston Road, London, NW1 3BH.

First published in US 1998 by NTC/Contemporary Publishing, 4255 West Touhy Avenue, Lincolnwood (Chicago), Illinois 60646–1975 U.S.A.

The 'Teach Yourself' name and logo are registered trade marks of Hodder & Stoughton Ltd.

Cover photo from Donald Cooper/Photostage

Typeset by Transet Limited, Coventry, England.
Printed in Great Britain for Hodder & Stoughton Educational, a division of Hodder Headline Plc, 338 Euston Road, London NW1 3BH by Cox & Wyman Ltd, Reading, Berkshire.

Impression number   10 9 8 7 6 5 4 3 2 1
Year   2002 2001 2000 1999 1998

CONTENTS

Introduction _____ ix

How to Use this Book _____ xi

PART ONE
THE HISTORY OF MUSICAL THEATRE

1   Early Days _____ 3

2   Gilbert and Sullivan; the Savoy Operas __ 19

3   Into the Twentieth Century_____ 47

4   Lights on for Broadway _____ 58

THE HISTORY OF THE MUSICAL

5   America; the Golden Years –
    Moving into the 1930s_____ 72

6   Meanwhile in Europe _____ 90

7   Rodgers and Hammerstein _____ 100

8   The 1950s, 1960s and 1970s_____ 110

9   The Musicals of Andrew Lloyd Webber __ 136

10 The 1980s, 1990s and into the Future ____ 149

PART TWO
A CLOSER LOOK AT SIX MUSICALS

11 Showboat (1927) _____ 157

12 My Fair Lady (1956) _____ 167

13 | West Side Story (1957) _____ 175

14 | The Sound of Music (1959) _____ 183

15 | Oliver! (1960) _____ 190

16 | Les Miserables (1980);
     English Version (1985) _____ 197

   PART THREE

17 | More Personalities from the World
     of Music Theatre _____ 209

   Answers to self-test questions _____ 231

   Bibliography_____ 235

   Index _____ 236

For Steve with love.

ACKNOWLEDGEMENTS

Music is my passion and for that I thank everyone whose own enthusiasm has touched me. My family, friends and the team at Hodders have, as usual, been unstinting in their support – without which nothing would ever get done.

INTRODUCTION

Music theatre is a vibrant art form that re-invents itself constantly and by doing so remains relevant to each new generation.

'Musical' is the name by which we recognise a twentieth-century phenomenon, but the English 'ballad' operas of the eighteenth century attracted a broad public and were certainly the 'musicals' of their day. German Komische oper, French and Austrian operetta, the Savoy Operas of Gilbert and Sullivan, as well as the many long-running musicals on Broadway and in the West End have all been successful because their musical and dramatic language is direct, relevant and, above all, entertaining.

Popular musical theatre is commercially led and aims to appeal to the widest possible audience in a style consistent with the musical and dramatic fashions of the day. The main objective is to entertain and this is achieved in a number of ways including memorable music, fabulous costumes, stage spectacle and great stories, but this doesn't mean that some of the world's greatest writers have been busy producing froth. Frivolity has its place certainly, but alongside the merriment, every human emotion and sometimes political satire and social commentary can be expressed using the powerful medium of music theatre.

The universal appeal of good theatre has rarely been more clearly demonstrated than by *Les Miserables*. With the power to communicate its theme across cultural boundaries, this musical has provoked countless acts of charity, rekindling the flame lit by its French author, Victor Hugo, whose nineteenth-century images of the struggle against oppression and social iniquity have real resonance for the audience of today.

This is a particularly exciting time for musical theatre, when brave voices are declaring that the day of the 'blockbuster' musical, with all its technical wizardry, is at an end. Since stage spectaculars have been around since at least the seventeenth century, it seems unlikely that this format will die out altogether, but with the advent of small productions from established composers, many more writers will have the opportunity to show what they can do in this comparatively low budget arena.

In whatever form, there is no doubt that musical theatre will continue to thrive, for as Samuel Jonson said in the eighteenth century, 'The stage but echoes back the public voice.'

I wish you well on your own journey of discovery and share with you the certain pleasure of that very special moment when the stage echoes back *your* voice ...

Susan Sutherland 1998

HOW TO USE
THIS BOOK

In *Teach Yourself About Musicals* you will find sections that allow you to broaden your knowledge in various ways.

The History of the Musical provides a background to the development of the style and shows how influences from different cultures have played their part in the shows we now enjoy.

A Closer Look at Six Musicals involves you more closely, not only in the actual show, but in the fascinating characters, on both sides of the curtain, who create, produce and perform for our pleasure. The hectic, sometimes humorous, always exciting atmosphere surrounding the birth of a show is evoked through familiarity with its detail, as well as through the anecdotes that bring back-stage gossip to life for you.

More Personalities from the World of Music Theatre was the most frustrating section of all to write, simply because of the many outstanding contributors for whom space could not be found, but there are still plenty of intriguing personalities to be discovered, so use this section as a spur to further discovery.

At the end of each main chapter you will find some questions (answers are given at the end of the book on pages 231–234). Use these to pick out the main points and also as a starting point for further study if you feel you would like to go into a particular topic in greater depth. Read through, or dip into, the choice is yours – there is certainly no wrong way to approach *Teach Yourself About Musicals*.

Part 1

The History of Musical Theatre

1 | EARLY DAYS

*'he cometh to you with words set in delightful proportion,
accompanied with the well enchanting skill of music; and with a
tale forsooth he cometh unto you, with a tale which holdeth
children from play and old men from the chimney corner.'*

The Defense of Poesy, Sir Philip Sidney, 1595

With civilisation comes entertainment and from the earliest times man has
learned, laughed and empathised with dramatic imagery. When music is
added to the mix, the message is intensified. Some early performances
were reserved for the educated classes, but travelling players visited
towns and villages providing entertainment for all, in the streets, or on the
village green.

In the tenth century *jongleurs* or minstrels travelled about Europe,
spreading news and telling stories, both fiction and fact, through music,
dance and song (see *Teach Yourself Opera*). Secular music owes much of
its development to troupes like these whose traditions and music formed
the basis of an aural library that became known as the music of the
troubadours or trouvères.

Sixteenth century

The Church was one of the first bodies to recognise the communication
potential of music and song. Every means possible was employed to
spread the Christian message; word of mouth, in picture form through
stained glass windows and in dramatic recreations often containing music.
Some musical presentations, however, became tainted with worldly
material and between 1545 and 1563, the Council of Trent, assembled in
Trent, Northern Italy by the Roman Catholic Church, ordered the removal
of all secular reference from church music.

By driving out some of the more adventurous performers and composers, the Church helped inadvertently to promote the development of secular music.

During the reign of Elizabeth I (1533–1603) the English language and culture was enriched by an unprecedented increase in exploration, foreign trade and travel. These in turn fostered developments in the performing arts. In educated circles, proficiency in music composition, singing and other artistic pursuits was considered a normal requirement, but the enjoyment of entertainment was not limited to a privileged few. Pageants held in celebration of some great occasion might last hours, or even days and contain several musical theatre presentations.

■ Between 9–25 July 1575, Robert Dudley, Earl of Leicester, expended a fortune on a series of entertainments for Queen Elizabeth I of England. As a further expression of his devotion, all the clocks and timepieces at Kenilworth Castle were stopped, so that time itself stood still during the Queen's visit. This memorable event was recalled in song some time later by the celebrated English composer John Dowland (1563–1626) in his composition 'Time stands still'.

Seventeenth century

The masque, which might form part of entertainments such as these, flourished in Tudor times and on through the reigns of James I and Charles I, even surviving in discreet performance during the period of the Commonwealth (1649–60). In fact one of the most significant masques, *Cupid and Death* (1653), written by Matthew Locke and Christopher Gibbons, was composed well into the rule of the restrictive Puritan government.

The tone of this must have been carefully judged, for the Arch-Puritan, William Prynne, declared that masques and plays were 'the work of the devil', whereas music itself was 'lawful, useful and commendable'.

Generally speaking, a masque might contain many of the elements we now expect to find in a musical; music, singing, drama and visual effects. In addition there could be interplay with the audience too, blurring the divide line between performer and spectator.

Eighteenth century

In the eighteenth century, musical theatre in England and Europe was well established. The rise of a prosperous middle class and the increasing availability of printed music led to a burgeoning interest in all types of music. At one extreme the comic operas, *opéra comique* in France, or *singspiel* in Germany, were practically indistinguishable from the fast-growing opera style of the day. At the other extreme, boisterous shows containing a pastiche of work enjoyed great popular appeal. One of the most notable of these, premiered at Lincoln's Inn Fields, London, was John Gay's *The Beggar's Opera* (1728) (see *Teach Yourself Opera*). Italian opera, considered a 'foreign import' by many in England, was gaining rather too strong a foothold for comfort. 'Exotic and irrational' was how it was described by Dr Johnson, so John Gay's irreverant words, lampooning the worst excesses of opera as well as, and no surprise here, jibing at the Prime Minister of the day, Sir Robert Walpole, hit the mark. The public loved it and though the topical references may be a little obscure now, *The Beggar's Opera* continues to entertain audiences right up to the present day.

Nineteenth century

By the middle of the nineteenth century, Great Britain, France and Germany had, apart from opera and ballet, music theatre in two distinct styles. The pastiche, often topical show that found success in its country of origin and the newly composed light opera, or operetta, forerunner of the musical, whose music at least knew no national boundaries.

Confusingly, the distinction between opera and operetta could be extremely vague. Melodies extracted from Donizetti's opera, *La Fille du Regiment* (Paris 1840), for example, became the 'pop' songs of their day, although the complex nature of some of the arias and orchestral work certainly place it within the opera genre. Apart from original works of operetta and translations of these, there was much poaching of ideas, story-lines and tunes across national boundaries. 'Hits' enjoying international acclaim in this era included those by the French composer, Adolphe Adam (1803–56), who declared that his only intention was to write music that 'is easy to understand and amusing to the public'. This he accomplished with *Le Chalet* (1834), and perhaps the most famous of all his works, *Le Postillon de Lonjumeau* (1836).

In Germany, Albert Lortzing (1801–51), actor, singer, composer, possessed all the qualities necessary for producing popular music theatre and this he achieved most ably with a number of works. Most successful of these was the light-hearted *Zar und Zimmermann* (Leipzig 1837), which placed the Tsar of Russia, incognito, working in a German shipyard.

Two Irish composers, Michael Balfe (1808–70) and Vincent Wallace (1812–65) also caused a stir among the theatre-going public: Balfe with *The Bohemian Girl* (London 1843), and Wallace with *Maritana* (London 1845).

Wallace, a violin virtuoso and inveterate traveller, found instant success with *Maritana* which was soon playing in theatres across Europe and America. Songs such as 'I dreamt that I dwelt in Marble Halls', were on everyone's lips, ensuring the enduring popularity of these early musicals.

Michael Balfe also found fame as the creator of the baritone role Papageno the bird catcher in the first London performance of Mozart's opera *The Magic Flute* (see *Teach Yourself Opera*).

Hervé (1825–92)

French singer, conductor, composer and 'jack of all trades' in the entertainment world, Florimond Ronger Hervé, preferred, in his theatrical career, to call himself by his last name, Hervé. An eccentric genius, Hervé produced more than 100 short entertainments, rather like mini-operettas, to form part of what might best be described as a variety show.

Trained in Paris with another significant French composer, Daniel Francois Esprit Auber, Hervé's zany lyrics and engaging music quickly gained a following with the public. Royal approval allowed him to open his own theatre, where he was able to indulge his talents, taking on at will the task of actor-manager, director, composer, singer and producer. In 1878, in a revival of Offenbach's *Orpheus*, Hervé was invited by the composer himself to play the leading role of Jupiter. This he accepted on the condition that the ailing Offenbach would conduct.

Neither man could have paid the other a greater compliment.

Hervé's most notable works include *Don Quichotte* (Paris 1848), *Les folies dramatiques* (Paris 1853), *Aladdin the Second* (London 1870) and *Mam'zelle Nitouche* (Paris 1882).

Jacques (Jacob) Offenbach (1819–80)

Engaging tunes, sheer exhilaration in his musical style and a great energy
for composition allowed Offenbach to become one of the most dominant
forces in popular music in the nineteenth century. Through his work in
particular, operetta became an accepted, even essential part of the cultural
scene, paving the way for the twentieth-century musical.

Born in Cologne into a warm and loving musical family, Offenbach was
the son of a synagogue cantor. His grandfather, Juda Eberst, a fine tenor,
had taken a new name from Offenbach-am-Main where he had settled and
become a music teacher. In 1833 Offenbach's father sent him to Paris
where it was believed a Jew might prosper without prejudice. Here, the
gifted youth won a coveted place at the Music Conservatoire, a privilege
normally reserved for native born Frenchmen. This came about through
the auspices of professor and composer Luigi Cherubini, who took up
Offenbach's cause after hearing him play only part-way through his
audition pieces on the cello.

Offenbach's student days at the Conservatoire were not as happy as might
have been expected. He found the discipline imposed by an academic
approach to music tiresome and spent only a year suffering under such
constraints.

Maybe it was the type of music he had performed as a child that drew him
towards the world of popular entertainment, for to eke out the family
income, Jacob (who would come to be called Jacques in Paris), with two of
his nine siblings, older brother Julius and sister Isabella, had formed a trio
that played locally and specialised in all the popular tunes of the time.

The Conservatoire may not have suited him, but Offenbach took his
studies seriously and continued to study composition with the man who
also taught Bizet, Jacques Halevy. He also continued to have private
lessons on the cello with the great performer and teacher, Norblin.
Gaining a reputation as something of a virtuoso on the cello, and with his
intense style of performance, slight build and arresting, almost ugly, if
fascinating features, Offenbach came to the attention of the cartoonists of
the day. Their interest was more than welcome, for it provided him with
free publicity throughout his career.

In 1834, he joined the *Opéra Comique* orchestra as a cellist and in 1840
he became involved in a broader sense with the *Comedie Française*.

During this time Offenbach wrote several operettas, but had no luck finding a theatre management prepared to back his work. The only solution, he decided, was to emulate Hervé and stage these productions himself. In 1855 he leased the tiny, 50-seat Théâtre Marigny on the Champs Elysées, a decision that proved to be the turning point in his career.

Offenbach's timing was perfect, as the great international Exhibition being held nearby provided him with an extra pool of potential theatre-goers. Now known as the home of Les Bouffes Parisiens, the theatre went on to host a season of light-hearted operettas, including works by Adam and Delibes, as well as *Les Deux Aveugles* and *Le Violoneux* by Offenbach. The success of this venture was such that even when the Exhibition closed, Offenbach was able to transfer Les Bouffes Parisiens to the larger Théâtre des Jeunes Elèves in the centre of Paris. The composer Saint-Saëns described this venue as being a place where 'One could laugh with the waistcoat unbuttoned.'

The opening presentation was Offenbach's own *Ba-ta-clan* (1855), a romp depicting ship-wrecked Parisiens attempting to cope with life on oriental shores. He followed this with a high profile operetta competition, proving once again that he knew how to keep his preferred style in the public eye. The top award was split between Georges Bizet, who would go on to write one of the most popular operas of all time, *Carmen*, and Charles Lecocq who would find his own success with operettas such as *La Fille de Madame Angot*. Offenbach wrote at great speed, with a number of librettists and by the middle of the 1850s he had formalised an operetta style. The audience could now expect regular ingredients like the landler, waltz, polka, gallop, can-can, as well as some military allusion and the 'patter song', so ably taken up by Gilbert and Sullivan. Offenbach enjoyed a happy marriage (in 1844) to Herminie d'Alcain, the daughter of a wealthy socialite, and was an extremely gregarious man. He entertained regularly, with guests like Bizet and Delibes being drawn into his hilarious musical games. Offenbach even liked people around him while he composed and declared his work to be 'a mutual insurance company for the defeat of boredom'. Rossini went further, dubbing him 'The Mozart of the Champs Elysées'.

In 1857 Offenbach's company made a successful visit to London, but though he was now earning considerable sums, he showed little sense in practical matters, overspending on lavish productions and equally lavish hospitality.

The following year he returned to Paris and experienced his greatest success to date with his first venture into the newly liberated* world of French musical theatre. (*Previously, the French government had imposed strict controls upon commercial houses to protect their own state-run theatre productions, which tended towards huge casts and much spectacle. These attracted a great deal of interest from the theatre-going public, so in order to keep commercial ventures less appealing, the government devised a rule whereby only three speaking or singing characters would be permitted in each commercial production.)

These restrictions hardly troubled Offenbach, who proved with every one of his early operettas that 'size isn't everything'. Having been shown to be unworkable, the restrictions were withdrawn. Offenbach appears to have exacted a sweet revenge with his reworking of one of Paris Opera's most cherished classical themes, *Orpheus ed Euridice* (Paris 1858; 2 acts. Paris 1874; 4 acts). His pungent treatment of a familiar theme would become a recurring motif in the life of this mischievous composer. In Offenbach's interpretation, *Orpheus ed Euridice* became *Orphee aux enfers*, or *Orpheus in the Underworld*. Poignancy turns to humour, trust to lust and the whole delightful romp is enhanced by the most engaging music and a large cast of endearing, if over-sexed, characters. The can-can, previously reserved for lewd performance in low places, was rendered respectable in its new setting, but still caused a sensation, as Offenbach must have known it would.

Opening night was a crazy affair, with bailiffs at the door, a burst gas main in the street and principals who refused point-blank to put on their costumes. Fortunately, the moral indignation that greeted the forward publicity ensured that every seat in the house was full.

Although *Orpheus in the Underworld* remains one of Offenbach's most popular and enduring works, there are several more wonderful pieces; *La belle Hélène* (1864), *La vie Parisienne* (1866), *La Grande-Duchesse de Gerolstein* (1867) and *Les Contes d'Hoffmann* (1881), to name just a few of more than a dozen operetta.

■ The recording by Joan Sutherland from *La Grande-Duchesse de Gerolstein* of 'Vous aimez le danger…Ah! que j'aime les militaires!' is a 'must have' for any collection.

■ Offenbach's original star, Hortense Schneider, became the darling of her day when she created the role of a very saucy duchess.

Offenbach was all the rage in Vienna too, where, in 1863, he was invited to write a waltz for the 1864 Journalist's Ball. Johann Strauss was also invited to make a contribution and he named his waltz 'Morgenblatter' (Morning papers), to compliment Offenbach's 'Abendblatter' (Evening papers). Offenbach's piece enjoyed immediate success, although history has judged the waltz by Strauss to be the more successful.

Money troubles were never too far away and by 1875 Offenbach was bankrupt. His old colleagues Meilhac and Halevy on the other hand, were doing well, collaborating with Bizet on *Carmen* and with Strauss on *Die Fledermaus*. The fickle public went crazy for *Die Fledermaus* and though many pointed out that Offenbach was the father of operetta, this gave little comfort to a man whose career was suffering a definite set-back.

As a final insult, after a life-long feud with the composer Richard Wagner, during which each derided the other's work, Offenbach saw his old enemy gaining in popularity.

Redemption came from an unlikely source when Offenbach was invited to the Philadelphia exhibition in America in 1876. He greeted this opportunity with a flurry of work, collaborating once again with Meilhac and Halevy. The resulting shows were only moderately successful, but no matter, America and a large pay-cheque beckoned. Offenbach the man scarcely lived up to the expectations of the American public, who had anticipated a composer as ebullient as his music. With his unprepossessing features, slight physique and mild public manner, he was not at all what they had imagined. Nonetheless, he was well treated and his fame spread.

When he returned to France in July of that year, more works and several revivals were to come before another masterpiece emerged, but this time, Offenbach would not live to enjoy the success of the finished piece. Good living and overwork had finally taken their toll and some of the orchestration of *Les contes d'Hoffmann* (1881) had to be completed after his death from gout of the heart, by the French composer Ernest Guiraud. *Les contes d'Hoffmann* is a rather more serious work than the rest, but earns its place in the modern repertoire.

Apart from his immense contribution to operetta, Offenbach completed numerous other compositions during his life-time, including five ballets, dozens of pieces of incidental music, songs, dances and orchestral music, but it is for his invaluable contribution to the joyous world of light music theatre in particular that Jacques Offenbach will be remembered.

Late nineteenth-century French music theatre

It is perhaps not surprising that the French public, having been plunged into an era of street riots and war, were hungry for some light relief.

- After a series of violent street battles in February 1848, supporters of universal suffrage, led by Louis Blanc, overthrew King Louis Philippe of France (see *Les Miserables*, page 197). The Second Republic was established and Louis Napoleon, a nephew of Napoleon I, was elected President of France. (He declared himself Emperor in 1852.)

- On 24 June 1859 the battle of Solferino was fought at the village of the same name in Lombardy, Northern Italy. The French and Sardinian troops under the command of Louis Napoleon, now Napoleon III, defeated the Austrians, commanded by their Emperor, Francis Joseph I. The terrible suffering on this day led to a campaign by the Swiss humanitarian, Jean Henri Dunant, for the setting up of the Red Cross society. This organisation was one of many elements established to preserve the rights of prisoners and the wounded in war, to be ratified by the Geneva Convention in 1864.

- To provoke Napoleon III to battle, Chancellor Bismarck of Prussia put forward a German candidate for the vacant Spanish throne. The French were defeated at the battle of Sedan in 1870.

The 1870s appeared to reward not only the French people, but the whole theatre-going public, for their forbearance during these troubled times. French music theatre was now awash with great productions and one of the best of these was *La Fille de Madame Angot* (1872) by Charles Lecocq.

Charles Lecocq (1832–1918)

This French composer studied with Halevy at the Paris Conservatoire where, in 1850, he won first prize for harmony and accompaniment. With the operetta *Le Docteur Miracle* (1857), he was joint winner, with Bizet, of the operetta competition sponsored by Offenbach, but would wait several years before receiving proper recognition. In 1868 his three-act operetta *Fleur-de-thé* achieved the long-awaited success and more than 40 works in a similar style would follow.

In the 1870s Lecocq lived in Brussels, where many of his works were staged before transferring to Paris. *La Fille de Madame Angot* (1872) was his most successful work, running for over 500 consecutive nights following its premiere in Brussels.

His last work, a serious opera, *Plutus* (1886), was not a success, but this scarcely dented the reputation of a composer whose big hit, *La Fille de Madame Angot*, delighted the theatre-going public worldwide during the 1870s and 1880s. The original Belgian company played to huge acclaim in London, where at one time, no fewer than three versions of the show were playing in the West End at the same time. The magic of this show consists of a melodious and memorable score, with two barnstorming parts for the ladies, strongly drawn characters for the men, nimble chorus work and a waltz to rival Strauss. And if that wasn't enough, the plot features the most irresistible combination known to man; sex and politics.

Jacques Francois Halevy (1799–1862)

Although as not well known nowadays as some other composers, teacher, composer, librettist and author, Jacques Halevy, taught a few of the very best. He was a pupil of Cherubini at the Paris Conservatoire and then in his turn became teacher to luminaries like Bizet, Lecocq, Saint-Saëns and Gounod, etc. Amongst others, he was joint librettist with Meilhac for Bizet's opera, *Carmen*.

Vienna

Franz von Suppé (1819–95)

Born in Split in the then Dalmatia, von Suppé was taken to Vienna as a boy. Here he settled and was in the vanguard of the drive to establish a Viennese operetta tradition to rival the French.

In 1840 von Suppé became director of music at the Theater in der Josefstadt, moving to the Theater an der Wien in 1845. In 1856 two of Offenbach's operettas, *Le Violoneux* and *Les Deux Aveugles* were presented in the original French in Vienna, and two years later a German language version of Offenbach's *Le Mariage aux Lanternes* recognised the growing enthusiasm for this style of entertainment in Vienna. It could only be a matter of time before a local composer put up a challenge and it was Carl Conradin who stepped forward with his opera-bouffe *Flodoardo Wuprahall* in 1859. *Flodoardo Wuprahall* enjoyed some success, but it was von Suppé's romp, *Das Pensionat*, staged at the Theater an der Wien in 1860, that generally gets the credit for starting up an operetta tradition equal to the French in every way, yet typically Viennese.

By this time von Suppé had left the Theater an der Wien, moving in 1862 to the Theater am Franz-Josefs-Kai and then in 1865 to the Carltheater.

The Theater an der Wien held his loyalty, however, and for almost the last 30 years of his life, von Suppé was in charge of music at this prestigious theatre.

A prolific composer, he would complete more than 150 operettas and operas, most of them successful in Vienna in their time. Of these *Boccaccio* (1879) enjoyed huge success, not just in Vienna, but in both Europe and America. It is still heard occasionally, but his overtures *Poet and Peasant* and *Light Cavalry* have remained justifiably popular to the present day.

Johann Strauss II (1825–99)

Viennese violinist, conductor and composer of one of the greatest operettas of all time, *Die Fledermaus*, Johann Strauss II was the famous son of a famous father. Johann I was renowned for his glittering waltzes, stirring tunes such as the 'Radetzky March' and the scintillating performances of his orchestra. He had three composer sons of whom Johann II was the most distinguished. By 1844 Johann II had gone into competition with his father and this was to last until 1849 when the two orchestras merged.

European tours between 1856 and 1886, plus a tour of the United States in 1872, cemented Johann II's reputation. His countless memorable waltz tunes soon saw him dubbed 'The King of the Waltz'. A further endorsement came from the Imperial Court when he was given the highly prestigious post of Director of Music for Balls 1863–71.

It's hard to imagine that the man who for 25 years enjoyed such musical celebrity, who wrote 'The Blue Danube' waltz and who would go on to write the crowning glory of all operettas, *Die Fledermaus*, could have had anything less than a glorious beginning to his career as an operetta composer.

However, such was the case when, prompted by friends, colleagues and a theatre manager with an eye for the main chance, Strauss II turned his talents in the direction of music theatre. His fame alone ensured a short run for the first offering, *Indigo und die vierzig Rauber (Indigo and the Forty Thieves)* (1871). The work was even staged abroad, but despite later revisions, its success was fleeting.

Strauss II persisted with the style and went on to write 17 operettas in total. Most of these didn't come close to achieving the type of success he had enjoyed with his famous waltzes, but two works have remained justifiably prominent; *Die Zigeuner-baron (The Gypsy Baron)* (1885) and *Die Fledermaus (The Bat)* (1874).

Die Fledermaus (1874)

Sentimental, sophisticated, sensual, with gloriously slow solos and Prince Orlofsky played by a comely maiden. With the brash drunken comedy of Frosch, the jailor, the Hungarian passion of Rosalinda's Czardas and Adele's famous 'laughing song', not forgetting the haunting chorus 'Bruderlein und Schwesterlein' (Brother mine and Sister mine) led by a mischievous Falke, *Die Fledermaus* has every ingredient necessary for a smash hit and continues to delight audiences as much today as it did in Vienna, Berlin and New York in 1874, London in 1876 and Paris in 1877.

- ■ A must for any collector of the world's most popular music.
- ■ Johann Strauss and family are not related to the German classical composer Richard Strauss 1864–1949.

Carl Zeller (1842–98)

A chorister at the imperial chapel, Carl Zeller later studied law at the university of Vienna. He then went on to the Ministry of Education and Culture, but his career was cut short by scandal.

For a fresh start, Zeller turned to his musical background and produced an operetta, *Jocande* (Vienna 1876). This met with some success, but it was with his next piece *Der Vogelhandler* (Vienna 1891) that he was to achieve lasting fame.

Unusual for its time in that it took gentle country matters as a theme, rather than glamorous society, or military topics, *Der Vogelhandler* contained a wealth of melody and enchanted audiences across Europe. Interestingly enough, though this work is renowned as Zeller's most significant contribution to the catalogue of Viennese operetta, it is hardly staged today. Most familiar of all his melodies, in fact, is a tune for soprano from a less successful operetta, *Die Oberstieger*, called 'Don't Be Cross'.

Karl Millocker (1842–99)

Together with von Suppé, Strauss and Zeller, the Viennese-born Millocker, though perhaps a less familiar name, is an equally significant composer in the founding of the Viennese operetta tradition.

At the age of just 16 he joined the orchestra of the Theater in der Josefstadt as a flautist and on von Suppé's recommendation was appointed conductor at the Theater Thalia in Graz in 1864, where he began to experiment with operetta composition. In 1866 he conducted at the Theater an der Wien, travelling next to the German Theatre in Budapest in 1868, before returning to Vienna in 1869.

Several operettas followed, bringing him some success, but it was with *Der Bettelstudent* (The beggar student) in 1882 that he achieved real renown. The success of this piece in both Europe and America was enormous and it survives in the German and Austrian repertoire to the present day.

British Music Hall

Music Hall encouraged people from all walks of life to visit the theatre. The audience was able to enjoy a heady mix of amusing patter, topical satire, sentimentality and often bawdy humour, presented to them by personalities who enjoyed celebrity status comparable to a modern-day soap star. British Music Hall was mother to a style that would evolve gradually over a number of years.

Georgian coffee houses often had glee clubs or singing groups to amuse their customers and the huge number of taverns offered a variety of diversions as well as providing somewhere for songwriters to sell their song sheets. Supper clubs frequently provided entertainment and one of the most successful of these was Evans in London's Covent Garden.

With popular music as vital as this, it was only a matter of time before many of the larger drinking or eating establishments saw the benefit of enlarging their premises to accommodate an ever-increasing audience.

Evan's success spawned a number of informal tavern-type Music Halls, where the emphasis shifted from dining with entertainment, to entertainment with refreshments. The prevalence of these venues ensured that the fame of local performers spread and by 1860 there were more than 700 ballad singers plying their trade in London alone. The custom for the more refined ballad singers to visit well-to-do homes after supper in order to provide the family with a little harmless entertainment was inevitably tainted by the increasingly familiar Music Hall tunes. These sometimes provided a fascinating view of working-class life, hitherto unknown to the folk above stairs.

Inspired by ballad, folk-song, topical events, nationalistic airs and opera, British Music Hall was responsible for attracting increasing numbers of people into the theatre, helping to establish the wide-ranging enthusiastic audiences that popular music enjoys today.

Pantomime

An off-shoot of the Music Hall tradition, pantomime (as the traditional Christmas-time entertainment is known in Britain today) was popularised by Augustus Harris who had the idea of bringing popular comedians from the Halls together for a Christmas extravaganza he called 'Pantomime'. The 'dame', a comic lady of a certain age, was played by a man and the 'principal boy' was played by a girl. This tradition survives lustily in Britain to the present day.

Music printing

The availability of a printed copy has determined the fate of many a melody and in the early days of Music Hall, many so-called reputable music publishers considered the style too vulgar to add to their list. However, most middle- and upper-class families owned a piano and there was a strong demand for sheet music of the most popular tunes, forcing the publishers to relent.

To begin with, the cover was simply printed as the first page in a book, but by the late 1850s full-colour covers added greatly to the appeal of the product. Fortuitously, the size of the song copy fitted perfectly into the pane of glass in a shop window, fuelling competition between rival publishers to achieve the most eye-catching cover.

Music theatre cross-over

If you already love the catchy tunes and sheer entertainment value of the musical, this is a very good time to look back to an era when what we now call opera was the light entertainment of its day. Of course, there were serious operas but there were other productions that contained tunes every bit as memorable as those you may have enjoyed in more recent times. In some of these works, sung speech called *recitative* takes the place of spoken dialogue. This is not always very tuneful and is always more helpful if it is in a language you understand. Be patient, because at the end of the recitative there should be a good tune! Some of these works are happy, some sad, but all of them have wonderful music for you to explore (see *Teach Yourself Opera*).

The Magic Flute, 1791, Mozart
The Barber of Seville, 1816, Rossini
The Daughter of the Regiment, 1840, Donizetti
Faust, 1859, Gounod
Carmen, 1875, Bizet
The Tales of Hoffmann, 1881, Offenbach
Lakme, 1883, Delibes
Cavalleria Rusticana, 1890, Mascagni
I Pagliacci, 1892, Leoncavallo
Hansel and Gretel, 1893, Humperdinck
Andre Chenier, 1896, Giordano
La Boheme, 1896, Puccini
Der Rosenkavalier, 1911, Strauss

Recorded highlights are another great way to explore popular music theatre of the past.

Self-test questions

1 What effect did the Council of Trent have upon secular music?

2 In the seventeenth century, who declared that masques and plays were 'the work of the devil'?

3 What was the name given to the boisterous early eighteenth-century entertainment written by John Gay?

4 Describe two types of music theatre that thrived in the nineteenth century.

5 What is *opéra comique*?

6 In a revival of Offenbach's *Orpheus in the Underworld*, what part was Hervé invited to play?

7 Who completed Offenbach's orchestration for his work *Les Contes d'Hoffmann*?

8 Charles Lecocq was the joint winner of an opera-writing competition sponsored by Offenbach; with whom did he share the prize?

9 Name a significant nineteenth-century Austrian composer of operetta whose career was cut short by scandal.

10 Who wrote *Die Fledermaus* (1874)?

2 | GILBERT AND SULLIVAN; THE SAVOY OPERAS

Overview

In the middle of the nineteenth century, London was lagging behind Paris and Vienna in the formulation of a popular opera style. Mainly English versions of foreign works played in London theatres and a national brand only evolved slowly, owing a great deal to the confidence of a theatrical family named the German Reeds. From modest beginnings in 1854 at St Martin's Hall, London, the German Reeds improved their stage productions and developed a following. By 1867 they were able to lease the St George's Hall, install a substantial orchestra and chorus and present Arthur Sullivan and F C Burnand's comic opera *La Contrabandista*. This production met with only modest success, but Sullivan and Bernand's next offering *Cox and Box* (1869), which, prudently, was staged by the German Reeds at their smaller facility the Royal Gallery of Illustration, was a hit. Appearing on the same programme, though for a shorter run, was a work called *No Cards*, with music by Thomas German Reed and a libretto by W S Gilbert. In his capacity as critic, Gilbert reviewed *Cox and Box* for the magazine *Fun*. He declared that, in his opinion, Sullivan's music was too good for the play. This may not have been meant as the outright compliment it appears since later, when Gilbert and Sullivan had formed their famous creative partnership, Gilbert was sometimes known to criticise Sullivan's music for being 'too good', or too classical in style for their type of entertainment.

In 1869 the German Reeds presented another of Gilbert's works, *Ages Ago*, with music, dedicated to Sullivan by one of his closest friends, Fred Clay. Surely it could only be a matter of time before fate took a hand ...

The famous pair are said to have been introduced to each other during rehearsals of Gilbert's *Ages Ago* in July 1870.

Francis C Burnand's fame rests today largely on the fact he collaborated with Arthur Sullivan on the comic opera *Cox and Box*, but he also created an English version of Offenbach's *La Belle Hélène* and contributed to many other popular shows of the time. Two works of his that stand apart from these lighter productions because they had music written specially for them by the composer and musical director Frank Musgrave are *Windsor Castle* and *L'Africaine*.

Burnand went on to become the editor of the magazine *Punch* and would claim in later life that he was responsible for the creation of English opera bouffe. We shall see how Gilbert and Sullivan took the notion of comic opera and transformed it into a quintessentially English art form.

Gilbert and Sullivan

Like the Beatles, the librettist, William Schwenck Gilbert and composer, Arthur Seymour Sullivan, created a catalogue of work that was a product of its time, yet retained a unique stamp. Richard D'Oyly Carte was their Brian Epstein, bringing what would become known as the Savoy Operas to the attention of the world.

William Schwenk Gilbert (1836–1911)

> *'I am an ill-tempered pig and I glory in it.'*
> W S Gilbert

William Gilbert, nick-named 'Bab' as a child, was the eldest of four and the only son of a naval surgeon and a doctor's daughter. He was born in London, where his family lived in comfortable circumstances in a house just off the Strand. He studied law at King's College, London, but left, aiming to gain a commission in the Royal Artillery, a desire that had been fired at the height of the Crimean War. Sadly for Gilbert, but happily for the rest of us, his patriotic fervour was not to be rewarded. The war ended suddenly, putting a stop to the recruitment drive, so Gilbert returned to his studies and, at the same time, began his apprenticeship as a man of the theatre. Audaciously, he transformed the King's College Scientific Society into a Dramatic Society, where fellow students and lecturers proved rich fodder for his sharp pen. Together with his literary exploits, Gilbert was also an accomplished artist and this skill proved particularly useful in allowing him to illustrate his thoughts on all the visual aspects of a production.

In 1857 he gained his degree and entered the Civil Service as a junior clerk, an occupation that didn't suit. He remained in this position for four long years, easing the tedium by becoming involved part-time with the 5th West Yorkshire Militia. His office of Ensign proved a great success and he moved on to become Captain in the Royal Aberdeenshire Militia in 1865.

A tall, good-looking man with fair hair and blue eyes, Gilbert retained a military bearing and a penchant for things military all his life. Good looking he was, successful, certainly, but his character was not liked by all. The editor of the first edition of the *Dictionary of Music and Musicians*, Sir George Grove, described Gilbert at the height of his powers as being 'a bitter, narrow, selfish creature'.

Eccentric certainly, irascible often (see The Carpet Affair on p. 43) yet affable when it suited him, Gilbert must have been a difficult partner at times for the genial Sullivan. Nonetheless, the partnership survived, as did Gilbert's long, though childless marriage to Lucy Turner, the daughter of an army officer, whom he married when she was just 17 and he 31.

'Write about what you know,' is a regular admonishment to writers and Gilbert's work often reflects this maxim. He found humour in most situations and his skill as a wordsmith was exceptional. His biting wit spared nothing and no one and neither hallowed institutions nor current fashions escaped his attention. He also made clever use of certain events in his own life. We can only speculate as to which middle-aged lady, or ladies, so infuriated the young Gilbert that he found sending-up unattractive ladies of a certain age so irresistible. Another influence must have been a dramatic event in his own young life, when he was kidnapped briefly in Naples. Mix-ups involving children occur several times in the Savoy Operas. Whatever twists and turns taken by Gilbert's imagination, his brilliance was indisputable. His 'patter songs', where speed of delivery is everything, made clear and significant points, rather than relying on mere showy performance and it would be hard, if not impossible, to find their equal.

Leaving aside for a moment the great partnership of Gilbert and Sullivan, Gilbert was also a prolific poet, playwright and librettist for other composers. The play *Dulcamara* or, *The Little Duck and the Great Quack* was his parody of Donizetti's opera *L'elisir d'amore (The Love Potion)* and was to prove another valuable journey for him along the learning curve of stagecraft. The play's producer, Tom Robertson, had set new standards in dramatic discipline in his own works by giving actors specific moves to make, rather than allowing them to act with total spontaneity. He also had them performing everyday tasks on-stage, promoting an increased empathy with the audience, who could relate more easily to this type of natural behaviour.

When Gilbert finally met Sullivan in July 1870, he was poised on the brink of a more triumphant career than he could ever have imagined. All the ingredients for success were assembled and waiting for the fuse to be lit. An eventful life, fertile mind and sound theatrical grounding would prove invaluable assets in the partnership, which certainly proved to be a meeting of minds, if not of temperaments. Gilbert was sensitive to criticism of his work to such a degree that he would fire off a writ at the slightest provocation, and such a perfectionist in production that he drove his colleagues to distraction, but this same man had a long and successful marriage, kept a small zoo of pet animals on his estate and invited the gentlemen to retire at the end of dinner so that he could enjoy the company of the ladies. There are further examples of a warmer side to his nature on the day he died in May 1911. He visited a sick friend in the morning and in the afternoon had arranged to give a swimming lesson to two young women in the lake at his home, Grim's Dyke. When one of the young women got into trouble, Gilbert swam out to help her. A gallant act for an elderly gentleman of 74, but sadly the attempt was to prove fatal.

Whereas Sullivan was much admired by Queen Victoria and by society in general, Gilbert was something of a maverick and would wait until 1907 for his knighthood, whereas Sullivan received his on 22 May 1883. Gilbert was cremated at Golder's Green crematorium and buried in the churchyard at Great Stanmore close to his home. Sullivan's funeral service was held in the Chapel Royal at St James's Palace where he had once served as a chorister and he was buried in the crypt at St Paul's Cathedral.

There is a memorial to Gilbert from his wife 'Kitten' in Harrow Weald Church and also a memorial from the nation on the embankment in London, not too far from Sullivan's. The inscription on the London memorial tells us all we need to know about Gilbert's professional manner. It reads, 'His Foe Was Folly and His Weapon Wit'.

Bab Ballads

These poems, some illustrated, were written by Gilbert using his childhood family nickname, 'Bab'. The first Bab Ballads appeared in 1869 and the success of these ensured that a further collection was published in 1873. A selection of Babs was published in 1877, but public opinion required them to be revised in 1882, to include some omissions from the early editions. There are in total 139 poems and the complete collection was published in 1970 by Belknap Press of Cambridge, Massachusetts, USA; *The Bab Ballads by W S Gilbert*, edited by James Ellis.

Arthur Seymour Sullivan (1842–1900)

'I have chosen music, because nothing in the world would ever interest me so much.'

Arthur Sullivan, aged fourteen

Arthur Sullivan was born in south London, the younger of two sons of an Irish musician, Thomas Sullivan. Money was short and his mother, Maria, was at times forced to accept employment as a governess in order to make ends meet.

Fortunately, Sullivan's father was a talented musician and the family's fortunes saw a small improvement when Thomas was appointed Bandmaster at the Military College, Sandhurst, and again when he became Professor of the Clarinet at the Royal Military School of Music. Even so, Sullivan's background was quite modest in comparison to Gilbert's.

Musically gifted and with a beautiful voice, Sullivan left for boarding school at the age of eight, becoming a chorister at the Chapel Royal at the age of twelve. One year later in 1855, his first song, 'O Israel', was published by Novello. The following year, facing stiff competition from older entrants, Sullivan won the prestigious Mendelssohn scholarship. He held this for three years and it enabled him to attend the Royal Academy of Music. Here it was decided that he should go on to study at the Conservatoire founded by Mendelssohn in Leipzig. His fellow students in Leipzig included the founder of the famous touring opera company, Carl Rosa, and the Norwegian composer, Edvard Grieg. His two years in Leipzig were coming to an end when Sullivan was invited to stay on for another few months. At first the onus of paying both tuition fees and living expenses fell solely on the hard pressed Thomas Sullivan, who took on extra teaching work in the evenings so that his son might continue his studies. Eventually the Conservatoire waived Sullivan's fees, easing this burden considerably.

'I will work very hard,' Sullivan wrote home, 'in order that you may see that all your sacrifices (which I know you make) have not been to no purpose.'

In Leipzig, Sullivan was acclaimed for his incidental music for Shakespeare's play, *The Tempest* and this work attracted the interest of Sir George Grove who arranged for a performance at the Crystal Palace in England in 1862. The style of this piece, reminiscent of Mendelssohn's own music, found Sullivan an even more significant admirer in the person of the Queen. Queen Victoria invited Sullivan to compose an anthem for the wedding of her son and later he was appointed Master of the Queen's Music. This was not the first occasion that Sullivan had attracted the admiration of the Royal family, for as a boy chorister at the Chapel Royal, his singing had earned him ten shillings from Prince Albert. How pleased the Queen must have been to note the development of this young musician and in a style that accorded so well with her taste. Now Sullivan was to teach the boys of the Chapel Royal, as well as giving lessons at the Crystal Palace School of Art in piano and singing. To bolster his meagre income still further, he also accepted the post of organist at St Michael's Church in Chester Square, London. This last position augured well for the future Savoy Operas and *The Pirates of Penzance* in particular, for in order to improve the thin male tone in the chorus, Sullivan recruited local policemen. The notion of Pirates' Sergeant of Police and his comical, if somewhat more restrained forerunners of the Key-Stone Cops, certainly arose from this as Sullivan himself later admitted. This modest degree of financial security allowed Sullivan to put the sale of his compositions on a more business-like footing and slowly, but surely, he was able to develop, both as a composer and a man of means.

By the late 1860s Sullivan was much in demand across the length and breadth of Great Britain both to compose for and to conduct his works at countless music festivals. He was appointed by the Queen to correct the musical outpourings of her husband and was also organist at the fashionable church of St Peter in Cranley Gardens, London. A number of serious works improved his standing still further in the musical community. Ballads, hymns, oratorio, opera, ballet, incidental music, orchestral works; Sullivan had all the appearances of becoming the foremost British composer of classical music of his day and this situation was further endorsed by his appointment, at an early age of 24, to the Professorship of Composition at the Royal Academy. Here he found teaching to be a tedious occupation and though he was already an accomplished mimic of musical styles, there was still no real sign that this utterly conventional darling of society was destined to become the master of musical fun. The heritage of his years as church organist, however, have not been lost and continue to bring pleasure to all those who love singing. His most famous compositions in this style include the rousing hymn 'Onward Christian Soldiers' and the very beautiful carol 'It came upon the midnight clear'.

A chance meeting with the librettist F C Burnand led to the first real comic opera, *Cox and Box*. Taken from J Maddison Morton's play, *Box and Cox*, this was to be a private production between friends in Burnand's house. Sullivan and his friend, Fred Clay, both had beautiful singing voices and took the leading roles of Box and Cox respectively and another musical chum, Norman Scott Russell, took the part of Bouncer. These amateur theatricals proved so successful that a public performance was arranged at the Adelphi Theatre.

The enthusiasm with which this venture was received took everyone by surprise and the show had to be performed over and over again in an attempt to assuage the public appetite for such a long-awaited event. Admittedly miniature, it was undeniable that here at last was a thoroughly British comic opera. Prophetically, on the same bill, appeared the name W S Gilbert, who provided the words to a piece called *No Cards* with music by Thomas German Reed.

A second collaboration between Burnand and Sullivan resulted in *La Contrabandista*, but this more clearly revealed the mismatch between clever composer and merely able librettist. What was needed was a happy marriage of words and music and the relationship between Sullivan and Burnand was merely a brief engagement.

Meanwhile, Fred Clay was also embarked upon his own brief engagement with none other than W S Gilbert. The two men were involved in presenting an operetta called *Ages Ago*, with music written by Clay and dedicated to his friend Sullivan. It was only natural that Sullivan should call in to see how rehearsals were progressing. He received a typically cranky greeting from the perverse librettist, whose jokes were sometimes known only to himself, but in spite of this the two men survived the introduction and found their paths crossing several times more in the interval between this initial meeting and the forming of their partnership.

Establishing a real British alternative to the popular French and Viennese comic operas wasn't to be without teething problems, even with these two creative geniuses at the helm. Boxing Day 1861 at the old Gaiety Theatre on the Strand, *Thespis* or *The Gods Grown Old* was an interesting first collaboration for Gilbert and Sullivan. Unusually, the public weren't keen, whilst the critics were full of admiration. The two men learned some basic truths from this first attempt – it helps if the performers sing in tune and first nights must run smoothly, without endless embarrassing delays.

Furthermore, the British theatre-going public wanted an easily digested storyline, with characters with whom they were familiar, or at least could more reasonably imagine, rather than exalted gods and goddesses of whom they had never heard before. Even so, *Thespis* ran for 64 performances, though the music has been lost; possibly destroyed by Sullivan, and Gilbert in later years was also reluctant to demonstrate any support for this, the first fruit of their partnership. This was not the end of the story, however, but just the beginning, for artists' manager, composer and impressario, Richard D'Oyly Carte, or 'Oily Carte', as the lampoonists of the day dubbed him, saw *Thespis* at the Gaiety and recognised its potential. This man's driving ambition was to see the establishment of an English operatic tradition that would surpass any foreign import and now he knew that time was at hand.

Arthur Sullivan scarcely required a knighthood to raise him any higher in the eyes of his countrymen, for he lived life at the pinnacle of public approval. He seems to have been a genial man, popular with the ladies and enjoying many friendships. He never married and perhaps the rather predatory attentions in his youth of Rachel Scott Russell and, to a lesser extent the attentions of her two sisters, combined with his mother, the ever-present Maria Sullivan, who moved in with her son when his father died, left him little inclination to embark upon marriage. In any event, Sullivan was secure in the adoration of his public, if not a wife. There is no doubt that his collaboration with Gilbert awoke something in him that allowed all the careful years of study to be put to work in the most unique, exciting and unexpected way. In a letter to his father he writes, 'How can I thank you sufficiently, my dearest Father, for the opportunity you have given me of continuing my studies…' I am sure that Thomas Sullivan would be the first to agree that the wonderful catalogue of music known as the Savoy Operas is thanks enough.

Richard D'Oyly Carte (1844–1901)

'The starting of English comic opera in a theatre devoted to that alone was the scheme of my life.'
Richard D'Oyly Carte 1869

Gilbert and Sullivan had genius, of that there is no doubt, but with Gilbert's irascibility and Sullivan's laid-back manner, without a driving force to unit the two, the establishment of a British tradition in music theatre might have waited a lot longer. Richard D'Oyly Carte was to prove as essential to the success of this venture as Gilbert and Sullivan themselves.

Born in comfortable circumstances in London, Richard D'Oyly Carte's father was a flautist and partner in a firm making musical instruments. His mother was a clergyman's daughter who had travelled extensively for the times and who encouraged the speaking of French in the home several times a week. Richard D'Oyly Carte was encouraged to join the family business after university, but this was not to his taste. He was already a minor composer of operetta and songs and in 1870 he set up as a theatrical agent in Charing Cross Road. He was extremely successful and eventually represented such luminaries as the singer Adelina Patti, the poet Malcolm Arnold, the composer Charles Gounod (see *Teach Yourself Opera*) and even Oscar Wilde. He knew Gilbert and Sullivan individually and since seeing *Thespis* had harboured the desire to see the pair working together again. The opportunity finally arose when Gilbert showed him a script that he intended to work on with the composer Carl Rosa. D'Oyly Carte agreed to back the idea on the condition that Gilbert worked with Sullivan instead. Gilbert duly took the manuscript to Sullivan's house where his manner of reading it suggested he might fly into a rage if it was not well received.

He need not have worried for Sullivan loved the piece and would go on to prove that he too could work at speed when sufficiently inspired. Three weeks later *Trial by Jury* was ready. Truly a miniature gem, D'Oyly Carte had every right to congratulate himself on his good judgement. That same judgement would steer the good ship *Pinafore* and the rest of the operas through the tricky passage of temperament and ego, with unfailing firmness and sound business sense.

The Savoy Theatre

The Savoy Theatre was a novelty in itself, because the new building was to be lit by electricity. At first the generator proved insufficient to the task and the stage was still lit by gas light, but within a matter of months this was rectified, sparing audience and players alike the stale air and heat that had been usual in small theatres up to this time. The Savoy was Richard D'Oyly Carte's brainchild and was built on the site of a medieval palace of one of the Princes of Savoy. It would seat 1,292 people. The first Gilbert and Sullivan opera to be staged at the Savoy was *Patience* on 10 October 1881. The Savoy Operas at that time referred to all music theatre productions at the Savoy Theatre, whether or not they were by Gilbert and Sullivan.

The D'Oyly Carte name

D'Oyly was a first name of Richard Carte's that joined forces with his surname, therefore, Mr R D O Carte became Mr R D'Oyly Carte.

Gilbert and Sullivan Operas

Title	Date of first performance	Venue
Thespis	26 December 1871	Gaiety Theatre, London
Trial by Jury	25 March 1875	Royalty Theatre, London
The Sorcerer	17 November 1877	Opera Comique, London
HMS Pinafore	25 May 1878	Opera Comique, London
The Pirates of Penzance	30 December 1879	Royal Bijou Theatre, Paignton
	31 December 1879	Fifth Avenue Theater, New York
	3 April 1880	Opera Comique, London
Patience	23 April 1881	Opera Comique, London
Iolanthe	25 November 1882	The Savoy Theatre, London
Princess Ida	5 January 1884	The Savoy Theatre, London
The Mikado	14 March 1885	The Savoy Theatre, London
Ruddigore	22 January 1887	The Savoy Theatre, London
The Yeomen of the Guard	3 October 1888	The Savoy Theatre, London
The Gondoliers	7 December 1889	The Savoy Theatre, London
Utopia Limited	7 October 1893	The Savoy Theatre, London
The Grand Duke	7 March 1896	The Savoy Theatre, London

Thespis or *The Gods Grown Old*

Billed as: An entirely original Grotesque* (*for today's understanding read ridiculous) opera in two acts.

Synopsis

Slipping standards on Mount Olympus prompts chaotic job-swop between gods and mortals.

Points of interest

- As the music to this opera at the time of writing is missing, it is difficult to be sure of the voice types required for all parts. It is certain that the standard of singing on the opening night left much to be desired, causing Sullivan to complain that, 'Few actors in the cast can sing, and of those who pretended to, hardly any could be said to compass more than six notes.' His brother Frederic, playing the part of Apollo, would have been a notable exception to such criticism. Frederic went on to create the role of The Learned Judge in *Trial by Jury* and, had he lived, the role of John Wellington Wells in *The Sorcerer* would have been his triumph, rather than George Grossmith's.

- Having given up a career as an architect to pursue a career on the stage, Frederic Sullivan quipped that he was 'still drawing large houses'.

Trial by Jury

Billed as: A novel and entirely original Dramatic Cantata.

Form: In one act.

Synopsis

With apologies to Gilbert… '…and the Court has convened to hear the pleas for this Breach of Promise of Marriage'.

Points of interest

- Originally conceived as a filler for an evening in which the main attraction was *La Perichole*, *Trial by Jury* was a great success for the Queen's favourite composer, Arthur Sullivan, and continued to run long after *La Perichole* had finished. There was less fuss about the librettist, even though Gilbert was by this time one of the foremost British writers of his day. Prophetically, *The Times* commented, 'It seems as though poem and music had proceeded simultaneously from the same brain.'

The Sorcerer

Billed as: An entirely new and original Modern Comic opera in two acts.

Synopsis

Love potion wreaks havoc in serene shires setting.

Points of interest

- Victorian propriety crept into Gilbert's thinking so that only unmarried people might be affected by the love potion.
- From this opera onwards, it seems that a formula for players had been devised: the lowest type of female voice, the contralto (see *Teach Yourself Opera*) became a regular inclusion, characterising older ladies desperately seeking husbands; the baritone comic or, as in *Yeoman*, whimsical role, that attracted many charismatic and skilled actor/singers, such as George Grossmith, Martin Green, John Reed, the 'patter song' where a great many words are sung at great speed – a popular inclusion for this category; at least one showpiece tenor role; ditto baritone; and bass to add some gravitas. Although not in this opera, there would be quite frequently a mezzo-soprano/contralto singer in the role of: funnier/older/less attractive, friend/relation of soprano lead or significant other, in light comedy/soubrette role, e.g. Hebe in *HMS Pinafore*, Pitti Sing in *The Mikado*. On occasion the mezzo-soprano or middle range female voice played a bigger part, e.g. Mad Margaret in *Ruddigore*, Iolanthe in *Iolanthe*. Showy soprano, e.g. Mabel in *Pirates*, Aline in *Sorcerer* and/or tending towards a more dramatic soprano voice, e.g. Josephine in *HMS Pinafore*, Elsie in *Yeoman*.

■ The chorus too plays a significant role in all the operas and Sullivan's writing in this case shows the benefit of all his previous training and experience. Note particularly the anthem-like, 'Hail Poetry' in *The Pirates of Penzance* and the truly operatic demands of the finale of *The Yeoman of the Guard*.

HMS Pinafore or The Lass that Loved a Sailor

Billed as: An entirely original Nautical Comic Opera in two acts.

Synopsis

Humble sailor loves a lady. All seems lost until mix-up at birth with his Captain is revealed.

Points of interest

■ Rousing choruses, including the opening 'We sail the ocean blue', which must have made an immediate impact; Glorious solos, e.g. Captain Corcoran's 'Fair moon, to thee I sing', clever catchy tunes, e.g. 'I am the Captain of the Pinafore' sung by Captain Corcoran, surpassed in status at least by Sir Joseph Porter's 'I am the Monarch of the Seas', not to mention Josephine's poignant 'Sorry her lot' and the patriotic anthem so in tune with its time, 'For he is an Englishman', all contrived to make this the first blockbuster for Gilbert and Sullivan.

■ Visually, the original production must have been as stunning as its words and music. Gilbert brought his artistic skills to bear, visiting Nelson's flagship, *Victory*, to provide sketches for his set builders, enabling them to build a sensational replica of the *Victory*'s deck on-stage.

■ The great success of this piece owed as much to its political comment as to the strength of its tunes, witty words and spectacular set. Although slow to begin with, due to unusually hot weather and muted critiques in the press, success when it came would endure to the present day. Gilbert's jibe at the still vigorously upheld British class system and his reference to a First Lord of the Admiralty who had never been to sea, in the person of Sir Joseph

Porter, rang gloriously true. The public loved him for it and as the word spread, they flocked to listen to his sharp observations and draw their own conclusions regarding the similarities between Sir Joseph and the real-life First Lord of the Admiralty in Disraeli's Government, W H Smith, founder of the booksellers. Predictably this 'nautical' luminary was soon dubbed 'Pinafore Smith'.

■ Sullivan advanced public awareness and popularity of his music by conducting orchestral concerts in which the latest tunes from the operas would be included. Ticket sales benefited enormously from this clever marketing ploy.

■ During the Christmas holiday period 1879–80, Gilbert staged a version of *HMS Pinafore* with a cast of children between the ages of 10 and 13. The music was re-set to suit young voices.

■ This work was taken up almost immediately by professional, semi-professional and amateur companies alike, fuelling an appetite for Gilbert and Sullivan that would never die. Woefully, there were also a number of 'pirate' versions, notably in the United States, some of which did no credit to the original. D'Oyly Carte was prompted into taking the London company to New York, complete with Sullivan conducting and Gilbert, heavily disguised beneath beard and whiskers in the chorus (at least for the opening night), to show the standards expected of the 'real thing'. The Americans loved it even more.

The Pirates of Penzance or *The Slave of Duty*

Billed as: A new and original melo-dramatic opera in two acts.

Synopsis

Careless Nanny apprentices her charge to a pirate, rather than a pilot. All is resolved when Pirates discover that they are after all, 'noblemen who have gone astray'.

Points of interest

■ Having been taken by surprise by the sheer number of misinterpreted and/or shoddy, pirate editions of *Pinafore* in

America, Gilbert and Sullivan decided to do everything possible to obtain a restrictive copyright in the USA for any new production. Working at top speed, Sullivan managed to finish the score just in time for the opening night. Rehearsals had been carried out in secret, as and when the music became available.

■ A matinee performance was arranged in England the day before the American premiere, to be given by an official D'Oyly Carte touring company that happened to be appearing in Torquay for the Christmas season. The company presented a cobbled together version of *Pirates* at the Royal Bijou Theatre in Paignton, Devon. This was more of an emergency measure to secure British copyright than a considered premiere. Half the music was still missing, including the splendid overture, and Sir Joseph Porter was forced to speak, rather than sing his lines. The costumes were adapted from *Pinafore*.

■ The New York show was quite different, with glorious costumes and an overture finished in the early hours of the morning of the premiere by Sullivan and Alfred Cellier working flat out. The reception was rapturous.

■ In spite of all efforts to prevent them, including strict security for the new work, pirate versions of both *Pinafore* and *Pirates* persisted.

■ The 'proper' first night in England was held on 3 April 1880 at the Opera Comique. Once again comments were passed in the press regarding the exceptionally close creative relationship between Gilbert and Sullivan.

■ The ultra-clear diction required by Gilbert prompted a criticism that the players spoke too slowly.

■ Although hugely popular with its musical delights and Gilbert's pithy commentary on popular humorous topics like 'new money' and misplaced loyalties, the original London run was shorter than *Pinafore*, with 363 performances to *Pinafore's* magnificent total of 571.

Patience or Bunthorne's Bride

Billed as: A new and original aesthetic opera in two acts.

Synopsis

Aesthetes vie with Dragoon Guards for the attention of rapturous maidens. Patience, a milkmaid, more rustic than rapturous, out-manoeuvres the female competition.

Points of interest

- Opening at the Opera Comique, *Patience* was the first Gilbert and Sullivan work to be staged at the new Savoy Theatre. Electric light, still a great novelty, was used and lightbulbs featured in the programme illustrations for the Savoy Theatre production of *Patience*.

- *Patience* proved very popular and ran for 578 performances at the Savoy. Undoubtedly, the electric lighting contributed to this lengthy tenure, with the resulting improved air quality, more effective illumination and its sheer novelty value.

- Lampooning only the worst excesses of the aesthetic movement, *Patience* found favour with Oscar Wilde. Wilde looked quite the real-life aesthete and his approval raised interest levels in *Patience* still further. Oscar Wilde was also one of the many luminaries other than Gilbert and Sullivan who appeared at one time or another 'on the books' of Richard D'Oyly Carte's theatrical agency.

- It seems likely that Gilbert's penetrating wit influenced Wilde's writing to some degree and social commentary, that ruffler of critics' feathers who considered it out of place in light entertainment, was certainly in tune with the Irish dramatist, George Bernard Shaw's approach. Shaw enjoyed a long life (1856–1950), was an early member of the socialist Fabian society and aimed to stimulate his audience's social conscience as well as to provoke an emotional response. Like Gilbert, he frequently achieved these intentions through comedy.

- Touring companies not only took productions of *Patience* throughout Great Britain and to America, but to Australia too.
- Pirate productions in all these countries provoked legal action by Gilbert, Sullivan and D'Oyly Carte. Their efforts were often unsuccessful, but this did not prevent them becoming extremely wealthy on the proceeds of properly licensed performances and music sales.

Iolanthe or *The Peer and the Peri*

Billed as: An original fairy opera in two acts.

Synopsis

Can there really be a 'Vacancy' sign in the House of Lords, when all the peers fly off to never-never land with the fairies? ...

Points of interest

- The first Gilbert and Sullivan opera to be written with performance at the Savoy Theatre in mind.
- Gilbert's view of the law in *Iolanthe* must have been coloured during his own early studies. His view of the aristocracy is also interesting, for though he lampoons this estate, he longed for the recognition and distinction that could be bestowed by a knighthood.
- *Iolanthe* provided Sullivan with a distraction and with focus following the death of his beloved mother.
- Gilbert had already toyed with the notion of a fairy marrying a mortal in one of the Bab Ballads, 'The Fairy Curate'.
- The secrecy in which the rehearsals were held fuelled public interest and rumour, adding greatly to ticket sales.
- The title *Iolanthe* was withheld from the cast until the last moment. As *Iolanthe* is repeated many times throughout the work, appearing almost like a Wagnerian *leit motiv* representing this particular character in a snatch of tune, the phrase 'Come Perola' was rehearsed instead. This led to fears that the correct version would not be remembered. Sullivan comforted his troops by reminding them that, unlike himself, Gilbert would be pacing up and down in the

street somewhere nervously awaiting the outcome of his latest show. As Gilbert and himself were the only ones who knew what should be sung, the cast could sing whatever they liked and the audience would be none the wiser.

■ The story-line was leaked, of course, and demand for tickets grew apace. The opening night didn't disappoint, in fact the finale to Act One had to be completely repeated to assuage the public's appetite. Libretti were provided for all the audience to follow the words and this was easily done in those days before it became customary for house lights to be extinguished completely.

■ The spectacle on-stage was enhanced by the elaborate robes of the peers and by the entrance of Iolanthe herself on a river of real water.

■ The premiere in New York was held on the same evening and because of the time difference, it was possible to send a cable from London relating the triumph of that production before the American show had even started.

■ The British Prime Minister, Gladstone, saw the show and the following spring, (1883) offered Sullivan a knighthood. A degree of fair play prevailed in real life, with Sullivan's mentor from his youth, George Grove, receiving his knighthood on the same occasion. Fair play proved illusive, however, where Gilbert was concerned and he would wait more than 20 years for his own knighthood in 1907.

■ Sales of music to the public exceeded all expectations. The satirical references to the House of Lords were particularly appreciated at a time when the Liberals had recently taken power, only to find their reforming zeal continually spiked by the opposing views and veto of the Upper House.

Princess Ida or Castle Adamant

Billed as: A respectful Operatic Per-Version of Tennyson's *The Princess* in a Prologue and two acts.

In fact this work is considered to contain three acts, making it similar in form to many of the more serious classical operas. (Opera Buffa usually contained two acts, which again helped to give the impression that

Princess Ida would be rather more serious in tone than previous works by Gilbert and Sullivan.) The length of *Princess Ida* was just one consideration that led to its exclusion for many years from the regular repertoire of the D'Oyly Carte Opera company.

On opening night, 5 January 1884, with prolonged intervals resulting from complicated scene changes, *Princess Ida* ran for three-and-a-half hours.

Synopsis

Brainy daughter of ghastly King, with three daft brothers, not surprisingly renounces men and retreats to Castle Adamant with other brainy ladies. Courageous male trio succeed in both breaking in and breaking down all female defences.

Points of interest

- The vocal parts and in particular the role of Princess Ida require voices with the stamina, power and range usually associated with main-stream opera. This, together with the length of the production, makes it an awkward inclusion in the standard repertoire of a light opera company.

- There are many principal parts, some of which are brief, yet demanding. This makes effective characterisation difficult for performers and creates practical difficulties for management and performers alike.

- Gilbert admitted to the first King Gama, George Grossmith, that he had modelled the character on his own professional demeanour.

- Sullivan was ill during final preparations, and on the first night of this work he needed morphine to enable him to conduct. Exhaustion, kidney infection and no doubt stress provoked both by deadlines and his heavy gambling, all contributed to his substantially less than usually euphoric mood. In spite of this, he was still able to write in his diary that *Princess Ida* had been a 'brilliant success'.

- Sullivan wrote to Gilbert shortly afterwards saying that he didn't want to write any more comic operas. Fortunately, D'Oyly Carte had previously contracted both of them to doing just that.

■ Act two, known as 'the string of pearls', contains one strong melody after another. Perhaps if the plot had sprung in its entirety from Gilbert's vigorous imagination, or been based on one of his own Bab Ballads rather than being tied to the germ of an idea from someone else's work, it would have possessed more of the spontaneous appeal so attractive in the other operas.

■ With an original run of 246 performances, *Princess Ida* fell well short of Gilbert and Sullivan's best loved works. Bookings had dropped by the beginning of 1884 and D'Oyly Carte informed the awkward duo that another work would be required within six months.

■ Living standards had to be maintained after all and both thrived artistically when humour could be brought to the mix. Agreement would have to be reached whatever stumbling blocks of ego stood in their way. Disagreement over whether they would, and if they did, what might be the subject, ended at last with an idea that inspired them both; *The Mikado*.

The Mikado or *The Town of Titipu*

Billed as: An entirely original Japanese Opera in two acts.

Synopsis

Cupid lands Mikado's son in trouble. Deception lands the Lord High Executioner in even more.

Points of interest

■ At 672 performances over two years, *The Mikado* enjoyed a longer original run than any other Gilbert and Sullivan opera. It met with ecstatic acclaim from all quarters.

■ A Japanese exhibition in Knightsbridge and a large Samurai sword, hanging in Gilbert's study (later used in actual performance by the original Ko-Ko), must have played some part in fuelling the creative thoughts that led to this masterpiece.

■ Gilbert proved himself demanding beyond anything the regular cast had come to expect from a man they knew to be a perfectionist. Reasonably, he considered his words of equal importance to Sullivan's music and complained that he could hear every note of the latter, whereas his words were sometimes indistinct. Diction, he demanded, must be faultless, as must all moves and gestures made with the added burden of unfamiliar oriental costumes. Some of these, such as Katisha's costume, were originals and more than 200 years old.

■ To enhance authenticity still further, Gilbert brought in Japanese women from the exhibition to instruct his cast on the use of a fan and how to appear graceful in the heavy costumes.

■ Rehearsals were relentless and by first night, Ko-Ko, played by George Grossmith, had lost his voice and his nerve. Nonetheless he coped with the unusually large comic role and took tranquillisers for some time afterwards to ease his stage fright.

■ Once again, snobbery becomes the butt of Gilbert's humour in the humour-less figure of Pooh Bah. He acknowledges the pressures assailing so many of his fellow men in the character Ko-Ko and with his favourite recurring theme advises vigilance when dealing with wily ladies of a certain age.

■ Rutland Barrington, who created the role of Pooh Bah, was notorious for singing out of tune. On opening night of *The Mikado*, however, he sang faultlessly throughout, prompting Gilbert to explain famously that this unexpected improvement was due to 'first night nerves'.

Ruddigore or *The Witch's Curse*

Billed as: A new and original Supernatural Opera in two acts.

Synopsis

Ghosts and curses abound in this Cornish village until common sense provides a solution.

Points of interest

■ With costly transformation scenes and elaborate costumes, *Ruddigore* proved to be one of the most expensive Gilbert and Sullivan productions to stage.

- Extreme excitement gripped Gilbert and Sullivan fans for the opening night of *Ruddygore* as it was titled originally. After a masterpiece like *The Mikado* it was not surprising that everyone's expectations were somewhat inflated. The new show was soon dubbed 'Bloody Gore', or worse, 'Bloody Bore', moving Gilbert to adjust the spelling of its title to read *Ruddigore*.

- Unbelievably, hisses broke out in the theatre on opening night, due largely to the weakness of the plot in the second act, preceded by a lengthy interval.

- Later in the run, the comic lead, George Grossmith, had a sudden attack of peritonitis, allowing his understudy Henry Lytton to take the stage as Robin Oakapple. From disappointment-led hostile silence to rapturous acclaim at the end of the show, Henry Lytton saw his destiny as a future principal of the D'Oyly Carte Opera Company confirmed that night.

- Richard D'Oyly Carte's beloved electricity enhanced the ghostly scenes in *Ruddigore* to an extent that would not have been possible with gaslight. The ability to turn lights up and down at will, even achieving complete black-outs, was a new and invaluable aid to theatrical presentation that provided additional novelty for the audience.

- *Ruddigore* ran for 288 performances, undoubtedly a disappointment after *The Mikado*'s barnstorming 672, but in anyone but Gilbert and Sullivan's terms, just short of 300 performances would have been counted a great success.

- Like *Princess Ida*, the music in *Ruddigore* comes very close at times to a truly operatic style.

- Although Gilbert would, in later life, claim *Ruddigore*, along with *Yeomen of the Guard* and *Utopia Limited*, to be a favourite work, neither he nor Sullivan appear to have been satisfied with it at the time. Gilbert blamed Sullivan's music, saying it was too classical in tone for a comic opera and Sullivan felt his music to have been swamped by Gilbert's book. They certainly made money from the venture, but possibly felt a bit flat after the public reaction to this work, after the clamour of approval that had greeted *The Mikado*.

The Yeomen of the Guard or *The Merryman and his Maid*

Billed as: A new and original Opera in two acts.

Synopsis

Very different in mood, *Yeoman* is poignant and stirring, rather than light-hearted and whimsical. Fairfax, falsely accused, is to die on Tower Green. Travelling players are drawn into a plot to free him with both distressing and passionate consequences.

Points of interest

- In a letter to Gilbert written in 1884, Sullivan wrote, 'I should like to set a story of human interest and probability, where the humorous words would (only) come in a humorous situation.' *The Yeomen of the Guard* fulfils this wish to the full with its more realistic story-line. The customary spectacle and attractive melodies remain, but satire and burlesque give way to real human emotions.

- Sullivan was relieved that Gilbert had come up with an idea with which he felt comfortable, rather than another light-hearted romp. He must have seen this as an opportunity to use his musical talents to some deeper purpose.

- Queen Victoria's Golden Jubilee in 1887 created an ideal atmosphere for entertainments with an historical and essentially British feel to them.

- *The Yeomen of the Guard* contains everything that is best about Gilbert and Sullivan, with rousing choruses, clever, witty songs, glorious melodies and now pathos added to the mix.

- The original Jack Point, George Grossmith, viewed himself as very much the comedian and felt his fans might think it one of his japes if he collapsed and died at the end of the work. He toned down his responses accordingly, but George Thorne, a D'Oyly Carte principal in the provinces, considered a more tragic ending appropriate. This has proved to be the most effective climax to one of the most interesting, if very different, collaborations between Gilbert and Sullivan.

- *The Yeomen of the Guard* ran for 432 performances following its premiere at the Savoy Theatre, London.

The Gondoliers or *The King of Barataria*

Billed as: An entirely original Comic Opera in two acts.

Synopsis

Two gondoliers learn that one of them is King of Barataria. Until it is known which of them is king, they must rule jointly. Casilda, daughter of the Duke of Plaza-Toro, longs to marry her father's drummer-attendant, Luiz. Family friction follows until it becomes clear that Luiz has prospects above the ordinary.

Points of interest

- Rumbles of discontent erupted yet again between Gilbert and Sullivan, with Sullivan feeling that his music was likely to be eclipsed by Gilbert's lyrics if he failed to stand his ground. Yet critics had not always been as fulsome in their praise of Gilbert as they were with Sullivan. It seems likely that Sullivan always harboured the suspicion that he could have achieved even more had he not been so successful with his comic operas.

- The idea of setting a light-hearted piece in Venice might seem the very last thing Sullivan would be interested in, yet he had recently visited the city and had like it immensely. At the same time Richard D'Oyly Carte invited him to compose a grand opera for the opening of his new theatre, the Royal English Opera House in Cambridge Circus. This would result in *Ivanhoe* which Sullivan wrote with the librettist, Julian Sturgis. This five act serious opera eased Sullivan's frustrations in that direction, freeing him to take up Gilbert's suggestion that they should now work on a new Savoy Opera they could both enjoy.

- The strain of composing both works at once was almost too much for Sullivan and even the usually difficult Gilbert became as accommodating as possible during the creative process. Melodies such as the winsome 'When a merry maiden marries' and the vibrant 'Dance a Cachucha' betrayed nothing of Sullivan's weariness.

■ Sullivan was granted the longed-for scope for his music and there is less spoken dialogue in this opera than the others. Even so, Gilbert's talent to amuse lost none of its bite.

■ Five days before the opening there was still no title for the piece. Although both Gilbert and Sullivan had kept up a leisurely pace during the initial stages, final rehearsals were as hectic as ever.

■ Frank Wyatt took over the comic role the Duke of Plaza-Toro from George Grossmith when that famous comedian decided to leave the company and return to a solo career in the Music Halls.

■ Following the great success of *The Gondoliers* Gilbert and Sullivan were as generous with their praise for each other as they had been with their past criticisms.

■ *The Gondoliers* ran for 554 performances and was performed before Queen Victoria at Windsor Castle in 1891. The Queen's diary shows that she found it 'quite charming throughout'.

■ **The Carpet Affair**   Calm waters between the two great men could never exist for long and their greatest fall-out to date soon occurred. The bombshell, when it came, was not a matter of egos, or creative freedom, but a row over the cost of a carpet for the Savoy. It seems that Sullivan had thought the matter of no consequence and said nothing when D'Oyly Carte went about the refurbishment. Gilbert meanwhile was on holiday with his wife and returned to find the replacement carpet a *fait accompli*. To the amazement of colleagues and public alike, Gilbert took the matter to court. It would be years rather than days before Gilbert was prepared to accept D'Oyly Carte's explanations and Sullivan's offers of reconciliation, but when the great partners did meet, it was inevitable that they should discuss the possibility of another opera.

Utopia Limited or *The Flowers of Progress*

Billed as: An original Comic Opera in two acts.

Synopsis

Country grinds to a halt when government achieves perfection.

Points of interest

- Like *The Gondoliers*, *Utopia Limited* has a number of small parts, enabling chorus members to take a more prominent role – ideal for keeping boredom at bay in a company like D'Oyly Carte.
- It's possible that the song 'A tenor all singers above' is better known than the show itself, and for good reason.
- Set on a South Sea Island, *Utopia Limited* demanded a high standard of singing from its soloists and a facility for comedy in many of the roles.
- By this time, both Gilbert and Sullivan were in poorer health than they had previously enjoyed. On the first night, Gilbert was recovering from a particularly unpleasant bout of gout and Sullivan had been granted the services of the personal physician of the Prince of Wales whilst on holiday, for stress and illness had rendered him prematurely aged.
- When criticised for the political nature of his jibes in *Utopia Limited*, Gilbert protested famously that there was nothing of a controversial political nature in the piece, since 'it didn't do to divide the house'.
- Perhaps the combined creative wells were running a little dry, or public tastes were changing; either way *Utopia Limited* failed to achieve the unconditional acclaim of most of its predecessors. Nonetheless, its original run of 245 performances would have been counted a great success for collaborators other than these.

The Grand Duke or The Statutory Duel

Billed as: An original Comic Opera in two acts.

Synopsis

A salutory tale about the risks of gambling.

Points of interest

- Twenty-five years after a group of players swopped places with the gods on Olympus in *Thespis*, the last Gilbert and Sullivan work saw theatricals once again turning matters topsy-turvy with their attempts to take over a kingdom.

- *The Grand Duke* had the shortest opening run of any of their works apart from *Thespis*; *The Grand Duke* with 123 performances and *Thespis* with 64.

- By this time three men, D'Oyly Carte, Sullivan and Gilbert were all suffering ill health.

- Several crowd-pulling cast members had left by now, including the comedian, George Grossmith, soubrette, Jessie Bond and creator of roles such as the Pirate King and the Mikado, Richard Temple.

- Gilbert's plot was unusually laboured for him, but Sullivan's music still held some magic, even if not with quite the same consistency as before.

- The critics were merciless in revealing facts that were now clear to all: 'The rich vein, worked for so many years, is at last dangerously near exhaustion'.

- D'Oyly Carte obtained the contract to produce revivals of the operas with fortunate consequences for fans of Gilbert and Sullivan everywhere.

The D'Oyly Carte Opera Company

Richard D'Oyly Carte was unquestionably the driving force behind the business life of Gilbert and Sullivan and, under his guidance, original productions of Gilbert and Sullivan operas were often presented almost simultaneously in several different places. With *Sorcerer*, the nucleus of a regular company was formed and with each successive opera, names were added to a cast list that remained constant, give or take a name or two, for more than a decade. This type of loyalty would become a feature of a company that provided a niche for performers whose voices did not quite fit the grand opera mould, or who were truly actor/singers in the best tradition, or who, in some cases, would have been hard pressed to forge a solo career outside the unique world created by Gilbert and Sullivan. That apart, there have been some outstanding performers from the 1870s right up to the company's close on Saturday, 27 February 1982.

A main Second Company was formed in 1919, but this lasted only eight years and was disbanded in 1927.

Author's note

If you are looking for a style full of tunes that has neither the dense texture of some operas nor the candy-floss content of some musicals, I urge you to give Gilbert and Sullivan a try. There are plenty of works to choose from; I would start with *Pinafore*, *Pirates* or *The Mikado* and just take it from there. Proceed with caution … you may become addicted.

Self-test questions

1 Name the three people who brought the Savoy Operas to the attention of the world.

2 What was Gilbert's boyhood nickname?

3 What were Bab Ballads?

4 What was the name of Sullivan's first collaboration with F C Burnand?

5 How many operas were written jointly by Gilbert and Sullivan?

6 Which of the Savoy Operas is set in Japan?

7 Which Savoy Opera is also known as *The Merryman and his Maid*?

8 In which of the Savoy Operas does the Duke of Plaza-Toro appear?

9 Which is the last opera to be written jointly by Gilbert and Sullivan?

10 What was the name given to the opera company that performed these works?

3 | INTO THE TWENTIETH CENTURY

Overview

The beginning of the twentieth century was marked by an increase in international tension that would culminate in the tragedy of the First World War. Out of this human catastrophe came a radical social upheaval and with the many adjustments that were having to be made, music was just one way in which change could be reflected. Preferred themes in music theatre might be idealised and wholesome, or brash and exhilarating, but either way, they offered a much-needed escape from reality.

Women too, many of whom had entered the workplace for the first time during the labour shortage created by the First World War, represented a new spending force and helped to foster a demand for family entertainment.

Repression in the form of dictatorships that sprang up between the two great wars in Russia, Italy and Germany provoked rebellion in thought as well as action and this challenge to accepted traditions manifested itself in musical experimentation in the arenas of both classical and light music. Censorship in both Germany and Russia after 1930, however, prevented these two countries from participating for a time in any new musical departures. The severe economic downturn in the 1930s, coupled with the rise of fascism, saw a reappraisal of moral and social issues take centre stage and by the time the Second World War had ended in 1945, the next major shift was close at hand. This came about through the rapid development of radio and television, together with the vastly improved quality of recorded sound, and would result in a type of global culture quite different from the nationalism of the nineteenth century.

France

In the dying years of the nineteenth century, Edmond Audran (1840–1901) became yet another established figure in the world of French operetta. With works like *Les noces d'Olivette* (1879), *La cigale et la fourmi* (1886) and most notably *La mascotte* (1880), he achieved international renown. The story-line of *La mascotte* gives some idea of the way things were heading in the sophisticated yet sensual and often titillating world of French music theatre. A young girl whose job is to care for turkeys – yes, turkeys – brings good luck to her employer as long as she remains a virgin. Naturally, everyone in the kingdom, from the King down, wants to employ this virtuous maid, but her boyfriend has something other than luck on his mind. Will she? Won't she? That is the question... This type of rather suggestive material proved extremely popular all over Europe and productions to please the home market, rather than the world at large, also flourished. Change was coming, however, and in the capable hands of André Messager (1853–1929), French music theatre entered a gentler and altogether more refined era. With teachers who included Fauré and Saint-Saëns, Messager was a noted conductor as well as composer, pianist and administrator. His works *Veronique* (1898) and *Les P'tites Michu* were romantic rather than suggestive and proved as popular on the English-speaking stage as in France. In particular, the song 'Trot Here, Trot There' from *Veronique* became extremely and enduringly popular. In spite of these notable triumphs, the era of France as world leader in the arena of music theatre was rapidly being overtaken by the exciting developments in both Vienna and England, but before too long these countries too would come under the influence of an irresistible force; a force that was in itself a product of all these countries, for the United States of America owes its musical heritage to immigrants from all over the globe.

Vienna

The glorious epoch of Viennese music, encompassing composers like Strauss, von Suppé and Millocker, seemed to dim at the end of the nineteenth century. Several minor composers, such as the conductor and critic Richard Heuberger, made significant, if fleeting impressions with their output, but the German-speaking people were waiting for their own blockbuster to rival works like England's *H M S Pinafore*. They needn't have worried, for when it came, their contender, *Die lustige Witwe*, was every bit the triumph and every bit as long lived as anything produced by the rest of Europe.

Franz Lehár (1870–1948)

This Austro-Hungarian military band conductor became a prolific composer who scored bullseyes with a significant number of works. The serious opera *Kukuska* was a success and his 'Gold and Silver' waltz has remained a firm favourite to the present day. When Lehár left the army in 1902 he turned his hand to operetta and his first two, *Wiener Frauen* (1902) and *Der Rastelbinder* (1902), were so well received that he decided to devote himself to composing. Two failures followed, but undaunted, Lehár went on to compose one of the most popular works of all time, *Die lustige Witwe* (1905) known in English-speaking countries as *The Merry Widow*.

An incredible 30 more similar works flowed from his pen, although none of them achieved quite the same success as *The Merry Widow*. Lacking a strong 'follow-up' to the *Widow* caused Lehar's popularity to wane in the short-term and this decline was halted largely through the efforts of the Austrian-born British tenor, Richard Tauber. A fine conductor and outstanding operatic tenor, Tauber championed Lehár's music and, in turn, Lehár wrote several roles for him.

Today, extracts from Lehár's works are more usually heard than his operettas, although of these *The Merry Widow* is revived with great frequency and is not only a great pleasure to listen to, but also marks the revival of the Viennese operetta tradition in the twentieth century.

The Merry Widow (1905)

With a story based upon the French dramatist, Henri Meilhac's comedy *L'Attaché d'ambassade*, this operetta in three acts has a complicated plot that really doesn't matter, for the mood is clear enough and the music ravishing. A wealthy widow is wooed with the single intent of using her money to help the debt-stricken country of Pontevedria. Of course, nothing is really that simple and neither is the widow. Songs like 'Vilia' became 'hits' in their own right and the combination of comedy, pathos, rousing military strains and romance ensured an enthusiastic reception for this work that has never waned. Two more Lehár works worth investigating are *Der Graf von Luxemburg* (*The Count of Luxemburg*) (1909) and *Zigeurnerliebe* (*Gypsy Love*) (1910).

- Broadway revivals ran on to the 1940s, so it comes as no surprise to find that Hollywood would also become attracted to the theme.
- A silent film version of the story was released as early as 1925.
- In October 1934, the Hollywood movie version of *The Merry Widow* was premièred, featuring Maurice Chevalier, whose star was on the wane as far as playing young romantic leads was concerned, and the lovely Jeanette MacDonald, prior to her memorable partnership with Nelson Eddy.
- This 1934 film of *The Merry Widow* was the most expensive movie musical of its time and was the most expensive film to be produced by MGM since *Ben-Hur*.
- Some sophisticated new lyrics were written for this film by the gifted American lyricist, Lorenz Hart.
- Another film was made in 1952, starring Lana Turner and Fernando Lamas.

Oscar Straus (1870–1954)

This Austrian conductor and composer was an experienced writer for the cabaret circuit in Berlin around the beginning of the twentieth century. His first success on the music theatre stage was with *Ein Waltzertraum* (*A Waltz Dream*) (1907); a work that remains a favourite in Europe and especially in France, to the present day. The show that gave Straus his greatest success on the English-speaking stage was *The Chocolate Soldier*. Originally known as *Der Tapfere Soldat* (1908) or *The Brave Soldier*, this production was a hit in the United Kingdom and the United States as well as Europe. Of as many as 40 more works by Oscar Straus in a similar vein, none would achieve the heights of these two, although extracts are still enjoyed along with his many other compositions which include cabaret songs and film scores.

England

The Gaiety Theatre and George Edwardes

There was a time when not to have heard of, longed to be, or indeed longed to be *with* one of 'The Gaiety Girls' was inconceivable. The fact that the Gaiety Theatre achieved such a colourful reputation without the benefit of today's media hype, is due largely to one man, George Edwardes. Edwardes's past experience included managing productions for W S Gilbert and he had also been business manager at the Savoy Theatre for Richard D'Oyly Carte. By bringing the traditions of musical theatre up to date, Edwardes would, for a time, surpass even the D'Oyly Carte Opera Company's success. He achieved this by shunning the bawdy, sometimes banal vehicle of burlesque in his main productions, whilst retaining the glamour, and brought his shows closer in form to a musical play. This approach proved popular and Edwardes would be remembered as the 'father' of musical comedy.

His very first show of this sort, *In Town*, would appear to a modern audience to have been more of a variety show than a musical, but it was still a departure for the public and one they welcomed. Written by Jimmy Tanner, Frank Osmond and Adrian Ross (of whom more later) and starting life at The Prince of Wales Theatre before moving to the Gaiety, this production boasted a chorus of beautiful young women dressed in the latest fashions and, as word got around, they alone proved a great draw. Apart from this innovative attraction, a well-known comedian, Arthur Roberts, and the popular soprano, Florence St John, headed the cast of a show that clearly set a trend and enjoyed a run of 292 performances.

The success of this production provoked a great deal of competition and the audacious idea of bringing some of the more daring aspects of the burlesque, or music hall, into the theatre proper, took hold. 'Respectable' folk could now visit 'respectable' theatres and enjoy some previously forbidden fruits.

The writers behind these innovations were not, as might be supposed, merely modestly educated, enthusiastic young chancers, but the literary young turks of their day, like Arthur Ropes, winner of Cambridge University's most prestigious prize for poetry. As his alter ego, Adrian Ross, Arthur Ropes was not only co-creator of *In Town*, but also wrote the words for the colourfully titled *Morocco Bound* which, with its first part more closely resembling current notions of a musical and a second half that allowed its principals to perform their own act, tried to give the audience the best of both worlds. This 'variety musical' style proved extremely popular in England in the 1890s, but Edwardes was already thinking ahead. His next major presentation, *The Gaiety Girl*, with music by Sidney Jones and words by a younger lawyer who called himself Owen Hall, moved closer still to the modern notion of the musical. There was witty dialogue and more of a tale that ran throughout the production.

Ivan Caryll (1861–1921)

Born in Belgium, Ivan Caryll studied at the Liège Conservatoire and then became conductor at London's Lyric Theatre. He worked in both the United States and in England, and during the late-nineteenth and early-twentieth centuries completed a great many compositions for the stage. As a writer of hit shows he could be compared to a modern composer such as Andrew Lloyd Webber and there were further similarities in the fact that Caryll also had several productions running in the West End at one time. Not that Caryll's productions were reserved for the home market alone; his export of prime musical material provided yet another similarity to Lloyd Webber.

From the first of his songs for *Little Christopher Columbus* in the early 1890s, Caryll went on to contribute to numerous Gaiety hits and eventually, his was one of *the* names to dominate the billboards of London's West End. None of his productions was flimsy, yet their entertainment value did not suffer for that. Perhaps his most notable work was *The Duchess of Dantzic*, based on the French play, *Madame Sans-Gene* by Sardou. This habit of looking to France for creative inspiration would colour the output of writers for some time yet.

The Shop Girl (1894)

This show contained a wealth of tunes that could stand alone. One of the most popular of these had not been written by the show's main composers, Ivan Caryll or Lionel Monckton, nor even by Adrian Ross, who contributed more of the music, but by an Irish composer, Felix McGlennon. In those days, it was quite usual for a promising song to be brought into a show to give a leading player a 'show stopper'. Sung by the male juvenile lead, Seymour Hicks, 'Her Golden Hair was Hanging Down her Back' scored a huge hit and the show ran for more than 500 performances. A revival in the 1920s ran for more than 300 performances.

Lionel Monckton (1861–1924)

One of the most prolific composers of 'hit' songs and songs for shows generally, Lionel Monckton was born in London and studied law at Oxford. He began his professional life as a barrister, but his musical interests burgeoned and the step from part-time music critic to full-time composer was a short one, to the lasting good fortune of audiences everywhere.

His name ranks alongside that of Ivan Caryll and apart from his valuable contributions to many shows, Lionel Monckton's own productions and, in particular, *The Arcadians* (1909) and *The Quaker Girl* (1910), are outstanding.

The Geisha (1896)

With music by Sidney Jones and some songs by the 'soon to be hugely famous' Lionel Monckton and another composer, James Philip, play by Owen Hall and lyrics by Harry Greenbank, not to mention a star cast, including the debonair Hayden Coffin, this show was certain to succeed. Like many shows before or since, it introduced songs that live on long after anyone can recall where they came from. An example of this was Huntley Wright's comic song 'Chin Chin Chinaman Chop Chop Chop'.

In the role of Wun-hi, Wright was able through this one number to eclipse even the adored Coffin's performance and it was his infectious account of a Chinese man's woeful lot in Japan that got the nation's feet tapping. Soon the whole theatre-going world was singing along and the Daly's Theatre run of 760 performances was augmented by productions worldwide.

A Country Girl (1902)

With music by Lionel Monckton, book by James T Tanner and lyrics by Adrian Ross of *The Shop Girl* fame, *A Country Girl* also included some musical numbers by the popular songwriter, Paul Rubens, who would go on to achieve even more fame with, amongst others, his hit songs for the musical *Floradora*. Opening at Daly's Theatre, London in January 1902,

A Country Girl concerns the home-coming of Geoffrey Challoner, who is accompanied by a couple of exotic new pals. Challoner manfully resists the charms of Princess Mehelaneh and returns eventually to the arms of his 'country girl', the appropriately named Marjorie Joy. With the part of The Rajah of Bhong played by none other than Savoy Opera stalwart, Rutland Barrington, and Challoner played by Hayden Coffin, whose debonair good looks assured him of most of the worthwhile male leads on the West End stage at this time, success was assured.

During the 729 performances many revisions and improvements took place, enabling the show to score additional success in both New York, where it opened in 1902 and again in 1911 and Paris, where it was staged at L'Olympia in 1904.

Clinging to the past

There would always be an audience for the more straightforward musical tale, but the new century brought with it a hunger for novelty and a fresh approach. In spite of this, many of the older style shows did draw the crowds and some remain popular to the present day, or are remembered for a particular tune, character or star performer. Basil Hood and Arthur Sullivan's *The Rose of Persia* (1899) and *The Emerald Isle* (1901), completed by the English composer Sir Edward German, were notable in their day and another work by German, *Merrie England*, which he wrote in collaboration with Basil Hood, achieved considerable success. *Tom Jones* (1907), is another piece by German that deserves mention.

Another fashionable show was *Miss Hook of Holland* (1907) and this had a score by Paul Rubens, who also collaborated on the book with Austen Hurgon.

Lionel Monckton was far from idle and *The Country Girl* (1902) and *The Quaker Girl* boasted the same winning team of Adrian Ross writing lyrics, as well as the popular performer Hayden Coffin for the ladies, but it was *The Arcadians* in collaboration with lyricist Arthur Wimperis and starring Dan Rolyat that really boasted some winning tunes.

The Arcadians (1909)

Lionel Monckton had clearly tapped into public taste with his music and with this work he achieved one of his greatest triumphs. The plot was about as clear as mud, but nothing as trivial as a leaky plot was going to prevent audiences from flocking to hear the glorious tunes time and time again. Howard Talbot was responsible for some of the music and the lyrics were provided by Arthur Wimperis. Songs like 'The Pipes of Pan' and 'Arcady is Ever Young', combined with the strongest of casts, assured a triumphant run for this show. Amongst the cast, names like Florence Smithson, Phyllis Dare, Alfred Lister and Harry Welchman (who would go on to score an enormous personal triumph in the musical *Desert Song*), would help to make the reputation of the West End. Even stars of the stature of Cecily Courtneidge would later boast that they too had played a part at some time in a West End production of *The Arcadians*. Revivals, a silent film version and even a CD recording as recently as 1993, with some tracks by the original cast, ensures that Arcady, whilst ever young will never die.

The Quaker Girl (1910)

With lyrics by Adrian Ross and Percy Greenbank, Lionel Monckton's new hit followed hot on the heels of *The Arcadians*. A mere 18 months later in fact, this show, presented by George Edwardes, opened at the Adelphi Theatre in the West End. Based on a book by James T Tanner and Gertie Miller, the story centres around the young English Quaker girl, Prudence, who is tempted for a while by the high life in Paris. More glorious music, most notably the lovely 'Come, come to the ball' assured Lionel Monckton of another monster hit on both sides of the Atlantic. Revivals have continued to the present day, especially in amateur companies.

In spite of his huge success as a composer for music theatre, Lionel Monckton by no means held a monopoly on the most popular shows of this era.

Floradora (1911)

The music theatre production *Floradora* created a sensation after its opening at the Lyric Theatre, London, in November 1911. The show ran for 455 performances and the Floradora Girls, a sextette of lovelies who, with six handsome young gentlemen, provided an eye-catching enhancement to the tale, proved a huge draw. Their most popular song 'Tell me pretty maiden (are there any more like you at home?)' was *the* number one hit of its time. In New York *Floradora* achieved even more success, running for 553 performances at the New Casino Theater. Other musical items from the show, like 'The Silver Star of Love' and 'I Want to Be a Military Man' became enormously popular on both sides of the Atlantic and the show enjoyed a run of 549 nights on Broadway. Its songs became hits independent from the show, whilst its performers and in particular the Floradora Girls went on to become full-blown celebrities. The show revived to great acclaim in London in 1915 and 1931 and in New York in 1920. Offering the audience every type of visual delight, the title *Floradora* is taken from an exotic island and from the perfume manufactured there by a wealthy American, Cyrus Gilfain. The plot features his romantic entanglements and the setting moves from the island to a castle in Wales. To a deliciously named private investigator, Arthur Tweedlepunch, falls the daunting task of untangling the inevitable confusion and ensuring that everyone ends up with the right partner. Leslie Stuart, a popular song writer, wrote much of the music as well as some of the lyrics and other lyrics were provided by Ernest Boyd-Jones, Alfred Murray, Fred A Clement and Paul Rubens, who also wrote the songs 'Tact' and 'I've an Inkling'.

Chu Chin Chow (1916)

One of the longest-running British musicals of all time opened in the middle of the First World War. The public was desperate for a respite from the ghastly news brought to them daily by newspapers in page after page of closely typed names of the dead and this show's unprecedented triumph proved to be a piece that was right for the moment. It failed to sustain anything like the same level of interest after the war. With music by Frederic Norton and words by the Australian Oscar Asche, the glamorous production, starring the beautiful Josie Collins, provided the perfect venue for a soldier to take his mind off his next destination and so the show became a hallowed institution, rather than a real milestone in the history of music theatre.

The Maid of the Mountains (1917)

This backbone of every amateur company's repertoire was first staged at Daly's Theatre, London on 10 February 1917.

With Harold Fraser-Simpson handling most of the orchestration and James Tate providing most of the music, apart from some inclusions by songwriters F Clifford Harris, James W Tate and Arthur Valentine,

Frederick Lonsdale's swashbuckling book scored an even greater triumph in the war years than *Chu Chin Chow*.

The Maid of the Mountains' enduring popularity is almost certainly due to the strength of its music which includes such tunes as 'Bachelor Gay' and the ultimate in romantic melodies 'A Paradise for Two.'

Demand was growing, however, for something more in line with the faster pace of the new century and in the USA creative forces were poised to provide that in plenty.

Self-test questions

1 From which work by André Messager did the popular song 'Trot Here, Trot There' come?

2 Who wrote *The Merry Widow* and what was his nationality?

3 What was the name of the tenor who championed this composer's work?

4 What was the name of the most popular work to be written by the Austrian composer, Oscar Straus?

5 With which theatre was George Edwardes most closely associated?

6 What name did Arthur Ropes use when writing for the stage?

7 Name the show in which each of these composers was involved
   a Ivan Caryll; with a work based upon a French play.
   b Lionel Monckton; with a show containing the pipes of pan.

8 What was the name of the comic song made famous by Huntley Wright in *The Geisha*?

9 Can you name a hit song from the musical comedy *Floradora*?

10 From which hit show of 1917 did the romantic melody 'A Paradise For Two' come?

4 | LIGHTS ON FOR BROADWAY

Overview

In the United States with its young, thrusting economy, the demand for light entertainment grew apace during the nineteenth century, but clear divides along national lines still existed in society. Clinging to 'the old world' whilst forging the new was one of the main reasons why the United States lagged behind Europe in establishing its own style of music theatre. Foreign language productions were often imported and appealed in the main to a particular section of the population, but as the years passed and the various national groups intermingled, a need grew for a style that had resonance for all the people, rather than any single group.

The 1890s saw the first real shift in American public taste, when on 28 October 1887 the unveiling ceremony of the Statue of Liberty on Bedloe's Island was witnessed by more than a million people, for whom that moment encapsulated everything they expected to find in the New World; hope, freedom and unity.

Nineteenth century

To see how change set in, almost imperceptibly at first and then gathering pace as confidence in a national identity grew, it is necessary to look back a little further to one of the first 'home-grown' American exports, *The Doctor of Alcantara*. This show was produced in Boston in 1862. Described on the playbill as an opera bouffe, it was written by two new Americans; Benjamin Woolf, who wrote the libretto, was from London and Julius Eichberg, composer of the music, from Dusseldorf. Flagging up for the first time the exciting cross-cultural impulses that would make the American musical such a vibrant art form, it was still very much a first 'toe in the water'. Commercial pressures and the writers' understandable caution meant that *The Doctor of Alcantara* clung substantially to the Old European traditions. Nevertheless, it was staged successfully in both England and Australia following its premiere in Boston.

The Black Crook 1867

Scantily clad, good-looking girls, cavorting on stage in a 'near the knuckle' production is guaranteed to draw the crowds and *The Black Crook* promised all of these. It was in fact a musical entertainment where the story was immaterial, for what the audience had really come to see was at best spectacular effects and at worst titillating tableaux. Based loosely on the legend of Faust, there was original music, together with a few old chestnuts and some of the main performers had been imported from Europe just to add extra appeal.

The learning curve

Alongside this type of 'adults only' music theatre, musical hall, known as vaudeville in the USA, also thrived. Anything that involved France was expected to be saucy and so guaranteed to draw an audience, until 'refinement' arrived in the guise of Offenbach's *La Grande Duchesse de Gerolstein* in 1867. Here was the genuine article from France, delivered in an altogether more tasteful manner, but still rather too close to opera in style and so falling short of the growing requirement for true family entertainment. The following year, 1868, saw a burlesque troupe from the United Kingdom, headed by the beautiful Lydia Thompson and her chorus of 'British blondes' enjoying huge success with clever repartee and subtle innuendo, rather than vulgar display.

The lesson of entertainment with mass appeal – though as yet strictly for adults – based on good story-lines and strong music, was not lost on the melting pot of creative forces in the New World.

Evangeline (1874)

Edward E Rice achieved public acclaim with his show, *Evangeline* or *The Belle of Arcadia*. Based on Longfellow's poem, the setting is relocated from Arcadia to nineteenth-century Nova Scotia and tells the poignant story of Evangeline Bellefontaine's life-time's devotion to Gabriel Lajeunesse: The young love-birds are separated, leaving Evangeline with no alternative but to become a nun. They are only reunited when Gabriel lies dying of the plague. Described by the composer as a 'burlesque diversion', unlikely as it may seem, the show was given a humorous treatment, but more importantly was considered suitable entertainment for the whole family.

Rice went on to make his name by producing more shows like *Evangeline* that families could attend with complete confidence.

The star

In America home-grown star performers were beginning to emerge. One of the first was J K Emmet who played the part of Fritz in the musical *Fritz, Our Cousin German*. The significance of this musical comedy/ melodrama lies more in the success it engendered for J K Emmet than in anything else and Emmet would always be associated with the role. Another performer who became inseparably linked with a part was Henry Dixey who played Adonis in the show of the same name. Dixey's wit, comic timing and above all his good looks and manly physique – displayed to best advantage in a pair of body-hugging tights – assured him the kind of popularity enjoyed by pop stars today.

Harrigan and Hart

Harrigan and Hart were two more significant names in American music theatre in the 1880s and 1890s. Ned Harrigan in particular was famed for the sketches he wrote for himself and his partner, Tony Hart. In the main these were based on the 'old country' characteristics that made immigrant Americans so amusing to each other.

Harrigan transplanted the characters he created from show to show and one of the most popular of these was his irrepressible Irish-American character, Dan Mulligan. The music in Harrigan's productions was 'kept in the family' by his father-in-law, Dave Braham. Braham's expertise complimented Harrigan's own nose for a 'hit' song and some of these achieved lasting success, both in their home country and as far afield as London. The sketches, however, being comic observations on the idiosyncrasies of the new Americans, did not travel so well.

My Sweetheart (1884)

Several more American shows like *My Sweetheart*, starring the perennial teenager Minnie Palmer, opened in London in 1884 and travelled abroad successfully, but the world of music theatre still awaited a distinctive American work that would 'set the world alight'.

A Trip to Chinatown (1891)

The next landmark, to be launched by a man called Charles Hoyt in 1891, was called *A Trip to Chinatown*. With music by Percy Gaunt, the show's musical director, and set in Chinatown, San Francisco, this show enjoyed a successful tour of over a year before settling into a lengthy run of some 657 performances on Broadway. Although Hoyt and Gaunt were responsible for almost all of the music, the most enduring melody from this hugely popular show turned out to be by another composer called Charles K Harris. Harris's song was adopted by Hoyt and Gaunt simply because it suited a certain moment in the show to perfection, but it went on to become a worldwide hit. Forty years on, this song proved to have the same appeal for Jerome Kern, who, when there was a need for a period song in his musical *Show Boat*, chose Charles K Harris's 'After the Ball'.

Dawn of a new age

On the cusp of the twentieth century, America broke through with a work written by a journalist from New York, Charles Morton Stewart McLellan. Calling himself simply Hugh Morton for his work in the theatre, he had plenty of experience in both adapting and presenting works to suit the tastes of an American audience. The music was written by Gustave Kerker, a successful professional musician. *The Belle of New York* was cast very much in the mould of a variety musical, with a fairly cohesive plot in the first part and with plenty of opportunity for the various leading performers to show off their respective talents in the second. Perhaps most interesting of all is the fact that *The Belle of New York* had been devised with the express intention of appealing to an American audience, and by Hugh Morton, an experienced practitioner in the field. America, however, deemed it 'old-hat', whilst in Europe the response was quite different.

The Belle of New York (1897)

Now we might surmise that the Americans were waiting for a voice that expressed their unified society. To them *The Belle of New York* was just too European; too 'old country' in style. They may not have been quite sure what was needed to speak for the new Americans, but they'd know it when they heard it, and they hadn't heard it yet.

On the other side of the Atlantic the novelty of an American production, with its robust approach and insight into facets of life across the sea, proved irresistible.

From dragging its feet with a mere 56 performances on Broadway, *The Belle of New York* chalked up a resounding 657 performances in London's West End, as well as taking the theatre-going public by storm in all the major European capitals. It is still revived with considerable enthusiasm today, albeit mainly by amateur companies.

Briefly, the story concerns a ne'er do well young man from the provinces who fritters away his allowances on high living and pretty girls. On learning of this, his father disinherits him, leaving his fortune instead to a demure young girl in the Salvation Army, who is the daughter of his business partner. With plenty of wise-cracking and side-tracking by colourful minor characters along the way, the two young people are finally united, just as the two older men had wanted all along.

Black culture

The influence of black culture, already a force in cabaret, was beginning to make itself felt on the orthodox stage and although many shows with all-black casts played before an all-black audience in particular theatres, there was one show that had all the making of a hit that could transcend such arbitrary divisions.

In Dahomey (1903)

Book; Jesse A Shippe. Comedy; Bert Williams and George M Walker. Music; Will Marion Cook. Libretto; Paul Lawrence Dunbar.

Conceived around the successful black Vaudeville team of Williams and Walker, this show was written largely by black Americans for black Americans to perform, but it was believed to possess all the qualities necessary for commercial success in front of a wider audience. Perhaps this idea was before its time, but the tongue-in-cheek humour of a group of Boston swindlers, with their plan to bamboozle an elderly millionaire out of his fortune so they could take over Africa, failed to ignite Broadway. Once again, London embraced what America spurned and audiences were keen to experience the outstanding dance skills and vibrant spirit of the company, not to mention seeing for themselves the celebrated 'cake-walk'. In fact the most eagerly anticipated moment of all came when the audience was invited to judge the performers as they danced along to this syncopated forerunner of rag-time.

In Dahomey's triumph in London was topped-off with a command performance before the Royal family at Buckingham Palace.

***

Also in 1903 Gustave Luders, an American from Germany, caused a ripple of international as well as home-grown excitement with his productions, and most notable of these was *The Prince of Pilsen* which opened in New York in 1903, followed in 1904 by *The Sho-Gun*. Luders's star was soon on the wane, but Victor Herbert was more than ready to step into the breach. Then, in his turn, Herbert made a temporary bow to a Broadway newcomer from Prague, Rudolf Friml, who seized his opportunity when Victor Herbert refused to have anything more to do with writing a new part for his difficult star from *Naughty Marietta*, Emma Trentini.

Naughty Marietta (1910)

Music; Victor Herbert. Book and lyrics; Rida Johnson Young. Starring: Emma Trentini as Marietta d'Altena and Orville Harrold as Captain Dick Warrington.

Two young people searching for love find that they have been dreaming above the same love song 'Ah! Sweet Mystery of Life'.

Victor Herbert was one of the most important composers in American music theatre at this time but until film giants MGM transferred his musical *Naughty Marietta* to the screen more than 20 years after its Broadway opening, hardly anyone outside America was familiar with his music. With the inspired first-time casting of Jeanette MacDonald and Nelson Eddy, MGM scored a major triumph in 1910, catapulting Victor Herbert into the international limelight. Songs like the rousing 'Tramp, Tramp, Tramp the Boys Are Marching' and the passionate 'Ah! Sweet Mystery of Life', were sung, hummed and whistled by Herbert fans worldwide.

As if to prove that the old European traditions of operetta were not about to lay down and die, in 1911 Ivan Caryll came up with a peach of a show:

The Pink Lady (1911)

Book and lyrics; C M S McLellan. Music; Ivan Caryll.

Almost a play with music, *The Pink Lady* benefited from a strong, cohesive story-line and memorable tunes and the songs sprang naturally from the drama, very much in the style we have come to expect from a latter-day musical. Ivan Caryll had enjoyed success writing music for the London stage around the turn of the twentieth century and having emigrated to America in 1910, his collaboration with C M S McLellan, librettist of *The Belle of New York*, proved even more successful. Modelling their productions on the French world of music theatre, their second along these lines, *The Pink Lady*, was the most notable. With a well-told, flirtatious story that centres around a courtesan, exquisitely portrayed in the original production by Hazel Dawn and Caryll's glorious score, it is hardly surprising that this show became a great international hit, travelling as far afield as Australia and Hungary.

The Firefly (1912)

Rudolf Friml may have had the misfortune to inherit Herbert's temperamental leading lady from *Naughty Marietta*, a woman whose tantrums would eventually render her unemployable, but he wrote a score full of good tunes to Otto Harbach's libretto for *The Firefly*. The show opened at the Lyric Theater, New York on 2 December 1912 and ran for 120 performances, marking the start of an association between Friml and Harbach that would endure for ten productions.

Twenty-five years later, when his musical transferred to the screen, Friml added one of the most popular songs of all time in a film 'The Donkey Serenade'. The film of *The Firefly* is also interesting in that it starred Jeanette MacDonald with Allan Jones, rather than Nelson Eddy. Jones went on to land one of the leading roles in the film of Jerome Kern's musical *Show Boat*, showing himself to be a formidable rival for Eddy, but it was the partnership of Jeanette MacDonald and Nelson Eddy that possessed the type of indefinable chemistry the public wanted.

Friml went on to score another enormous success with the film version of his work *Rose-Marie*. After being given the 'Hollywood treatment' it bore little resemblance to his original musical, but *Rose-Marie* will endure forever, if only because it provided Jeanette MacDonald and Nelson Eddy with their signature tune 'The Indian Love Call'.

Alongside these romantic musical comedies, another more 'in-your-face' American style was flourishing under the inspired direction of one George M Cohan.

George M Cohan (1878–1942)

An American Jack of each and every theatrical trade; writer, composer, star performer, producer, etc., like Ned Harrigan before him, Cohan's inspiration could be found on his own door-step. With a background in Vaudeville, Cohan, together with his incredible catalogue of more than 500 songs and numerous full-scale musical productions, was larger than life. Numbers like 'Yankee Doodle Dandy' and 'Give My Regards to Broadway' from his show *Little Johnny Jones* encapsulated an era and conveyed a great sense of national pride to the American people more directly than any scholarly text. *Little Johnny Jones* was more of a play with songs and enjoyed only limited commercial success, although its strength of plot, combined with memorable music, presented within an unmistakably American framework, marks it out as a founding work of the great American musical. It was re-produced as a silent movie in 1923 and another film version appeared in 1930. The songs, however, became anthems and Cohan dominated Broadway right up to the start of the First World War. In 1917 his 'war' song 'Over There' plucked heart strings right up to the very highest in the land and he was awarded the Congressional medal for this song. In the year he died, Jimmy Cagney gave an unforgettable portrayal of Cohan in a film of his life, *Yankee Doodle Dandy*, winning Cagney an Academy Award and the 'best actor' award from the society of New York Drama Critics. This alerted a wider public to the exciting gifts of George M Cohan, the father of the American musical and it comes as no surprise to find his statue overlooking Times Square and theatre-land, a domain he made his own.

Al Jolson (c. 1885–1950)

The man who would be billed as 'America's Greatest Entertainer' was born in Lithuania and named Asa Yoelson. The family emigrated to the States, living first in Washington DC and then, when Asa's mother died and his father remarried, Asa followed his brother Hirsch, another promising performer, to New York.

The brothers changed their names to Harry and Al and formed a double act, although Al was forced to retire briefly from performance when his voice began to break. This was only a temporary set-back and he was soon back on stage whistling whilst Harry sang.

A trio formed by the brothers and Joe Palmer was short-lived and soon Al was working alone. He became famous (even before President Reagan) for the immortal phrase 'You ain't heard nothin' yet' and began to wow audiences coast to coast. His natural flamboyance made him a natural for the minstrel shows and it was here that he first became a major star. With a blacked-up face and rolling eyes, his stage persona could only cause offence today, but back then it brought Jolson's audience to their feet.

He made recordings as early as 1911 and became such a favourite that he frequently sent the cast off-stage, keeping the audience for himself. Legend has it that even the cast preferred to sit and watch him, rather than go home.

In 1918 he starred in the show *Sinbad* and brought Broadway audiences to their feet singing 'Swanee', 'Mammy' and 'Rockabye Your Baby With a Dixie Melody'. Many more shows followed and even a concert with the Boston symphony orchestra, which gives some idea of the esteem in which he was held. Eventually there would be a Jolson's 59th Street Theater and when songs like 'Toot Toot Tootsie' were added to his repertoire, it began to seem there were no more heights left for him to climb.

In 1916 he made a silent film – a risible concept for Jolson – and in 1929 *April Showers*, a short, experimental film, in which he sang three songs, captured by the new Vitaphone recording equipment. His real film breakthrough came in May 1926 when Jolson replaced the singer/comedian George Jessel in the film *The Jazz Singer*, possibly the most talked about musical ever committed to film. Jolson and one song in particular from this film would become 'joined at the hip', for who could imagine 'Mammy' emerging from the lips of any other man – and remember as you watch his histrionics that this was the man who had lost his own mother at an early age.

The film itself was not the masterpiece it was cracked up to be. Most of it was silent and crass subtitles appeared. It was riddled with clichés and 'corny' is far too kind a word, 'bad' is better, but *The Jazz Singer* does hint at a cohesive plot and one that is advanced by its music. Most importantly, it was a vehicle for Jolson, who makes no attempt to play anything but himself and this he accomplishes in no uncertain manner. The grating timbre of his voice, the emotional over-kill and facial grimaces seem at odds with sincerity and yet oddly this is what he conveys and with a power rarely equalled. 'Mother of Mine', 'Mammy', 'Dirty Hands, Dirty Face', 'Toot Toot Tootsie', 'Blue Skies' and 'Kol Nidre', are six songs that left early cinema audiences ecstatic … not for *The Jazz Singer*, but for Jolson. Jolson followed up *The Jazz Singer* with *The Singing Fool* (1928) and this, incredibly, brought him an even bigger hit with one of the first ever million sellers 'Sonny Boy'. It was his later films, however, like *Mammy* in 1930 and in the same year, *Big Boy*, that were said to most closely reflect his live performances.

Ruby Keeler was only one amongst four wives and he famously joined in with her from the stalls when she was starring in the musical *Show Girl*.

History records that she was not impressed, although they went on to make a film together in 1935, *Go into Your Dance*, in which Jolson sang 'About a Quarter to Nine'. Keeler's star was rising whilst Jolson's was sinking and the marriage ended in 1940, the year that Jolson returned to Broadway in the musical *Hold onto Your Hats*, but this was brought to a premature close when he contracted pneumonia.

On 7 December 1941, the Japanese attacked Pearl Harbor and Jolson immediately volunteered to entertain the troops. A whole new audience warmed to him and countless tours followed, but Jolson was now dogged by ill-health, culminating in an operation to remove part of his lung.

His career was boosted when a film of his life was released, starring Larry Parks. *The Jolson Story* (1946) was a huge hit and Jolson's records sales increased, he made radio appearances and guested on Bing Crosby's television show. Soon Jolson had his own television show and then the film *Jolson Sings Again* (1949) proved that the public were anything but tired of him and before long a new television series was under discussion. When the Korean war broke out, he was quick to volunteer his services again, but the work was too much for a man of fragile health and he died amongst friends from a heart attack. That night the lights went out on Broadway and Times Square came to a halt in tribute to a man whom even his rivals acknowledged to be the best.

What at first glance appears to have been a professional life built upon the grotesque, can be seen in reality to have been a professional life built upon a sincere desire to please and a totally selfless wish to serve an audience the best and only way Al Jolson knew how – with passion, integrity and unabashed emotion.

***

In 1923 America produced the first real challenge to Lehár's *Merry Widow*. Billed as a musical comedy in three acts and based on a book by Frank Mandel and Emil Nyitray called *My Lady Friends*, with a libretto by Irving Caesar, Otto Harbach and Frank Mandel and music by Vincent Youmans, *No, No, Nanette* would become an enduring worldwide hit.

No, No, Nanette (1923)

An out-of-town try-out at the Harris Theater, Chicago on 7 May 1923 was such a success that the show's touring company had scored an equally resounding triumph in London before a rather miffed Broadway got the chance to discover what all the fuss was about.

■ The show scarcely knew a break in performance and a revival in New York in 1971, starring Ruby Keeler, Helen Gallagher and Bobby Van, ran for two years.

■ Two film versions were made: in 1930, with Alexander Gray and Bernice Claire and again, most famously, in 1940, starring Anna Neagle and Victor Mature.

The legacy of *No, No, Nanette* is one of celebration and tragedy. The whole show and most especially songs like 'I Want to be Happy' and 'Tea for Two' would be celebrated across the world, whilst its young composer, Vincent Youmans, would be forced into premature retirement by tuberculosis in 1934, at the age of only 35.

Again using one of the world of music theatre's favourite themes of romantic confusion, the show bounces along with the characters fielding one misunderstanding after another with mixed success, but unfailing good humour. Girlfriends, wives and our 'hero', Jimmy Smith's ward, Nanette, all pitch up together in Atlantic City, where it falls to Jimmy's friend and lawyer, Billy, to sort out the muddle. Billy's efforts are not made any easier by the arrival of his own wife, Lucille, but on this sort of show, you can rest assured that something will turn up and by the end just about everyone is happy. 'Happy' certainly describes those first audiences and the show that had to stay put at its try-out venue in Chicago struck just the right chord everywhere it went, for with songs like 'Take A Little One Step', 'Tea for Two' and 'I Want to be Happy', *No, No, Nanette* had succeeded in capturing the spirit of an age.

Rose-Marie (1924)

Opening on 2 September 1924 at the Imperial Theater, Broadway, *Rose-Marie* was another collaboration between Rudolf Friml and Otto Harbach, with some additional music by Herbert Stothart and additional lyrics by Oscar Hammerstein II. Starring Mary Ellis and Dennis King, the show ran for 557 performances and boasted some memorable tunes including 'Rose-Marie' and the 'Indian Love Call'. Set in Canada, it tells the story of Rose-Marie La Flamme and her love for a Canadian Mountie, Jim Kenyon. The show was a huge success in London where it ran for more than two years and it also proved popular all over Europe. Revivals have continued on both the professional and amateur stage almost without interruption since the original production, and the film version with Jeanette MacDonald and Nelson Eddy was a classic of its time. Various other stars have become closely associated with the show including the singer David Whitfield on stage and Howard Keel in the 1954 film version in which he starred with Ann Blyth. The country singer Slim Whitman had a chart-topping hit for eleven weeks in 1955 with 'Rose-Marie', which he followed up with a second hit recording from the show, 'Indian Love Call'.

Sigmund Romberg (1887–1951)

Born in Hungary and a keen classical violinist, Romberg studied first to be an engineer and then served in the Hungarian army. Much of his time in the army was spent in Vienna and it was here, in his early twenties, that Romberg finally settled on music as his profession. Vienna was full of top class professional musicians, however, and America must have seemed to offer more opportunities to an aspiring young composer. Romberg moved to New York and his first show with lyrics by Harold Atteridge was called *The Whirl of the World* and opened in 1914. That same year, Romberg became an American citizen and more shows followed. In 1921 he drew upon his Viennese heritage and wrote *Blossom Time*, a show loosely based upon the life of Franz Schubert and containing what would become the extremely popular 'Song of Love'.

Success in this operetta-style musical convinced Romberg that he had discovered the perfect niche for his talents and in 1924 he followed *Blossom Time* with the enormously popular show, *The Student Prince*. Dorothy Donnelly wrote the lyrics for a wealth of glorious songs including 'Drinking Song', 'Deep In My Heart' and 'Serenade'. This major triumph was followed in 1926 by *The Desert Song* (see page 101) and *The New Moon* in 1928.

Although Romberg wrote more shows like *May Wine* (1935) and *Up in Central Park* (1945), and more lovely songs including 'When I Grow Too Old to Dream' with Oscar Hammerstein for the film *The Night is Young* (1934), he was fighting a hopeless battle against the rising tide of public taste for something fresh and new.

Anything that resembled the old-style operetta in which Sigmund Romberg excelled was considered old-fashioned, although time has proved his works to have the type of quality that can survive passing trends.

The New Moon (1928)

This show drew together some of the greatest forces in music theatre and not surprisingly went on to become a great success. The music was by Sigmund Romberg and the lyrics were by Oscar Hammerstein II, who had written the book together with Frank Mandel and Lawrence Schwab. No expense was spared and the original cast featured stars of the calibre of Robert Halliday and Evelyn Herbert in the Broadway production and Evelyn Laye and Howett Worster in the West End.

After a hesitant start in the American provinces, a thoroughly revised show opened at the Imperial Theater on 19 September 1928 and ran for more than 500 performances. The London production opened a year later and ran for 148 performances. Several revivals on both sides of the Atlantic enjoyed considerable success and there were two film versions: Grace Moore and Lawrence Tibbett took the leading roles in 1930 and, even more famously, Jeanette MacDonald and Nelson Eddy starred in the film version of 1940.

The songs were spectacularly good and included 'Softly, as in a Morning Sunrise', 'Lover Come Back to Me' and 'Stout-hearted Men'.

Self-test questions

1 Name one of the first American music theatre 'exports'.
2 Who wrote *Evangeline* and upon whose poem was the story loosely based?
3 J K Emmet was best known for playing a certain role. Which role and in which show?

4 Who was 'Dan Mulligan'?

5 For composing which song in particular was Charles K Harris famous?

6 What criticism did the American public level at *The Belle of New York*?

7 In which show did the celebrated 'cake walk' feature?

8 Can you name two famous musical numbers from *Naughty Marietta*, one involving a mystery and the other some marching?

9 Which American musical comedy is considered by some to rival Lehár's *Merry Widow*?

10 Name two outstanding shows written by Sigmund Romberg.

5 | AMERICA; THE GOLDEN YEARS – MOVING INTO THE 1930s

The arrival of 'the talkies' presented an exciting opportunity for the musical to transfer to, and in some cases to be written specifically for, this new medium.

A crop of gifted composers, the like of which the world of popular music had never known before, were gathering and rather than fighting to retain an individuality of background, they drew together the different strands, creating a musical era of unprecedented creativity. Increasingly, the racy jazz idiom came out of the cellar clubs and into mainstream shows, with its daring abandoned rhythms vying with a need for romance, that bounced between lust and wholesome with quirky charm. The use of all these diverse elements was utterly appropriate for a world that had known the terrible devastation of war, for if the horrors were to be obliterated for a time at least, escapism required a keener edge. Creativity prospered and continued to thrive throughout the Second World War, even leavening to some degree, at least from this great a distance in time, the blight of the Great Depression.

Climbing out of depression

The 1930s and 1940s

Between the woes of economic depression and the tragedy of the Second World War was an era of bread-lines, soup kitchens and unprecedented lawlessness.

The 1920s had been a time of great riches in the world of American music theatre with the emergence of the Gershwin brothers, Rodgers and Hart, Oscar Hammerstein II, Cole Porter, Irving Berkin and Jerome Kern, etc., but many of their works (with the notable exception of *Show Boat*, see page 159) had been a reflection of that giddy recovery following the first World War that helped dub those years the 'Roaring Twenties'.

Even leaving aside the effects of the Depression, the 1930s brought with them the realisation that everyday life could not continue with the same degree of optimism. Threats posed by Germany, Russia and Japan, civil war in Spain and unrest simmering in so many other countries cast an ever-darkening shadow and the Second World War 1939–45 would exact another terrible price from the peoples of the world.

Music theatre with its unique ability to provide relief, however temporary, from the growing tension possessed a powerful voice that crossed boundaries freely, and the awareness that an acid comment or witty observation could provide a telling commentary on world events was not lost upon the writers of the day.

Some musicals of the period remained as light-hearted and uplifting as ever, but increasingly, as the experiences of the war years took their toll, more audacious and contemporary themes were explored.

Film musicals and legends

The film musical added a vital ingredient to the increasing popularity of this art form. Now everyone had the opportunity to see top class productions, starring the very best performers in a succession of glamorous and entertaining stories set to music. Most of the stars had served long apprenticeships in live theatre before recording their skills for posterity and one of the most gifted of these was the dancer, singer and actor, Fred Astaire.

Fred Astaire (1899–1987)

One of the most elegant and seemingly effortless dancers of all time, Fred Astaire possessed little in the way of manly beauty, but everything in the way of grace and skill; an early screen test found him 'balding; can't act; can't sing; can dance a little'!

Although remembered chiefly for his dancing, Astaire was a fine actor and singer of his time and appeared in films with stars like Bing Crosby and Judy Garland. His on-film dance partners were numerous and included Leslie Caron, Cyd Charisse, Vera Ellen, Paulette Goddard, Rita Heyworth, Audrey Hepburn and Betty Hutton. In spite of this catalogue of beauties, his most successful partnership was with Ginger Rogers, another star whose personality and talent outshone mere physical perfection.

Fred Astaire was certainly a perfectionist, but he was highly regarded as a consummate professional whose artistry was presented with the minimum of fuss and whose manner, both on and off the screen, was direct and unassuming.

Gay Divorce (1932)

With lyrics and music by Cole Porter and featuring his glorious tune 'Night and Day', this was Fred Astaire's first outing as a star of a production without his sister, Adele, who retired in 1932. The show ran for 248 performances in New York

Flying Down To Rio (1933)

This saw the emergence of a major new force in musical film; Fred Astaire and Ginger Rogers.

Rogers had been consigned previously to small parts in films and usually the tarty types, since she wasn't a true beauty in the traditional leading lady mould.

In *Flying Down to Rio*, it became apparent that together, Astaire and Rogers possessed a special chemistry and although their part in the film was tiny, they made a huge impression.

The film is interesting in other ways, because numbers like 'Carioca' and 'Flying Down to Rio' provided something new for the audience. The choreography moved away from tightly scripted scenes, or pattern-like use of chorines. Instead some spectacular special effect sequences were introduced, where the girls appeared to be dancing on the wings of a plane – with one almost falling off, just to add a touch of realism!

The Wizard of Oz (Film version 1939; Show by the same name 1903)

The 1939 film, immortalised by Judy Garland and a supporting cast of understanding and endearing performers, had its Broadway predecessor and that show was adapted by the author L Frank Baum from his original novel *The Wonderful World of Oz* (1900).

Opening at the Majestic Theater, New York in January 1903, the re-named *Wizard of Oz* ran for 293 performances and was considered a great hit.

Anna Laughlin played Judy Garland's role of Dorothy and two popular comedians from the vaudeville stage, David Montgomery and Fred Stone, played the parts of Tin Woodman and The Scarecrow.

The score was quite different from the masterly piece created for the film by Harold Arlen and E Y (Yip) Harburg, being a hotch potch of pieces composed by a variety of composers. L Frank Baum was the main lyricist and A Baldwin Stone wrote much of the music.

The story must have been much the same, but those special characters that came to life in the film version with their unforgettable songs are what we remember today. The clever use of colour for all of Dorothy's dream sequence, after the black and white 'real life' opening, still creates a stunning visual impact and the effect on those early audiences can only be imagined.

Busby Berkeley

The man who to modern eyes seems to form a bridge between what a live musical *should* be and what a the film musical *could* be was undoubtedly Busby Berkeley. Though originally hired as a choreographer for the surprise hit film musical of 1930, *Whoopee!*, it was Berkeley's unique camera's eye view that introduced a totally new element to filmed dance in design and spectacle. There was nothing original about a large chorus line of beautiful girls, decked out in fantastic costumes and dancing with cutesy decorum, but what was new was the kaleidoscope-style camera technique. This transformed the chorus into abstract patterns that eddied and flowed across the screen, creating a visual feast for an audience that scarcely knew what to expect from the relatively new medium of film. Berkeley's dance designs for film became instantly identifiable and one of his most memorable settings was for the number 'Lullaby of Broadway' in the film *Gold Diggers of 1935*. (See *42nd Street*, page 150.)

Whoopee! was also noteworthy because of its star, Eddie Cantor, for whose wise-cracking, larger-than-life personality the Ziegfeld show of the same name had been a vehicle on Broadway. Now the exciting new film version confirmed him as one of the first major film stars, with a hundred thousand dollar fee and 10 per cent of the gross. The film was also brought to the attention of the world a pretty 13-year-old named Betty Grable.

Eddie Cantor (1892–1964)

The son of Russian immigrants, Edward Israel Iskowitz Cantor was born in New York and grew up to become one of the best loved gifted comedians and all-round entertainers America has ever produced. Nick-named 'Banjo Eyes' because of his mesmerising, rolling gaze, Cantor was orphaned while young and brought up by his grandmother. An instinctive entertainer, he busked in the streets before joining a group who blacked up their faces in the minstrel style for Gus Edward's show *Kid Cabaret* (1912). He served his apprenticeship in vaudeville, then progressed to Broadway, where he soon became a familiar face, starring in Florenz Ziegfeld's *Follies*. The show *Kid Boots* in 1923 introduced the public to two songs that would make Eddie Cantor famous around the world; 'Alabamy Bound' and 'If You Knew Susie'. In 1928, the Broadway show *Whoopee* based on a play by Owen Davis, was fashioned into the perfect vehicle for Cantor's talents and the film version in 1930, with added exclamation mark, *Whoopee!* (see page 75), featuring the song, 'Makin' Whoopee', established him as a top-earning Hollywood star. The film was destined for success, having every possible advantage, including the input of such masters of entertainment as Florenz Ziegfeld, Samuel Goldwyn, as producer, Busby Berkeley and the irrepressible Eddie Cantor as its star. Cantor was hit badly by plummeting share prices during the depression, but his career lost none of its impetus.

His films and radio broadcasts were numerous and the up-beat songs he became famous for were on everybody's lips. A few of the most popular include 'Yes Sir, That's My Baby', 'Dinah'', 'Keep Young and Beautiful', 'Ida, Sweet As Apple Cider', 'My Baby Just Cares For Me', 'You Must Have Been A Beautiful Baby'. He wrote song lyrics, too, as well as several books and was honoured by Hollywood in 1956 with an Oscar for his outstanding contribution to the world of entertainment.

Though she had a good ten years to go before she would become the Forces' pin-up, the young Grable made a sufficient impression on Sam Goldwyn, the film's producer, and Eddie Cantor himself, to feature in brief but significant moments throughout a film full of beautiful women. In the future she would lead the lovely Goldwyn Girls in a number of films, before becoming a major star in her own right. *Whoopee!* was a spectacular and expensive film for the time with a budget running at more than one and a half million dollars. It was filmed in technicolor and in 1930, with the depression running high, audiences needed entertaining like never before. Cantor gave them laughs in plenty and the film made him a star across the world.

Irving Berlin (1888–1989)

> *'Irving Berlin has no <u>place</u> in American music,*
> *he <u>is</u> American music ...'*
> Jerome Kern

The man who taught himself to play the piano became one of the greatest musicians America ever produced. With songs to inspire national pride, like the anthem 'God Bless America', proceeds of which he made over to the Boy Scouts and Girl Guides associations of America, or a song that grew to epitomise all that was good about the Christmas spirit, 'White Christmas', to one of the catchiest ragtime duets ever written, 'Play a Simple Melody'. Then there was 'Alexander's Ragtime Band' and 'A Pretty Girl is Like a Melody', which went on to become the signature tune of the Ziegfeld Follies, not to mention beauty contests ever after. The love songs he wrote for his second wife, Ellin Mackay, rank amongst his greatest and they include 'What'll I Do?' and 'Remember'.

The list of credits is formidable, and the number of shows and musical films in which Irving Berlin was involved make 'prolific' seem rather an inadequate word. Perhaps his greatest musical was *Annie Get Your Gun*, and with original cast members in London and New York including stars like Ethel Merman, Howard Keel, Betty Hutton and Dolores Gray, the 1940s were clearly nothing less than a golden age, in which Irving Berlin played an indispensable part.

His association with Fred Astaire and Ginger Rogers is part of Hollywood legend – who could forget the film *Top Hat* and the lovely song 'Cheek to Cheek'; then there was Bing Crosby and his recording of Berlin's 'White Christmas' that shot into the record books with an incredible 30 million sales, Marilyn Monroe's sizzling 'Heatwave' Judy Garland and Peter Lawford's endearing 'music hall' number 'We're a couple of Swells' from the film *Easter Parade*, not to mention Ronald Reagan and pals' rousing rendition of 'This is the Army, Mr Jones'.

Irving Berlin was not just one of the greatest songwriters of all time, he was the man you'd most want to write a song for you, because he knew instinctively what was needed to make each individual shine.

Born into a family of eight children, Israel Baline began life in Siberian Russia. When the pogroms reached their height, all but the two eldest Baline children fled to America where, in 1892, the family settled in New York's East Side. Moses Baline struggled to support his family the only way he knew how; teaching Hebrew, supervising Kosher meals and singing in the local synagogue. For a while his son Izzy joined Moses in the synagogue choir, but by the time Irving, as he would become known, was eight, Moses was dead. The young boy was left to sell newspapers or busk in the streets; anything to earn some money to feed the family. By the age of only 14, Irving had learned to make his own way, working as a song-plugger and even as a singing waiter. In fact his first real opportunity came from this last job, when a customer asked him to try his hand at writing a topical piece for his vaudeville act. Berlin chose to name the piece 'Dorando', a reference to the marathon runner who had been disqualified in the 1908 Olympic Games in London, because it was said the crowd's encouragement gave him an unfair advantage.

This was perhaps a little too abstruse for the vaudevillian, but not for the publisher, Ted Snyder, who was intrigued. Taken onto Snyder's staff, Berlin now earned the princely sum of 25 dollars a week.

1910 was a year that changed everything for him, elevating Irving Berlin to the ranks of most sought-after songwriters when his composition 'Alexander's Ragtime Band' captured the mood of the moment. Irresistibly foot-tapping though it was, this piece was not in the 'ragtime' style, but sufficiently connected by title at least with the new fashion to score a huge hit. Berlin did several authentic ragtime pieces, however, as well as the youth cult song of his day, 'Everybody's Doin' It'. Soon audiences everywhere were associating his name with the biggest fad of the decade, 'ragtime'.

In 1912 he married Dorothy Goetz, sister of a well-known producer on Broadway, Ray Goetz, but Dorothy died tragically from typhoid fever shortly after their honeymoon. Berlin's first Broadway score was completed by the time he was 26 and the show, *Watch Your Step*, contained the brilliantly contrived duet 'Play a Simple Melody'.

Drafted into the army during the First World War, Berlin was successful in persuading the hierarchy that he, and others like him, would be better employed entertaining the troops. He duly wrote a show, with an all-soldier cast, and named it after Yaphank, Long Island, where he was stationed. With songs like 'I Hate to Get Up in the Morning', *Yip Yip, Yaphank* scored a massive hit that not only assured full houses on Broadway, but repaid the army's top brass many times over financially for the faith they had placed in Berlin.

After the war, Berlin opened his own publishing company and also began his famous association with the Ziegfeld Follies. In 1921 he opened his own theatre, The Music Box, and so began the famous Music Box Revues. Soon he met the girl who, in the face of fierce parental disapproval, would become his second wife; Ellin Mackay. In defying her father, the wealthy businessman Clarence Mackay, Ellin assured the world of some of Berlin's most beautiful love songs.

The Depression hit Berlin both financially and psychologically and he declared himself to be 'dried up' in both respects. Fortunately, his many fans weren't left in denial for too long and 1932 witnessed his triumphant return, with better songs than ever, like the glorious 'How Deep is the Ocean'.

By 1935 Hollywood beckoned and Berlin began making the same kind of incalculable contribution to film music as he had already made to the stage.

For about the last 30 years of his life, Irving Berlin preferred to live quietly, modestly declining to receive the plaudits of either his fellow professionals, or the world at large.

Annie Get Your Gun (1946)

Annie Get Your Gun could scarcely fail with Irving Berlin's music and the experienced brother and sister team, Dorothy and Herbert Fields, handling the libretto. Based on a real-life love story from America's frontier days between members of Buffalo Bill's Wild West Show, Annie Oakley and Frank Butler, *Annie Get Your Gun* provides a real show-case for its leading lady and Ethel Merman, who starred in the original production, contributed in no small measure to the show's enormous success. Opening on 16 May 1946 at the Imperial Theater, New York, Merman's zingy performance, along with that of a strong cast, including Ray Middleton as Frank Butler and Marty Ray as Buffalo Bill, triumphed with songs outstanding even by Irving Berlin's standards and a production masterminded by Rodgers and Hammerstein. The show ran for 1,147 performances at the Imperial Theater and in 1947 the London production, starring Dolores Gray as Annie Oakley and Bill Johnson as Frank, broke even these records. In 1957 the show toured America with Mary Martin in the leading role and in 1966 Ethel Merman recreated her role on Broadway. By now the show included another Berlin song, 'An Old-Fashioned Wedding', and both song and show were rapturously received.

Berlin's songs from this, his masterpiece, are ingrained in the minds of anyone who loves the music of this era. There are so many, and each one is brilliant: 'There's No Business Like Showbusiness', 'I Got the Sun in the Morning', 'Doin' What Comes Natur'lly', 'They Say it's Wonderful', 'You Can't Get a Man With a Gun', 'The Girl That I Marry', 'I Got Lost in his Arms' and 'Anything You Can Do'.

A film version starring Howard Keel and Betty Hutton was released in 1950 and both professional and amateur revivals of the show occur frequently to the present day.

Cole Porter (1891–1964)

Yet one more outstanding figure in a remarkable era for American music, Cole Porter was born into a wealthy family and studied at both Yale and Harvard. His tutors at Harvard noted that he seemed less than enthusiastic about his law studies and advised the young man to concentrate on his first love, music, and this he did with conspicuous success. His vast catalogue of songs, for which he wrote both the words and the music, range from sophisticated word-plays like 'Its De-Lovely', the superlatives-song 'You're the Top', luscious love songs like 'In the Still of the Night' and the one song that is hard to imagine any other singer attempting once you have heard Frank Sinatra's version, 'I've Got You Under My Skin'.

Success didn't come immediately for the young Cole Porter and although some of his songs were used in Broadway productions even while he was still in college, his first attempt at a full score, *See America First* (1916), closed almost immediately. More attempts followed, but as would so often happen in the future, it was a Cole Porter song, rather than the show itself, that endured. This was the case in 1928 when 'Let's Do It' created a sensation in the show *Paris*.

The 1930s confirmed Cole Porter as a leading figure in American music theatre. His stage show *Anything Goes*, which famously conferred stardom on the flamboyant Ethel Merman (see page 225), opened on Broadway in 1934, and has been revived constantly. In 1936 there was a film version, starring Bing Crosby and Ethel Merman. The hit songs from this show alone are numerous: 'Anything Goes', 'You're the Top', 'I Get a Kick Out of You', 'All Through the Night', 'The Gypsy in Me', 'Blow Gabriel Blow'...

It was only natural that Cole Porter should be lured to Hollywood, although his stage work continued unabated.

In 1937 he suffered a serious injury following a riding accident which, after many years of pain, would result in amputation of his right leg in 1958. He never allowed this to stem the flow of truly wonderful music and we are all the richer for melodies like 'Ev'ry Time We Say Goodbye', 'Do I Love You?' and from his major Broadway hit *Kiss Me Kate*, 'Wunderbar', 'So In Love', 'Always True To You In My Fashion'. His music for the films *High Society* in 1956 and *Les Girls* the following year served to confirm the fact that Cole Porter was the consummate creator of songs far above the ordinary, since both the words and music were the handiwork of the same extraordinary man.

Anything Goes (1934)

At first glance it seems odd that at the eleventh hour the original book for *Anything Goes*, by P G Wodehouse and Guy Bolton, was mostly dumped in favour of a revised story-line by Howard Lindsey and Russell Crouse. These desperate measures were not taken simply to accommodate the tastes of a Broadway audience – a matter which could have been dealt with at a much earlier time – but to take account of a far more serious event. To base a musical production on the humorous consequences of a ship-wreck had been the brain-child of the Broadway producer, Vinton Freedway. He wasn't to know that only weeks before the opening, the *S S Morrow Castle* would go down. With time running out and expense running high, it was decided that the bones of the piece must be kept. The amorous high jinx would now take place during a crossing on-board a transatlantic liner and the new plot and dialogue was quickly learned and simply fitted around the existing music, sets, casts and costumes. The choice of new writers for the bulk of the re-writes was not a poor reflection on Wodehouse (whose last work it would be for the music theatre), for he was already engaged on other work. Guy Bolton had been rushed into hospital with acute appendicitis and so the urgent transformation fell to Howard Lindsey, who would also produce the show, and to another writer, Russel Crouse. Against all the odds the show opened on time, with just the sort of hype and glamour America needed to celebrate signs that the country was beginning to climb out of the Depression. Ethel Merman, in particular, who was on the books of Vinton Freedway and for whom *Anything Goes* was the perfect vehicle, seemed to personify the nation's optimism. Her co-stars were William Gaxton and Bettina Hall.

Songs like 'You're the Top', 'I Get a Kick Out of You', 'Blow Gabriel Blow', and 'Anything Goes' guaranteed a triumphant opening on 21 November 1934 and the show ran for 420 performances at the Alvin Theater. On 14 June the following year, *Anything Goes* opened in London at the Palace Theatre, where it was produced by C B Cochran.

In 1936 a black and white film version starred Bing Crosby, who would also star in the Technicolor re-make some 20 years later. Theatre revivals continue to the present day and one in particular, at the Lincoln Centre Theatre in 1987, was based on a new book by Timothy Crouse and John Weidman and brought in some more Cole Porter songs. Starring Patti LuPone in the part of Reno, this production ran for almost 800 performances and won three Tony awards.

Kiss Me Kate (1948)

William Shakespeare's play *The Taming of the Shrew* has surely never been presented in such an entertaining form as this 'play within a play'. In the adaption of Bella and Sam Spewack's book, action shifts between Shakespeare's Padua and a theatre company in Baltimore that has its own rivalries and love affairs to contend with. No one would deny that Shakespeare is a hard act to follow, but Cole Porter with his instinctive wit and impeccable timing proved equal to the task. His words and music not only enhanced the tale, but brought it bang up to date.

Broadway awaited the opening of *Kiss Me Kate* with the sort of enthusiasm reserved for a new Lloyd Webber, or Schoenberg and Boublil musical today. It opened at the New Century Theater on Broadway on 30 December 1948 and the public's confidence was amply rewarded by a veritable treasure trove of Cole Porter instant classics: 'Another Openin', Another Show', 'We Open In Venice', 'I Hate Men'.

Enjoying a phenomenal run of more than 1,000 performances, and winning a Tony award in the best musical category, *Kiss Me Kate* transferred to London with most of the original cast intact, including Alfred Drake playing one half of the battling duo, 'Fred/Petruchio' and Patricia Morison as 'Lilli/Kate', the other half. A triumphant run of over 500 performances at the London Coliseum resulted and successful revivals continued to thrive, most notably in London's West End in 1970, with Emil Belcourt and Ann Howard. There would be more revivals, in London in 1987 and New York in 1956 and 1965, as well as numerous performances in other major centres across the world.

The version that carried this marvellous amalgam of classic genius old and new to the widest possible audience was of course the 1953 film, starring the inimitable Howard Keel and a feisty Kathryn Grayson in the roles of Fred and Lilli. With the addition of Ann Miller's spectacular dancing and a new song to the production, 'From This Moment On', *Kiss Me Kate* began a whole new life and one that remains as vigorous and entertaining to a modern audience as it did to the film-goers of the 1950s.

George Gershwin (1898–1937)

The piano in the Gershwin household had been bought for George's older brother, Ira, but fate gave George the lion's share of musical talent, whilst Ira's gift lay with words. At 14, George was a professional musician, working mainly as a song-plugger and perfecting his technique, both as pianist and composer. He was soon attracting attention at the highest levels and in 1917 he was hired as a rehearsal pianist for a Broadway show written by Jerome Kern. His songs continued to be published, using either his brother Ira as lyricist, or other writers , including Irving Caesar. 'Swanee', one of Gershwin's most successful numbers, was written with Caesar and although a hit in the first instance for the Arthur Prior Band, this number would become identified with Al Jolson, following his unforgettable performance in the 1918 show *Sinbad*.

George, with his brother Ira and Buddy De Silva as lyricists, wrote the music for the *George White Scandals of 1919* and introduced the world of music theatre to classics like 'I'll Build a Stairway to Paradise'. Countless hits followed, mostly in partnership with Ira, and then Gershwin showed himself capable of bringing innovation and jazz idioms closer to the classical music world with 'Rhapsody in Blue' composed for Paul Whiteman. There would be more classical pieces, including 'Concerto in F', 'An American in Paris', 'Second Rhapsody' and eventually Gershwin's folk opera *Porgy and Bess* (1935) (see *Teach Yourself Opera*).

Gershwin wrote more than 20 complete scores for music theatre, most in collaboration with his brother, Ira, and these include: *Oh, Kay!* (1926); *Funny Face* (1927) starring Fred Astaire with his sister, Adele; *Rosalie* in 1928, with some contributions from the writer P G Wodehouse and the composer, Sigmund Romberg; *Strike up The Band* in 1930 and in the same year, *Girl Crazy*, starring Ethel Merman singing, 'I got Rhythm' and Ginger Rogers 'But Not For Me'; not forgetting the lovely duet 'Embraceable You'. Having conquered Broadway with a dazzling succession of hits, the Gershwin brothers took their talents to Hollywood in 1936 where they continued their amazing run of success with songs like 'Let's Call the Whole Thing Off', 'They Can't Take That Away From Me' and 'Nice Work If You Can Get It'.

In spite of the decline he must have endured from the effects of a brain tumour, Gershwin's last compositions were amongst his best. These include 'Love Walked In' and 'Love is Here to Stay', the songs he wrote for the film *The Goldwyn Follies* (1937).

At the very pinnacle of success, and only in his late thirties, George Gershwin died leaving a catalogue of music of such diversity, quality and sheer volume, it hardly seems possible that it was completed by one man in such a brief life.

Gershwin's ability to bring together all the strands of his multicultured nation allowed him to speak for the American people in the language of music and with a fluency that has never been surpassed.

Rodgers (1902–79) and Hart (1895–1943)

Richard Rodgers was born on Long Island, New York and whilst still a teenager he began composing songs that were good enough for a family friend to introduce him to the already established Lorenz Hart.

The two gifted young men struck up a partnership and in 1925 they wrote 'Manhattan' and 'Sentimental Me' for the *Garrick Gaieties* revue. That same year they produced their first full-length show, *Dearest Enemy* and the following year another show entitled *The Girl Friend*.

Hit songs were flowing and these included 'Here in My Arms', 'Mountain Greenery', 'Thou Swell','With a Song in My Heart', 'Lover' and 'The Most Beautiful Girl in the World'. Some of their best-loved numbers include 'The Lady is a Tramp', 'Falling in Love with Love', 'This Can't Be Love' and 'Bewitched, Bothered and Bewildered'.

The partnership broke up in 1942 when Hart, whose nervous personality was adversely affected by his increasing reliance on alcohol, announced his decision to retire from professional life. His lyrics endure and serve as a fitting tribute to one of the greatest wordsmiths America has ever produced.

The partnership of Rodgers and Hart may never have achieved the same celebrity as the partnership between Rodgers and Hammerstein, but their musical *Pal Joey* in particular is a significant milestone in that it broke with tradition; imposing gritty realism where there had mostly been escapism. The value of their contribution to the world of popular song is, of course, incalculable.

Pal Joey (1940)

A musical by Rodgers and Hart opening on Christmas day 1940 might inspire certain expectations, but these would be swiftly dispelled. In an art form where escapism ruled, *Pal Joey* was a new and gritty departure. The score was as rich as usual, but now songs like 'Bewitched, Bothered and Bewildered', 'I Could Write A Book' and 'The Flower Garden of My Heart', helped to advance the story, preceding Bernstein's masterpiece *West Side Story* by 17 years in this respect.

Far from being a family-style Christmas show, *Pal Joey* was an adult drama played out to music. The libretto, written by John O'Hara, was based on his own book of short stories and the characters confronted issues like sex and blackmail, albeit with a good dose of humour thrown in. This new format took time to find favour, although the songs became favourites almost immediately.

The show ran for 374 performances at the Ethel Barrymore Theater in New York, with a cast including Gene Kelly, Leila Ernst, June Havoc, Van Johnson and Vivienne Segal. A revival in 1952, when perhaps the world was better prepared for this original approach, ran for 542 performances, winning Tonys for Helen Gallagher as best actress, Robert Alton the choreographer and for the musical director, Max Meth. The cast also included Harold Land, Vivienne Segal and Elaine Stritch. There have been several successful revivals over the years and a film version was released in 1957, starring Rita Hayworth, Kim Novak and Frank Sinatra.

***

In 1944 another musical proved that although realism provided a refreshing change from time to time, escapism was still very much in demand and especially so during the war years. Closer to the old style operetta in form and requiring performers who could sing as well as they could act, *Song of Norway* secured a lasting place in the hearts of the public.

Song of Norway (1944)

This was the first show in which George Forrest and Robert Wright adapted music by classical composers to suit the format of a music theatre production. In this case they used the music of the Norwegian composer Edvard Grieg, and the book by Milton Lazarus, based on a play by Homer Curran, takes the essence of Grieg's life and spins some fanciful tales around it. The show opened on Broadway on 21 August 1944 at the Imperial Theater, after previews presented by the opera companies of both San Francisco and Los Angeles. The role of Grieg was played by Lawrence Brooks, the prima donna Louisa Giovanni by Irra Petina and the composer's friend, Rikard Nordraak, by Robert Shafer. A run of 860 performances made the show one of wartime's biggest hits. The 1946 London production ran for over a year and a film version was released in 1970, starring Florence Henderson and Toralv Maurstad. *Song of Norway* is in parts a vocally demanding piece, but revivals continue and there was a good recording made of the complete score in 1992, featuring Valerie Masterson (see *Teach Yourself Opera*), Diana Montague, David Rendall and Donald Maxwell.

Lerner and Loewe

Many of the most famous creative partnerships endured through decades of change in both the social and musical sense. One of these was the association between Alan J Lerner and Frederick Loewe, who produced works of great popular and commercial worth over a number of years. The two men came from different backgrounds, but complemented each other perfectly.

Alan J Lerner (1918–88) was born in New York and studied at the English public school, Bedales, and the renowned Julliard School of Music in New York. He went on to take a Bachelor of Science Degree at Harvard and his early work as a journalist and radio script-writer led in turn to his memorable collaborations, primarily with Frederick Loewe, on musicals like *Brigadoon* (1947), *Paint Your Wagon* (1951), *My Fair Lady* (1956), *Gigi* (1958) and *Camelot* (1960). He worked with Kurt Weill (see *Teach Yourself Opera*) on the musical production *Love Life* (1948) and with Burton Lane on *Royal Wedding* (1951), *On a Clear Day You Can See Forever* (1965) and *Carmelina* (1979). In 1951 he wrote the screen play for brothers George and Ira Gershwin's film *An American in Paris*. Other notable partnerships included those with André Previn, with whom he wrote *Coco* (1969) and Leonard Bernstein, *1600 Pennsylvania Avenue* (1976). His last musical, *Dance a Little Closer* (1983), starred his eighth wife, Liz Robertson, but closed after the opening night.

If Alan Lerner was the respected establishment figure, then **Frederick Loewe** (1901–88) was the buccaneer. Born in Vienna, his musical pedigree was impeccable. His father sang professionally and Loewe made his own concert appearances as a pianist with orchestras of the calibre of the Berlin Symphony. It was whilst accompanying his father on a tour of the United States that fate took a hand, when quite unexpectedly and tragically, Loewe's father died, leaving the young man to fend for himself as best he could.

It wasn't so easy to break into the American music scene at the type of level Loewe was accustomed to, but he took the opportunity to turn adversity into adventure, travelling around the States, picking up employment wherever and whenever he could. This period saw him working as a cowhand, prospecting for precious metals and playing the piano in bars and restaurants. By the 1930s, he was back in New York writing songs, but these failed to make any impression, possibly because they were considered too old-fashioned for his newly adopted homeland.

In 1942, his collaboration with Lerner began, but they would wait until 1947 for their first major hit, *Brigadoon*.

Brigadoon (1947)

A fanciful tale, *Brigadoon* is set in an idealised Scottish village that exists for a single day each century. Two American tourists, Tommy and Jeff, are unwittingly drawn into this mystical world and Tommy falls in love with one of the villagers, Fiona MacLaren. Tommy returns home to end his relationship with his American fiancée, knowing that he must return to Scotland to find Fiona. His love is so strong that the 'once a century' rule is broken, allowing him to re-enter Brigadoon and claim his bride. There are many lovely atmospheric songs in this musical, and their apparently Scottish flavour do credit to their Viennese and American creators. 'Almost Like Being in Love' is certainly the best known and could carry any show on its own, but 'The Heather on the Hill', 'I'll Go Home with Bonny Jean' and 'Waitin' For My Dearie' are amongst those that convey a real sense of Scotland, albeit a rather idealised view. *Brigadoon* opened at the Ziegfeld Theater, Broadway on 13 March 1947 and ran for almost 600 performances. Unfortunately, another show with a supernatural theme, *Finian's Rainbow* by Yip Harburg and Burton Lane, had opened a couple of months earlier (10 January 1947), stealing some of *Brigadoon*'s thunder. *Finian's Rainbow* boasted the soon to be regarded as classic number 'Old Devil Moon' and would outsell *Brigadoon* on Broadway. In 1949, however, London took *Brigadoon* to its heart and the show ran for almost 700 performances at His Majesty's Theatre. Revivals followed right up to recent times and like *Finian's Rainbow*, a film version of *Brigadoon* was made. The film of *Finian's Rainbow* was made in 1968 and starred Fred Astaire, Petula Clark and Tommy Steele. The film version of *Brigadoon* starred Gene Kelly and Cyd Charisse and was made in 1954.

Self-test questions

1 In which film did Fred Astaire first appear in a starring role?
2 Who was billed as 'America's greatest entertainer'?
3 What was the name of Irving Berlin's most famous musical?
4 Whose star status was confirmed by her performances in the Cole Porter musical *Anything Goes*?
5 What was the name given to the Cole Porter musical based on Shakespeare's play *The Taming of the Shrew*?
6 Name the musical and composer from which the song 'You're the Top' originates?

7 Who was Richard Rodgers's main partner before Oscar Hammerstein II?

8 From which of their musicals did the song 'Bewitched, Bothered and Bewildered' come from?

9 Upon which classical composer's music was the show *Song of Norway* based?

10 Who wrote 'I Got Rhythm'?

6 | MEANWHILE IN EUROPE

Charles B Cochran (1872–1951)

The master showman of the London Theatre in the 1920s and 1930s, Cochran was not flattered by the sobriquet 'The English Ziegfeld', for he considered himself, and justifiably, to be a power in his own right. There were many similarities, even to the 'Ziegfeld Girls', neatly countered by the far more refined sounding, 'Mr Cochran's Young Ladies', but Cochran's area of theatrical expertise covered a far more diverse field than Ziegfeld's. From 'Flea Circus' to the Royal Albert Hall, Charles B Cochran had a finger in every pie in entertainment's larder. One of his greatest gifts was his ability to spot a future star and this knack enabled him to bring names like John Mills, Anna Neagle, Jessie Matthews, Larry Adler, Hermione Baddeley, Gertrude Lawrence, Alice Delysia, Elizabeth Welch, Beatrice Lillie and Douglas Byng to the attention of the world. From the start of their first collaboration on the revue *On with the Dance* in 1925, Cochran's association with Noel Coward brought great credit to them both. Cochran went on to produce some of Coward's most outstanding works, although they fell out over royalty payments in 1934. Both men went on to further their careers without each other and Cochran scored countless hits with productions like *Half-Past Eight*, *Phi-Phi*, *Music Box Revue*, *Anything Goes* and *Bless The Bride*, not to mention his own lavish spectaculars, the *Cochran Revues*.

Noel Coward (1899–1973)

> *'I was born into a generation that took light music seriously.'*
> Noel Coward

A contemporary of Irving Berlin, Noel Coward appeared to be the quintessence of English aristocracy, but he was born in Teddington,

Middlesex, an undistinguished part of England, in comfortable, through far from palatial circumstances.

Coward set his sights high and his unique talent allowed him to achieve much, culminating in a knighthood in 1970 for his services to the theatre. His skills as a word-smith compared with the great Gilbert, but Coward could also write the most memorable tunes. Drawing skills enabled him to record his impressions on paper, just as Gilbert had done so often before him, and one of the very best examples of this appears on the opening night souvenir programme for his 1961 production *Sail Away*. His illustration shows the choreographer, Joe Layton, in rehearsal with the dancers.

Coward was also an accomplished actor, the best man in many instances to take a leading role in one of his own works, and he frequently produced and directed these too. His skills on the piano were as idiosyncratic as Berlin's but in Coward's case, he preferred to play in the key of E flat and lamented the poor performance of his left hand which never quite mastered moving in a different scheme to the right. He also declared that, 'keys with sharps frighten me to death'.

Coward never subscribed to some airy dismissals of Berlin and referred to him as 'that superlative genius of light music', saying 'conservative musical opinion was shocked and horrified by such alien noises and, instead of saluting the new order and welcoming the new vitality, turned up its patrician nose and retired from the arena.'

Coward never lost confidence in his own ideas for a moment and set about establishing a unique style at a rapid, though to all outward appearances apparently languid, pace. His theatrical career had begun as a child actor and in 1918 he appeared in W D Griffith's film, *Hearts of the World*, starring the Gish sisters, Dorothy and Lillian. Just a few years later he progressed to writing plays and songs and was only in his early twenties when his revue *London Calling!* (1923) caused a sensation on the West End stage. This show starred Gertrude Lawrence, whose verve and charm added so greatly to the parts she played and who had met Coward when he was a young boy and she, barely a teenager, at the Italia Conti stage school in London.

In *London Calling!*, they danced and sang together and 'You Were Meant For Me', had been choreographed for them by Fred Astaire. A song that has not stood the test of time so well, 'Parisian Parrot', was another great hit for Gertrude Lawrence.

In 1924, Coward revealed the full extent of the versatility that would mark him out as one of the leading figures of the British theatre. His play, *The Vortex*, opened the door wide on the subject of drug addiction, causing a sensation nationally and later on Broadway. He wrote several other plays, including *Hay Fever*, *Fallen Angel* and *Easy Virtue*. These were elegant, intimate pieces, in stark contrast to the declamatory style of theatre that had gone before and were sometimes laced with a pithy wit that revealed the flaws lurking beneath a character's veneer of apparent sophistication.

Not all his works by any means were centred around lofty folk and their complicated lives and his writing for revues continued apace. Then in the 1920s and 1930s his music peaked gloriously with stage productions like *Bitter Sweet*, which opened in London in 1921; a film version was released in 1940.

Set in late-nineteenth-century Vienna and with much of the story told in flashbacks, this was romantic musical comedy at its best and contains some ravishing tunes, including the ever poignant, 'I'll See You Again'. More works from this golden era include *Cavalcade*, which was made into a film in 1933, *Private Lives; Words and Music*, from which came the evocative song 'Mad About the Boy'; *Hands Across the Sea*; *Design for Living*; *Conversation Piece*; *Fumed Oak*; *Tonight at Eight-Thirty*; *Present Laughter* and *This Happy Breed*. His play with music, *Blithe Spirit*, written and produced towards the end of the Second World War, captured the mood of the moment to perfection and the song 'London Pride' in particular struck a chord with a world that was slowly emerging from the pain of too much loss. Coward's screenplay and music for the David Lean film *In Which We Serve* (1942), which he co-directed with Lean as well as taking one of the leading roles, again had a theme that underlined the resilience of the human spirit and for this he received an Academy award. Films of some of his stage works followed, but by the 1950s a wind of change was blowing and Coward's plays with music were beginning to be regarded as old fashioned. *Relative Values* (1951) had some success, but nothing like the level of popular acclaim his earlier works had achieved. Never at a loss, Coward turned to cabaret and delighted audiences, both with his wonderful music and witty banter. Appearances followed at the Café de Paris and then, improbably enough, at the Desert Inn, Las Vegas, where his intimate and worldly act transferred itself seamlessly and with enormous success to that vast brashness within the Nevada Desert. A live album was produced, *Noel Coward at Las Vegas*, celebrating this extraordinary triumph.

Television appearances followed and, with this upsurge in interest, more stage productions ensued in the 1960s like *Nude With Violin* and *Just a Song At Twilight*. Amongst the exciting performers who brought Coward's work to life, Beatrice Lillie immortalised, 'I Went to a Marvellous Party' (from *Set To Music*, 1939), José Ferrer gave the acting profession a model upon which the loveable roué would always be based after he appeared in *The Girl Who Came To Supper* (1963). This also starred Florence Henderson and the ebullient Tessie O'Shea, who didn't just sing, 'London', she *was* London. Elaine Stritch's shrewdly timed barbs revealed a sense of theatre that very nearly matched the Master's own and numerous Coward songs delighted the world including 'We Must All Be Very Kind to Aunty Jessie' (1938), and 'Don't Put Your Daughter on the Stage, Mrs Worthington' (1935).

Coward's wit may have been biting, but it was never undeserved, nor did he falter from taking a humorous tilt at 'plummy voiced' Englishmen like himself. As with Irving Berlin, the catalogue of his plays with music, revues and songs is outstanding as well as extensive and varied enough to merit further study.

Me and my Girl (1937)

One of the most successful musicals of all time, with music by Noel Gay and book and lyrics by Douglas Furber and L Arthur Rose. In the beginning, to think of *Me and my Girl* was to think of one man – Lupino Lane.

Lupino Lane (1892–1959)

This hugely popular entertainer was born into a theatrical dynasty in London that could trace its connections back to the seventeenth century, numbering the famous clown, Grimaldi, amongst its relations. There seems to have been no skill that the young Lupino failed to master, but it was for his portrayal of a lovable cockney rogue with trade-mark bowler hat that the public loved him best. He starred in numerous productions, but *Me and my Girl* with its cockney anthem 'The Lambeth Walk' provided him with the ideal vehicle for his talents.

The show opened at the Victoria Palace, London, on 16 December 1937 and ran until June 1940, racking up 1,646 performances. A film in 1939, again starring Lupino Lane, brought the show to a wider audience, as did a televised version, which had the distinction of being the first ever West End show to be recorded in this way.

Revivals have kept the show in the public eye and the production adapted by Stephen Fry in 1985 brought in two more hits by the show's original composer, Noel Gay; 'The Sun Has Got His Hat On' and the old George Formby hit, 'I'm Leaning on a Lamp Post at the Corner of the Street'. Fry's production ran for eight years at the Adelphi Theatre in the West End, breaking countless records and winning the coveted Lawrence Olivier Award for best musical, with Robert Lindsay, who would repeat his West End triumph on Broadway, winning the award for the best actor. Lindsay, his co-star, Maryann Plunkett and Gillian Gregory, the choreographer, all won Tony Awards for their outstanding contributions to this great show.

Ivor Novello (1893–1951)

Dubbed the British answer to Richard Rodgers, David Ivor Davies was born in Cardiff, Wales. Later he would take the name of his mother, Madame Clara Novello Davies, who was a celebrated singer and singing teacher.

Madame Novello was the ideal person to encourage the young Ivor on both the piano and with his voice, and at the age of ten, he won first prize singing in his age group at the National Eisteddfod. A singing scholarship followed to Magdalen College School Oxford, where he also studied the organ, together with music theory, harmony and counterpoint.

His first song, 'Spring of the Year', was published in 1909 and while he was still 17 he set a poem by the American writer, Lena Guilbert Ford, to music which resulted in the song, 'Keep the Home Fires Burning'. Tapping in so keenly to the mood of a nation at war brought him to the attention of the world, but in spite of this early triumph, Novello continued to pursue his film career, whilst honing his skills as a composer.

In 1921, he wrote a piece called *The Golden Moth* with P G Wodehouse, but this was not a success and then in the same year he was part composer with Helen Trix of a show called, *A to Z*. This starred Gertrude Lawrence, Jack Buchanan and the Trix Sisters and contained the song 'And Her

Mother Came Too'. More acting appearances followed and he wrote a successful play with Constance Collier, entitled *The Rat*.

In 1927 Ivor Davies changed his name by deed poll to Ivor Novello and continued to write, star in and produce works for the theatre. His play *Fresh Fields* was a particular success and ran for 464 performances.

Novello now pursued the impresario H M Tennent and succeeded in persuading him that some response was needed to counter the flood of musical works from America. Noel Coward was enjoying conspicuous success in this field and Tennent was looking for a suitable production to stage at one of his London theatres ...

Glamorous Night opened at the Theatre Royal, Drury Lane, London on 2 May 1935, with Ivor Novello in the non-singing role of Anthony Allen and the lovely Mary Ellis played the female lead, Militza Hajos. The lyrics were written by the actor-writer, Christopher Hassall, who had been appearing in Novello's play, *Murder in Mayfair*. He would become Novello's regular partner, writing lyrics for many similar enterprises.

The reception for this lyrical and beautifully staged piece of Ruritanian nonsense was rapturous, aided no doubt by the handsome presence of Novello, who soon built up a fanatical female following in spite of the fact that he was homosexual. Sets were by the distinguished designer Oliver Messell and the director was Leontine Sagan. The irresistible melodies included songs like 'Fold Your Wings', 'Glamorous Night', 'Shine Through My Dreams' and 'When the Gypsy Played'. The show was forced to close at Christmas to allow for a prior pantomime booking, but a successful tour followed and then *Glamorous Night* returned in 1936 for a season at the London Coliseum. In 1937 a film version was released, starring Mary Ellis, Otto Kruger and Barry MacKay.

Careless Rapture followed, opening at the Theatre Royal, Drury Lane on 11 September 1936. With lyrics by Christopher Hassall, this time the romantic action was set in London and China, with leading roles taken by Ivor Novello, Dorothy Dickson, Zena Dare, Ivan Samson and Olive Gilbert.

The show ran for 295 performances, but the music showed some sign of being constructed in haste and fewer songs than might have been expected became popular with the public. 'Music in May' is perhaps one of the most engaging and the others included 'Love Made the Song', 'The Manchuko', and 'Why is there Ever Goodbye?'

Crest of the Wave opened at the Drury Lane Theatre on 1 September 1937. This was a cheeky view of Hollywood concerning the adventures, amorous and otherwise, of a group of actors and producers. Once again Ivor Novello both wrote the music and starred in the show. Lyrics were by Christopher Hassall and the cast also included Peter Graves, Dorothy Dickson and Olive Gilbert. The song 'Rose of England' emerged as the overall success story of the show and was performed widely over the years. Other songs from this production included 'The Haven of Your Heart', 'If You Only Knew', 'Used to You' and 'Why Isn't It You?'

The Dancing Years opened at the Drury Lane Theatre on 23 March 1939 and would be recognised as one of the greatest shows ever devised and written by Ivor Novello; the lyrics were again by Christopher Hassall. Forced to close prematurely in September 1939 because of the impending outbreak of the Second World War, the following year there was a tour of the UK before the show returned to the West End, where it opened at the Adelphi Theatre on 14 March 1942. It was the most popular musical of the war years, running for 969 performances, and the cast included Ivor Novello, Mary Ellis, Roma Beaumont, Olive Gilbert, Peter Graves and Anthony Nicholls.

There were numerous revivals and a film version in 1950 starred Dennis Price. Once again, love was the theme and the story was now set in Vienna, allowing full rein to be given to glorious waltz tunes and romantic music in general.

Of the many sensational songs written by Ivor Novello, 'I Can Give You the Starlight', 'My Life Belongs to You', 'Waltz of My Heart', 'My Dearest Dear' and 'The Wings of Sleep' from *The Dancing Years* are amongst the best.

Perchance to Dream opened at the London Hippodrome on 21 April 1945, with book, words and music all conceived and written by Ivor Novello. The theme was romance and glamour and the plot traced the story of a family over several generations from Regency times. Close in style to Viennese operetta, Novello had judged the mood of his public perfectly, for they were still reeling in the aftermath of war and his escapist entertainment was exactly what was needed. Taking people out of themselves for a few hours proved a hugely successful formula and the show ran for 1,022 performances. Novello starred and with him was the redoubtable actress, Margaret Rutherford, as well as the ever-popular Roma Beaumont and Muriel Barron. 'We'll Gather Lilacs' would become as familiar to the British people as the national anthem, but there were other beautiful songs in this show including 'The Path My Lady Walks', 'A Woman's Heart' and 'Love is My Reason for Living'.

King's Rhapsody, devised, written and composed by Ivor Novello and with Lyrics by Christopher Hassall, would be the last show in which Novello appeared. The production opened at the Palace Theatre, London on 15 September 1949, with Ivor Novello, Vanessa Lee, Zena Dare, Olive Gilbert and Phyllis Dare in the cast. *King's Rhapsody* ran for 839 performances and was tragically curtailed when Novello died from a thrombosis only hours after making a speech on the night of 5 March, in response to the cheers of an ecstatic audience. The critics had been cool in their reception of *King's Rhapsody*, almost certainly because they felt that creative works should now be moving away from an operetta heritage.

The flood of new-style works from America only served to emphasise this notion, but Novello was a master in his own right and had built up a huge following amongst the theatre-going public. They knew what they liked and even if the plots were a bit thin, with this one set at the royal court of 'Murania', a night of light entertainment was guaranteed, as was fabulous music. By now the cast was practically Novello's repertory company and the audience must have greeted them like old friends.

A film version of this show came four years later and the songs have become classics in their own right; 'Fly Home Little Heart', 'The Violin Began to Play', 'If This Were Love' and 'Some Day My Heart Will Awake'.

Gay's the Word was written by Novello during the run of *King's Rhapsody*. He could not appear in this show since he was still appearing in *King's Rhapsody* and, of course, less than a month after the opening of *Gay's the Word*, he was dead. The show opened at the Saville Theatre on 16 February 1951 with Cicely Courtneidge, Lizbeth Webb and Thorley Walters in leading roles. The book and music were by Novello and more pithy lyrics than ever before were provided by Alan Melville. Set in modern times, the show featured the 57-year-old Courtneidge as an old trouper who opens a theatre school by the seaside. In some ways the show proved a vehicle for Courtneidge and it was her last role in a musical comedy, although she would star in several more revues. She ended her musical comedy career on a high, with songs like 'Vitality' and 'It's Bound to be Right on the Night'.

Gay's the Word ran for 504 performances and was considered a great hit as well as a fitting finale to the outstanding career of Ivor Novello.

Vivien Ellis (1904–)

Vivien Ellis's heyday as a composer and lyricist extended from the 1920s to the 1950s, but his life as a creative genius in other media lasted far longer. He employed his wit and wisdom in later life as an author, writing books like How to Enjoy Your Operation and, more optimistically, How to Make Your Fortune on the Stock Exchange. As a young man, he attended the Royal Academy of Music in London, taking lessons with the renowned concert pianist, Dame Myra Hess, in whose footsteps he hoped to follow.

Starting out as a composer for revues, filmtracks and other popular music outlets, Ellis had his first real success in 1929 with the musical comedy *Mr Cinders*. 'Ev'ry Little Moment' and 'Spread A Little Happiness', performed by Binnie Hale in the original production, made a lasting impression and Vivien Ellis was on his way.

His progress was impeded temporarily by ill health, but when he returned it was his contribution to C B Cochran's revue of 1930 in particular that re-launched his career and by 1938, Ellis had three hits running in the West End at the same time; *The Fleet's Lit Up*, *Running Riot* and *Under Your Hat*.

Soon Hollywood beckoned and Ellis began writing songs for the sweet-voiced Deanna Durbin. When war broke out in 1939, he returned to serve his country and became involved with the Forces' entertainment agency, ENSA. When the war ended in 1945, Ellis resumed his collaboration with the writer A P Herbert and with C B Cochran. Their first production, *Big Ben* (1946), achieved modest success, but their next, *Bless the Bride* (1947) was a huge hit. Lovely melodies like the duet 'This is My Lovely Day', 'Ma Belle Marguerite' and 'I Was Never Kissed Before' were the very embodiment of old-fashioned romance and it's hard now to imagine that the American musical *Oklahoma!* opened in the West End that very same week.

Bless the Bride lost nothing in the competition for the public's heart and the delightful tale of Lucy Veracity Willow, apparently doomed to marry the noble numbskull Thomas Trout, only to discover true rapture in the person of dashing French actor Pierre Fontaine, ran at the Adelphi Theatre for almost 886 performances. Ellis and Herbert's next show *Tough at the Top* came nowhere near *Bless the Bride* in the popularity stakes and *And So To Bed* (1951) achieved about a third of *Bless the Bride*'s run. Ellis wrote many more works for music theatre, including *The Water Gipsies* (1955), which benefited from the charismatic performance of Dora Bryan, and his children's musical *Listen to the Wind* (1954). Many well-deserved honours followed, but for a man who was a contemporary of Noel Coward and Ivor Novello, it is perhaps more significant that revivals, together with the use of his tunes in a variety of media, including advertising jingles, show that the music of Vivien Ellis is as much appreciated today as ever.

Self-test questions

1 Who was known as 'The English Ziegfeld'?

2 In 1923 a revue caused a sensation on the British stage; who wrote it and what was it called?

3 Which female performer became identified with the song 'I Went to a Marvellous Party'?

4 Lupino Lane was famous for portraying what type of character?

5 Where was Ivor Novello born?

6 Can you name two of his shows – one with the word 'rapture' in the title and the other with the word 'rhapsody'?

7 Which was considered to be his greatest show and can you name the two songs from his work?

8 Who, apart from Ivor Novello himself, usually wrote lyrics for Ivor Novello productions?

9 Can you name the most popular show to be written by Vivien Ellis?

10 Which American musical was running in London's West End at the same time as this production?

7 | RODGERS AND HAMMERSTEIN

Richard Rodgers (1902–79) was meticulous and disciplined, but flexible in his approach to composition. Whereas during his partnership with the mercurial Hart, Rodgers first wrote the music to which he would then coax Hart into writing lyrics, with Hammerstein he adopted a different approach. Hammerstein's words drove the plot forward and were written first, then Rodgers's perfectly judged music was composed to complete the picture. Hart's lyrics were frequently masterpieces of poetry in their own right, whereas lyrics by Hammerstein were more like the lines in a play, the power of which lay in their simplicity and directness. Hammerstein, like Rodgers, was much more of a disciplined professional than Hart, but that takes nothing away from the outstanding catalogue of songs that resulted from the Rodgers and Hart partnership.

In Oscar Hammerstein, however, Rodgers had found a partner who allowed him to explore the widest reaches of music theatre and fulfil his full potential as a composer of world class musicals.

Oscar Hammerstein II (1895–1960) was born into a theatrical dynasty on the management side and in spite of initially choosing law for his own career path, the young man found himself increasingly drawn towards the theatre.

From assistant stage manager working for his uncle, Hammerstein moved into writing shows and one of his most influential early associations was with the writer Otto Harbach, whose work for the theatre formed a bridge between the older style operetta and musical comedy. Their show *Tickle Me* was staged in 1920 and in 1923 Hammerstein and Harbach joined with Vincent Youmans and Herbert Stothart in writing *Wildflower*.

Next came one of the most memorable and enduring of all the early musicals, *Rose-Marie* (1924), which had music by Rudolf Friml and Herbert Stothart and lyrics by Hammerstein and Harbach. Hammerstein's future collaborators would read like a who's who of music theatre; Jerome

Kern for *Sunny* (1925); George Gershwin on *Song of the Flame* (1926) and then, on 30 November 1926, the curtain rose on *The Desert Song*.

The Desert Song (1926)

With music by Sigmund Romberg and lyrics by Hammerstein, Harbach and Frank Mandel, this tale of daring-do in the deserts of North Africa proved a lasting hit with the public in spite of its initial panning by the New York theatre critics. It ran at the Casino Theater, Broadway for more than 450 performances and audiences in London were just as enthusiastic the following year. Film versions appeared in 1929, 1943 and 1953 and stage revivals continue unabated to the present day. Because the show provides such an outstanding 'showcase' role for its male lead as 'The Red Shadow', several singers have based their career on this part alone, most notably Harry Welchman and, of course, John Hanson, who formed his own company to tour this and other popular musical comedy/operetta-style works. The music of *Desert Song* is outstanding; who could forget 'One Alone', 'Romance' and, of course, 'The Desert Song' itself...

Just a year after *The Desert Song*, Hammerstein would be celebrating another theatrical triumph. On 27 December 1927, *Show Boat* (see page 157) opened at the Ziegfeld Theater, New York. This show was the fruit of another Hammerstein collaboration with the composer Jerome Kern; an association that would result in several more shows, producing outstanding classics like 'The Song is You' and 'All the Things you Are'.

Like every other Broadway maestro, in the 1930s Hammerstein was lured to Hollywood where he continued to produce some remarkable songs in partnership, amongst others, with Jerome Kern; 'The Folks Who Live on the Hill' and 'The Last Time I Saw Paris,' are just two of their many hits. Hammerstein also wrote 'When I Grow too Old to Dream' with the romantic Romberg and 'I Won't Dance' with Harbach and Kern, but even with this degree of success in his pocket, for Oscar Hammerstein II, the best was yet to come.

In the late 1920s and 1930s Hammerstein had done some work with Richard Rodgers, but now, with Lorenz Hart permanently out of action, fate was about to take a hand and, in 1943, the first major collaboration between Rodgers and Hammerstein, *Oklahoma!* roared onto the stage. The exclamation mark was scarcely needed to underscore the fact that a tidal wave known as the 'American Musical' had well and truly arrived.

Oklahoma! (1943)

Oscar Hammerstein based his book and lyrics for this two-act musical on a play by Lynn Riggs called *Green Grow the Lilacs*. With a formula that would remain reasonably constant throughout every Rodgers and Hammerstein musical, the main criteria was a larger than life response to every event and every emotion. With its big cheesy grins, boisterous hoe-down, frilly girl and gun-totin' tomboy girl, good guy and bad guy, not to mention (what might be deemed a weakness of some American musicals) plentiful repetition of hit songs – just in case you didn't get them first time around – plus lashings of colour, movement, dance and romance, what *Oklahoma!* lacked in subtlety, it certainly made up for in sheer *joie de vivre* and plenty of whistle-on-the-way-home tunes. Having said that, *Oklahoma!* did break the mould by opening with a solo song rather than the customary 'grab their attention' boisterous chorus and that in itself proved a far more original and effective way of intriguing the audience – but when you can write songs like 'Oh What a Beautiful Morning' a certain confidence is allowed.

As amazing as it might seem now, *Oklahoma!* opened at the St James Theater, New York, on 31 March 1943, to a house that was only half full. The reasons were surely that the new partnership was untried; the original play had been concerned with the rivalries between ranchers and farmers; the rivalries driven by their need to use the land in different ways for cattle, or for crops – and even if the show *had* been renamed, it was with the name of a State, for goodness sake, and one that only conjured up sleepy towns and wheat fields stretching into the middle distance – all in all, hardly cause for a stampede at the box office ...

Of course, the extraordinary success that greeted this work is now a matter of record. Even if The Theater Guild, the company chosen to present the work, was one of the most highly respected theatrical groups in the United States, how could anyone have anticipated the scintillating choreography of Agnes de Mille, who had been given a faultless cast to work with, or the instantly appealing songs that must have seemed to follow each other in an endless stream, leaving audiences then and ever after in a state of delighted disbelief that anything on the stage could actually be so good.

One of the main strengths of *Oklahoma!* is in the fact that through the romance and cheeriness of it all are woven some darker threads; the character of Jed, the first on-stage 'death' in a piece of 'light entertainment' and even the wilful if comic wanton that is Ado Annie. The hero, of course, sings lustily of his home state and of the great weather there, whilst the heroine with equal propriety dreams of her ideal man stepping 'Out of Her Dreams'; Ado Annie is rather more forthright, confessing, 'I Cain't Say No' and just when the 'The Farmer and the Cowman' hoe-down couldn't get any more competitive, the fighting any rougher, or the dancing any more energetic, the title song 'Oklahoma!' swings into action, lifting the mood through the roof.

The original cast with Alfred Drake as the upright hero, Curly, Joan Roberts as the winsome heroine, Laurey and Celeste Holm as Ado Annie Carnes, was good enough, but when they eventually stepped down, the name Howard Keel was to become synonymous with the lead role and other stars such as Shelley Winters and, in the 1955 film version, Gordon Macrae and Shirley Jones made considerable contributions to the story of a show that has never really stopped playing for more than 50 years. That first poorly attended opening night in New York led to a run of 2,248 performances, then a production starring Howard Keel opened in London in 1947 and ran for 1,151 performances.

There were major revivals in New York in 1951 and 1965 and another major revival was presented in London in 1980 by Cameron Macintosh, and on the show's fiftieth anniversary in 1993 it was awarded America's highest theatrical honour; a Tony.

Carmen Jones (1943)

Although not a product of the Rodgers and Hammerstein partnership, but of Oscar Hammerstein alone, *Carmen Jones* is one of the cleverest musicals never written, for in this show Hammerstein takes the French composer Georges Bizet's existing score for his opera *Carmen*, and by altering names and setting creates an entirely new and utterly credible work of art. A gutsier approach and use of the vernacular is all that separates *Carmen Jones* from its classical counterpart, yet *Carmen Jones* is a flamboyant piece of music theatre, whilst *Carmen* is most definitely an opera, albeit one of the most popular operas ever written. (See *Teach Yourself Opera*.)

From Spain, the setting moves to America, where *Carmen's* cigarette factory becomes a parachute factory and in *Carmen Jones* an all-black

cast plays out the familiar tale of love, loyalty and treachery within
Hammerstein's brilliant new version. Escamillo, the Toreador in *Carmen*,
becomes Husky Miller the prize-fighter and the 'Toreador's Song' from
Carmen becomes – as if it was always meant to be – 'Stan' Up and Fight'.
Sweet Micaela from the opera *Carmen* is now Cindy Lou and her
wandering sweetheart, Don José, is re-born as Corporal Joe.

Carmen Jones opened at the Broadway Theater, New York on 2
December 1943 and ran for more than 500 performances. The main roles
were double cast, with Muriel Smith and Muriel Rahn taking it in turns to
play the part of Carmen Jones and Napoleon Reed and Luther Saxon
playing her tragic admirer, Corporal Joe.

In 1954 a film version starring Harry Belafonte and Dorothy Dandridge
brought this exciting new reading of Bizet's music to a wider audience.
Belafonte's singing role was dubbed by La Vern Hutcherson and Dandridge's
voice was also dubbed, in her case by the mezzo-soprano Marilyn Horne, who
went on to enjoy a deservedly sensational career in opera.

The film benefited from a particularly strong cast, notably the inimitable
and ebullient Pearl Bailey who excelled in the role of Frankie.

Carousel (1945)

The success of *Oklahoma!* had been built around a play in the repertoire
of The Theater Guild, so it comes as no surprise that in seeking a new
subject to set to music, other Guild productions were considered by
Rodgers and Hammerstein. *Liliom*, a play written by Frederick Molnar
and set in Budapest, at first seems an unlikely choice, but then
Hammerstein was the man who could take Bizet's *Carmen* and
mastermind its re-birth as *Carmen Jones*, so transferring action from
Budapest to New England wasn't such a big deal after all.

If *Oklahoma!* surpassed the usual stage musical offering with its flood of
hit songs and unusually multi-stranded emotional content, *Carousel*
possessed a similar number of hit songs, but these were set now within a
score of exceptional merit by any standard and the story-line was both
tender and stirring, as well as buoyant and entertaining. The
choreographer Agnes de Mille was said to have excelled even her work on
Oklahoma! and songs like the unusually dramatic 'Soliloquy', or 'June is
Bustin' Out All Over', 'When the Children are Asleep', 'If I Loved You'

and 'You'll Never Walk Alone' made huge impact on a public fast becoming accustomed to the Rodgers-style score with its plethora of glorious tunes. 'You'll Never Walk Alone' in particular, with its reverent, anthem-like character, struck a chord with the public that has allowed it to acquire a relevance far outweighing even its part in the show, crucial though that is.

The story revolves around fairground barker, Billie Bigelow, and his sweetheart, young Julie Jordan. When they marry and Julie becomes pregnant, Billie becomes involved in a robbery in order to provide some extra money for the baby.

Finally, racked with guilt and despair, Billie kills himself and it is only years later that he is allowed a chance to redeem himself and earn his place in heaven by helping his own daughter, now 15, through her own troubles.

The seamless blend of strong book, powerful score and thrilling dance led to a run of 890 performances following the opening on 19 April 1945 at the Majestic Theater, New York. *Carousel* ran for 550 performances in London after opening in 1950 and there have been countless revivals over the years, with a film version in 1956 starring Gordon Macrae and Shirley Jones who took the leading roles.

Amongst many tributes, *Carousel* was awarded one of the first prizes ever to be granted by the newly formed New York Drama Critic's Circle, for Best Musical of 1944–5. This recognition came hot on the heels of many other accolades heaped on *Oklahoma!* including the prestigious Pulitzer Prize and confirmed Rodgers and Hammerstein, if such confirmation was needed, as one of the foremost theatrical partnerships of all time.

South Pacific (1949)

Although at first glance the musicals of Rodgers and Hammerstein appear to be nothing more than light-hearted entertainment, this is rarely the case. In *South Pacific* the issue of racism is confronted, but in such a straightforward manner and with such an absence of fuss that the mind can easily be distracted by the intriguing setting and by Rodgers's easily digested tunes, and by the deceptive directness of Hammerstein's book. Based on James Michener's Pulitzer Prize-winning book *Tales of the South Pacific*, and with some libretto contributed by Joshua Logan, the action of *South Pacific* takes place during the Second World War. A romance has developed between Nellie Forbush, an American army nurse and Emile de Becque, a middle-aged French plantation owner, who already has two children by his late Polynesian mistress. A secondary romance is featured between a young American serviceman and a Polynesian girl; the young soldier fears that the difference between their cultures will prove insuperable and breaks off their relationship just before he is killed in action.

Apart from these central characters, the smaller parts are sharply drawn and provide some wonderful moments in the show, and one of the most notable of these characters is Bloody Mary, mother of the young Polynesian girl.

The role of Emile was created by Richard Rodgers specifically for the great operatic bass, Enzio Pinza, and two of Emile's songs 'Some Enchanted Evening' and 'This Nearly Was Mine' must rank amongst the greatest songs ever written by Rodgers and Hammerstein. In fact the whole score is a masterpiece of variety and evocative melody. 'Bali Ha'i', for instance, the mysterious Island described by Bloody Mary, is just one example of a tune that lingers in the memory long after other details of the show have faded.

'Younger Than Springtime' is another; sung by the ill-fated Lieutenant to his Polynesian sweetheart it is heart-breaking in its innocence and in an entirely different style, yet equally compelling 'There is Nothing Like a Dame' captures perfectly the mood of the lusty Marines as they wait to be called back into action.

Within a week of opening night at the Majestic Theater, New York on 7 April 1949, *South Pacific* had won the New York Drama Critics Best Musical Award and would go on to win a 1949–50 Tony in every category for which it was entered. Critics and public alike were lost for superlatives sufficient enough to describe the show and Mary Martin and Enzio Pinza in particular were singled out for even more praise. The show ran for a staggering 1,925 performances and in 1951 Mary Martin recreated her role to great acclaim at the Drury Lane Theatre, London.

The choice of the Hawaiian island of Kauai for location shots for the 1958 film, coupled with a mood-enhancing use of colour filters, presented the cinema-going public with a sensational experience. The leading role of Nellie was played in the film by Mitzi Gaynor and Rossano Brazzi, who certainly looked the part but couldn't sing, took the role of Emile de Becque. Brazzi's voice was dubbed by Georgio Tozzi, an American operatic bass, and the voice of Bloody Mary, still played on-screen by Juanita Hall, who appeared in the stage version, was dubbed by Muriel Smith. The original cast recording remained in the charts for a number of years and is still superior in many ways to a much later interpretation in which the glorious but unquestionably mature voice of Kiri Te Kanawa, together with a transposition of the original bass role, now sung by the tenor José Carreras, loses everything Rodgers evoked in his vocal realisation of the older, rich-voiced de Becque and the youthful, light-voiced girl.

The King and I (1951)

Although *The King and I* was conceived initially as a vehicle for the star Gertrude Lawrence, the discovery and subsequent casting of a relatively inexperienced Yul Brynner in the role of the King of Siam was a masterly stroke. For one so young, he possessed a commanding stage presence and an enthralling appearance. Unusually for an untried movie personality, Hollywood took a chance on Yul Brynner in the 1956 film version, but 20th Century-Fox's confidence was amply repaid when Brynner in the role of the King won an Oscar for Best Actor. Deborah Kerr was his co-star in the role of the governess, Anna and her singing voice was dubbed by Marni Nixon.

The King and I opened at the St James Theater, New York on 29 March 1951 and ran for 1,246 performances. In 1953 it opened at the Drury Lane Theatre, London and ran for over 900 performances, with Valerie Hobson in the role of Anna and Herbert Lom as the King.

The story features the growing respect and love between the autocratic King of Siam and the demure yet determined English governess employed to teach his 67 children something of Western culture. The music is once again supremely evocative of every twist and turn in the plot, without ever once falling into the trap of becoming overtly oriental.

The ones that got away...

(For *The Sound of Music* (1959) see page 183.)

Before *South Pacific* in 1949, there had been another, far less successful show produced by Rodgers and Hammerstein called *Allegro* (1947) and after *The King and I* in 1951, another two about which little is heard, *Me and Juliet* (1953) and *Pipe Dreams* (1955).

Allegro was a rather more abstract experiment than anything that had gone before and though it was admired in some quarters and enjoyed a reasonable run, it was never a hit on the scale that Rodgers and Hammerstein were accustomed to.

Me and Juliet at least boasted the lovely song 'No other Love' and the sets by Mielziner were much admired. It ran for a year, but was considered a mediocre offering by the high-flying pair.

Pipe Dreams was based on a novel by John Steinbeck, but general sanitising of a story that had a prostitute as one of its central characters rendered the main theme ineffectual. The show opened at the Shubert Theater, New York on 30 November 1955 with ticket sales in advance of $1.2 million – the largest to date for a Rodgers and Hammerstein musical _ but ran for only 246 performances. This was a disaster in financial terms and clearly shows where Rodgers and Hammerstein's true genius lay – in writing family shows.

Self-test questions

1   Which famous lyricist was composer Richard Rodgers's partner before Oscar Hammerstein II?
2   What generally came first, Hammerstein's words or Rodgers's music?
3   Who wrote the music for *The Desert Song*?
4   Which first major collaboration between Rodgers and Hammerstein premiered in 1943?
5   What was unusual about the musical *Carmen Jones*?
6   In 1945 a Rodgers and Hammerstein musical premièred with a central character called Billie Bigelow. What was that musical?

7 Which character sang 'Bali H'ai' in the musical *South
Pacific*?

8 In what year did *The King and I* open in New York?

9 Who took the role of the King of Siam in both the original
stage production and the film version of *The King and I*?

10 Can you name two musicals by Rodgers and Hammerstein
that failed to make 'the big time'?

8 | THE 1950s, 1960s AND 1970s

Thriving in the 1950s

The 1950s were an exciting time for light music in general and in the world of music theatre, more traditional works like the musical *Kismet* (see page 112), which drew on the musical themes of the classical composer Borodin, co-existed happily alongside blatant expressions of the newly prominent youth culture, like *Expresso Bongo* (see page 116).

With television still in its infancy and musicals as diverse as *Guys and Dolls*, *The King and I* and *Salad Days* ensuring that there was something for everyone, more and more people became attracted to live theatre.

Creating a solid tradition of theatre-going in the face of burgeoning technology, with all its compelling attractions, meant that live theatre not only survived, but thrived as never before during the latter half of the twentieth century.

Frank Loesser (1910–69)

From the 1930s to the 1960s, Frank Leosser, a self-taught musician, was one of the leading songwriters in America. He began by writing lyrics, first for vaudeville and then Broadway, before finally Hollywood beckoned and he began to collaborate on songs for the movies with composers such as Hoagy Carmichael, Jule Styne and Arthur Schwartz.

Amongst the countless hits during this period of his career, 'Two Sleepy People' from the film *Thanks for the Memory*, sung by Bob Hope and Shirley Ross, and 'See What the Boys in the Back Room Will Have', sung by Marlene Dietrich in the film *Destry Rides Again*, show the calibre of his work.

During Loesser's Second World War military service he began writing words and music in earnest and in 1948 he wrote one of his biggest hits,

'On a Slow Boat to China'. In that same year, he wrote the score for an adaptation of Brandon Thomas's English farce, *Charley's Aunt*, which had first been staged in London more than 50 years previously, in 1892. This new version called *Where's Charley?* included the classic 'Once in Love With Amy' and ran for 792 performances after opening at the St James Theater, New York on 11 October 1948.

In 1949 he won an Oscar for 'Baby It's Cold Outside' from the film *Neptune's Daughter*, starring Esther Williams and Red Skelton and two years later he produced his masterpiece, *Guys and Dolls*.

In 1952 he wrote the music for one of the best children's films ever, *Hans Christian Anderson*, starring Danny Kaye and it's hard, if not impossible to imagine that lovelier or more appropriate music could have been composed for this movie. Next on Broadway came *The Most Happy Fella*, for which he wrote both music and words.

This show highlighted Loesser's versatility and included some songs which were vocally demanding like 'My Heart is So Full of You' and others, notably 'Standing on the Corner' that went straight to the top of the charts.

The Most Happy Fella opened at the Imperial Theater, Broadway on 3 May 1956 and ran for a creditable 676 performances; all the more impressive in the light of the fact that Lerner and Loewe's stunning show *My Fair Lady* was running at the same time.

Critics were at a loss to describe *The Most Happy Fella* since the scope of its music was so wide it was difficult to pigeon-hole the show, but with its sung-through style, it certainly resembled opera in form at least. In 1991, amongst many revivals over the years, the New York City Opera company gave further credence to this notion when they produced their own version of Loesser's show, starring Giorgio Tozzi in the leading role.

Another Loesser show, *Greenwillow*, staged in 1960, closed after 95 performances, but in 1961, *How to Succeed in Business Without Really Trying* more than made up for any losses that might have been incurred. Running for an impressive 1,417 performances, this show was Loesser's last Broadway show, but won the Pulitzer Prize for Drama in 1962, Tony Awards for Best Musical, for the lyrics, writers, for Abe Burrows as Best Director and for Robert Morse in the category of Best Actor.

Frank Loesser died from lung cancer, an unrepentant smoker. As well as being an unpredictable and fiery man, he was unquestionably an innovative talent, whose contribution to music theatre in particular ensured that it remained at the forefront of developments in the performing arts.

Guys and Dolls (1950)

Frank Loesser produced some of his very best music and lyrics for this show. It opened at the 46th Street Theater, New York on 24 November 1950, with a book by Abe Burrows and Jo Swerling, based on Damon Runyan's tales with their boldly drawn characters.

Out of town trials proved so successful that *Guys and Dolls* was hailed as a triumph before it even hit Broadway. It had a strong cast of actor/singers – the irrepressible Stubby Kaye, in particular, stopped the show night after night with his infectious rendition of 'Sit Down, You're Rocking the Boat' and Robert Alda in the role of Sky won an Oscar, as did Isabel Bigley in the role of Sarah, the director George S Kaufman and the choreographer, Michael Kidd.

Countless revivals followed and a film version in 1955 starred Marlon Brando, Jean Simmons and Frank Sinatra, again with Stubby Kaye and Vivian Blaine recreating their stage roles. The story-line features the love story between two gamblers and their ladies; Miss Adelaide, a dancer, and Miss Sarah Brown, a member of the 'Save a Soul Mission'.

Fast-moving action, larger-than-life characters and brilliant songs like 'If I Were a Bell', 'Luck Be a Lady Tonight', 'I've Never Been in Love Before' and 'Take Back Your Mink' place this work alongside the very best musicals of all time.

More favourites from the 1950s...

Because the 1950s was such a fertile and diverse era for the musical, it will be helpful to mention a few more of those works that show something of the variety offered to the theatre-going public – not forgetting that this was also the decade of *My Fair Lady*, *West Side Story* and *The Sound of Music* (see pages 167, 175 and 183.)

Kismet (1953)

The word Kismet means 'fate' and it was partly fate that guaranteed this show's success. When a newspaper strike prevented indifferent critiques from reaching the theatre-going public, word of mouth from the first audiences ensured that the show was a hit before the presses were rolling again.

With the classical composer Borodin's soaring melodies adapted for music theatre by George Forrest and Robert Wright, who also wrote the lyrics, and a book by Charles Lederer and Luther Davis, *Kismet* opened at the Ziegfeld Theater, New York on 3 December 1953.

Kismet was a glamorously exotic and light-hearted show, based on a play from 1911 written by Eddie Knoblock, and tells the story of a shrewd beggar who outwits a wicked Wazir in order to wed his own daughter to the handsome young Caliph. Songs like the Borodin-inspired 'Stranger in Paradise' and 'And this is My Beloved', together with catchy tunes like 'Baubles, Bangles and Beads' made an immediate impact.

It wasn't the first time that Forrest and Wright had poached elements of classical music to illustrate a piece of music theatre. One of Broadway's biggest wartime hits, *Song of Norway*, was based loosely on the life of the classical composer Edvard Grieg and featured their adaptation of Grieg's music.

Kismet ran for 583 performances and the cast included Alfred Drake, Richard Kiley and Doretta Morrow. Drake and Morrow also appeared in the London production in 1955 and this ran for 648 performances. That same year a film version was released starring Howard Keel, Ann Blyth, Dolores Gray and Vic Damone.

The Boy Friend (1954)

Born in Cheshire, England in 1924, Sandy Wilson, the creator of *The Boy Friend*, had been educated at Harrow School and Oxford University. His songs were already being used in the West End when, in 1953, he was asked to write the book, lyrics and music for a production at the Players' Theatre Club, lasting no more than one hour and to be based on the music of the 'roaring twenties'. The run was originally intended to be about three weeks and Sandy Wilson's musical 'interlude' was excepted to provide an alternative to the usual Victorian music hall fare generally served up by the Players' Theatre in their 'Late Joys' programme.

Sandy Wilson came up with *The Boy Friend*, an affectionate look back at the 1920s musicals and the idioms of that time. This production exceeded everyone's expectations, for after a respectable life as a one-hour entertainment, it moved to the Embassy Theatre and was then expanded to suit the requirements of London's West End, where it opened at Wyndham's Theatre on 14 January 1954. Here it ran for 2,084 performances over more than five years.

There were several memorable songs in the show, including 'It's Never Too Late to Fall in Love', 'I Could be Happy with You' and 'Room in Bloomsbury'. Apart from its own not inconsiderable qualities, *The Boy Friend* is also significant in having given Julie Andrews her first leading role on the New York stage, at the Royale Theater, where the show ran for 485 performances. Ken Russell made a film version in 1971 starring ex-model Twiggy, and future Broadway star, Tommy Tune.

Salad Days (1954)

Essentially a British phenomenon, *Salad Days* bombed in the United States. Perhaps the unlikely tale of two students hiring a piano belonging to a tramp, only to find that the instrument possesses the power to make everyone dance, proved a little naïve for American audiences, but the show has never lost its hold on the British public's affection.

Following its opening at the Bristol Old Vic on 5 August 1954, where it had been conceived originally to fill a three-week gap in that theatre's schedule, *Salad Days* transferred to the Vaudeville Theatre, London, where it ran for a triumphant 2,283 performances.

The significance of the Old Vic in the creation of this show, was that it housed what was essentially a repertory group, accustomed to putting on plays, rather than musicals. *Salad Days* was something of a departure for the company, but with music by Julian Slade, a member of the company, who also co-wrote the lyrics with Dorothy Renolds, another member, the restrictions within which they had to work were clear-cut. Some of the actors were not good singers and much of the music reflects this fact in its narrow vocal range. The flip side of the coin is of course that these predominantly limited demands on a performer's singing capabilities make this an ideal show for amateur production. Indeed revivals, both amateur and professional, of this quintessentially English show continue to the present day in Great Britain.

The Pajama Game (1954)

The Pajama Game became an unexpectedly big hit for its creators, Richard Bissell and George Abbott, who based the book on Bissell's own novel *7½ cents*. With music composed by Richard Adler and words by lyricist Jerry Ross, and set in the unlikely surroundings of a pyjama-making factory, the plot encompasses an industrial dispute as well as romance.

Humour, catchy songs and scintillating choreography, by the then relatively unknown Bob Fosse, all contributed to the success of a show that enjoyed a run of more than a thousand performances at the St James Theater, New York, where it opened on 13 May 1954.

Janis Paige, John Raitt and Carol Haney starred in the original production with Haney winning a Tony for Best Featured Actress, along with Bob Fosse for his outstanding choreography. The show itself won a Tony in the category Best Musical. There were several big hit songs including 'Hernando's Hideaway', 'Steam Heat', 'Hey There', 'There Once was a Man', 'Once a Year Day', 'Small Talk' and 'I'm Not at all in Love'.

The London production also boasted a distinguished cast including the inimitable Max Wall, Joy Nichols, Edmund Hockridge and Elizabeth Seal, but it was the film version in 1957, starring the vivacious Doris Day and John Raitt, that really took the musical-loving public by storm. A combination of lyrical ballads like 'Hey There, You with the Stars in Your Eyes' and irresistible dance rhythms, so ably interpreted by choreographer Fosse, raised the show, with its unpromising setting, to the very pinnacle of achievement in music theatre.

Bob Fosse (1927–87)

Born in Chicago, Bob Fosse was a dancer and actor, who became one of America's most distinguished choreographers and directors, winning no fewer than eight Tony Awards in the process.

He studied classical dance and tap as well as acrobatic dancing and appeared in vaudeville, before serving in the US Navy from 1945–7. After studying acting at the American Theater Wing in New York, he toured in the chorus of several shows, performed in the chorus on Broadway and made several television appearances, before finally arriving in Hollywood in the 1950s.

After playing small parts in three films, he received his first big break when George Abbott brought him in to choreograph *The Pajama Game*. This proved to be a huge success for Fosse and he then went on to choreograph several more shows, eventually became a director as well as choreographer and divided his time between his commitments in the theatre and those in Hollywood.

He both directed and choreographed the film *Sweet Charity* (1968) starring Shirley Maclaine, but was criticised for allowing Maclaine's cloying self-indulgence in the role of Charity, as well as for other corny gimmicks that did nothing to enhance his reputation.

His stunning interpretation of dance in the 1972 film version of the musical *Cabaret*, however, won him one of that production's eight Academy Awards and re-established his reputation as one of America's leading choreographers.

Expresso Bongo (1958)

Expresso Bongo gave the newly fledged world of 'pop' music and the attendant upsurge of 'youth culture' a hearing on the establishment stage of music theatre.

With a story based loosely around a young man who became Britain's first really big rock 'n' roll personality, Tommy Steele, the show charts his discovery in a coffee bar in 1956, along with the fascinating details of his make-over into a star.

With his name changed by manager John Kennedy and agent Larry Parnes from Thomas Hicks to Tommy Steele, the book by Wolf Mankowitz and Julian More looks at the young man's career path as he seeks a wider audience. The show's name is derived from the nickname of the leading character in the musical, Bongo Herbert, played by Steele – so-called because he plays the bongo drums rather than guitar – together with the name of Bongo's hit, 'Expresso Party'.

Expresso Bongo opened at the Saville Theatre on 23 April 1958 and with its candid view on the burgeoning of this new cultural force, provoked mixed reactions. The music was by David Heneker, who went on to write the score for the hit musical in which Tommy Steele would demonstrate his versatility, *Half a Sixpence* (1963) (see page 120), Monty Norman and Julian More. The pithy lyrics were by Norman and Heneker, who managed to capture the idioms of that era's youth with impressive perception.

Expresso Bongo went on to enjoy a respectable run and a film version in 1959, starring Laurence Harvey, Cliff Richard and Sylvia Syms, benefited from the addition of a powerful song, 'A Voice in the Wilderness', by Norrie Paramor and Bunny Lewis. This reached number two in the charts for Cliff Richard and the film generally made a big impact on its mainly teenage fans.

Lock Up Your Daughters (1959)

This bawdy adaptation of Henry Fielding's *Rape upon Rape* by the founder of the Mermaid Theatre, London, Bernard (later Sir Bernard) Miles, was a unique period farce amongst an outpouring of traditional musicals.

Opening the Mermaid Theatre on 28 May 1959 and starring Stephanie Voss as the 'innocent' maiden, Hilaret, Frederic Jaeger as the highly-sexed Ramble and Richard Wordsworth as lecherous Justice Squeezum, *Lock Up Your Daughters* ran for 330 performances.

A season in New Haven, America followed in 1960 and the show returned to the Mermaid in 1962, before transferring to the West End, where it ran at Her Majesty's Theatre for two years. There was another run at the Mermaid in 1969 and revivals have continued both in this country and abroad.

With music by Laurie Johnson and lyrics by Lionel Bart, the songs captured the lusty, gutsy mood of the story-line to perfection and included, along with the title song, 'When does the Ravishing Begin?', 'On a Sunny Sunday Morning' and 'Red Wine and a Wench'.

Swing into the 1960s

Pop music and the youth scene transformed London in particular into the hub of an increasingly fashion-conscious world. Music theatre took a little time to adapt to the changes and accept the fact that rather than ignore the youth market, it could actually be wooed back into the theatre.

There were some terrific musicals produced in the early 1960s, but these appealed in the main to an older audience and offered a traditional-style, family entertainment. The mid-1960s had arrived before America led the way with a musical that addressed issues relevant to young people and held nothing back in either its opinions, or in the delivery of those beliefs. *Hair* was a true product of the 'hippie' generation, with strong language, nudity and performers sporting flowing locks that demonstrated their desire to defy traditional standards of behaviour – even if some of them had to wear wigs until their own hair grew!

With subject-matter that confronted draft dodging, drug taking, free love and religion, here at last was an entertainment with which young people could identify and the quality of its music ensured that the show had mass appeal, not only because of its more outrageous aspects, but for its continuance of all that is best in music theatre; the joyous celebration of life.

What follows are a few examples of musicals from the 1960s: *Flower Drum Song* might be said to show an uncharacteristic lack of confidence on the part of the fabulous Rodgers and Hammerstein team. Certainly its values seem almost cringingly out-of-sync with the rapidly changing moral codes of the 1960s. Many of the others follow a tried and trusted formula, while *Fiddler on the Roof* caused a great stir, as well it might, with its fascinating insight into Jewish tradition and the sacrifices made by one generation for the benefit of another. *Sweet Charity* pushes out the boundaries of respectable family entertainment, with tone-in-cheek humour saving it from unwarranted accusations of sleaze and *Cabaret* is simply a jewel in the crown of music theatre. The selection ends with *Tommy*, a piece whose value should not be underestimated; even if that value runs the risk of being obscured by today's technical wizardry.

Flower Drum Song (1960)

The plot concerns the interaction between an Americanised Chinese family and Mei Li, a bride imported by mail-order from China.

With no Western character for the majority of a Western audience to relate to and running the very real risk of appearing patronising – not just today, but even when the show was premiered in 1960 – and lacking a truly memorable score, the *Flower Drum Song* tottered along for what would have been an extremely creditable 600 performances for any other writers, but for Rodgers and Hammerstein has to be considered a modest run.

Joseph Fields collaborated with Oscar Hammerstein on the libretto and for this, his first time as director of a Broadway show, Gene Kelly left the choreography to Carol Haney. Haney certainly wasn't overawed by the Master's presence and one of the best scenes in the show was attributed to her flair, where singer Anita Ellis performed her show-stopping number, 'Fan Tan Fannie'.

There were a number of pleasing songs and of these 'Sunday' made it to the charts and 'I Enjoy Being a Girl' was popular, but now seems rather arch and dated; 'You are Beautiful' and 'A Hundred Million Miracles' having stood the test of time better. After an initial 'out of town' run at the Shubert Theater in Boston, opening on 27 October 1958, the show transferred to the St James Theater, New York in 1960. There was a London run in 1960 and a film version was released in 1961.

Camelot (1960)

To follow *My Fair Lady* would have been a daunting prospect for any writing team, but Learner and Loewe launched *Camelot* on Broadway on 1 December 1960 whilst *My Fair Lady* was still at the peak of its popularity.

They were justifiably confident that nothing could knock Miss Eliza Dolittle and Co off the top spot, but this new look at the Arthurian legend, based on the book *The Once and Future King* by T H White, wowed Broadway with the sheer splendour of its sets, not to mention the considerable drawing power of a youthful Richard Burton in the role of King Arthur.

These attractions were further augmented by Julie Andrews, as an equally appealing Queen Guinevere, and a handsome young newcomer, Robert Goulet, in the role of Sir Lancelot. Goulet was 'discovered' as an exciting new singing talent and went on to build a successful career for himself as a solo performer.

Cute numbers like 'Camelot' and the would-be lovers' 'tip-sheet', 'How to Handle a Woman', were a match for anything on Broadway, but 'If Ever I Would Leave You' was a cut above most of the competition and would have brought in the public on its own.

Like the dreamy, romanticised film version that followed in 1967 starring Richard Harris, Vanessa Redgrave and David Hemmings, the original stage production of *Camelot* might have benefited from some judicious pruning, but in spite of only a moderate degree of enthusiasm from the critics, the first Broadway production found approval where it mattered – with the public – and ran for almost 900 performances. In 1964 there was a London production starring Laurence Harvey as King Arthur; a part that was taken over later by Paul Daneman.

In 1993 Robert Goulet starred as King Arthur in a Broadway revival and subsequent tour, but whatever lustre he had developed in the years following his success in the part of Sir Lancelot deserted him utterly. His portrayal of the King was severely panned by both critics and public alike.

Half a Sixpence (1963)

Apart from the obvious attraction of a colourful and fast-moving show based upon H G Wells's novel *Kipps*, *Half a Sixpence* was especially significant in providing the music theatre launch pad for a rock 'n' roll star who was about to prove himself an all-round entertainer.

Tommy Steele excelled in the role of Arthur Kipps, a young apprentice at Shalford's Drapery Emporium and the story, charting the development of this engaging character as he first inherits then loses a fortune, allowed Tommy Steele full scope to employ his considerable talents.

Half a Sixpence opened at the Cambridge Theatre, London on 21 March 1963, with Marti Webb playing the role of Arthur's childhood sweetheart Ann, and Anna Barry playing Helen, the girl Arthur favours when he has money to burn.

With a book by Beverly Cross and score by David Heneker, the show ran for 679 performances, before moving to the Broadhurst Theater, Broadway, where it ran for over a year.

There were a number of memorable songs including the winsome title song as well as the rumbustious 'Flash! Bang! Wallop!' A film version was released in 1967 in which Tommy Steele starred with Julia Foster and Cyril Ritchard.

Funny Girl (1964)

Funny Girl was the ideal vehicle for Barbra Streisand. With a story based on the life of the earlier Broadway superstar, Fanny Brice, the similarities between that lady and Streisand were uncanny. Clearly destined for the highest reaches of theatrical glory, Streisand had found herself a part that not only showed off her particular talents as both singer and actress, but allowed a vulnerability and comic element to be revealed that made her all the more endearing to the audience.

The opening in New York at the Winter Gardens on 26 March 1964 had been delayed while revisions on the book were carried out. These were never completely resolved, but a strong score, featuring music by Jule Styne and lyrics by Bob Merrill, allowed Streisand to raise the roof with numbers like 'Don't Rain on my Parade' and the poignant, but equally stunning 'People'. The last song became a hit for Streisand, who also won an Academy Award for her performance in the 1968 film version, in which she starred alongside Omar Sharif as the playboy and love of Fanny's life, Nicky Arnstein.

The Broadway show ran for 1,348 performances, with Streisand and Sydney Chaplin in the leading roles. Streisand also starred in the London production.

Hello Dolly! (1964)

The huge success of this show derives not only from a score of unusual appeal, but from the fact that in providing a show-case for its female lead, the fame of *Hello Dolly!* could only gather pace in direct relation to the number of gifted actresses who became associated with the role.

Carol Channing was the original Dolly in a production that opened on Broadway at the St James Theater on 16 January 1964. The show ran for 2,844 performances, with stars like Phyllis Diller, Betty Grable and Ethel Merman playing the role of Dolly at one time or another.

Touring companies saw Dorothy Lamour, Mary Martin and Eve Arden, amongst others, lend their spirit to the role and the 1969 film version starred Barbra Streisand at the very height of her powers, together with the strongest imaginable cast, including Walter Matthau and Michael Crawford.

Arguably, Carol Channing's interpretation remains definitive and she re-created the role of Dolly on Broadway in 1978 and then in London the following year.

Based on Thornton Wilder's play *The Matchmaker*, Michael Stewart's book takes an affectionate view of the shenanigans surrounding self-appointed matchmaker, Dolly Gallagher Levi, along with the love-life of a less complex, if equally lovable character, the young clerk, Cornelius Hackl.

Jerry Herman's music was outstanding and Louis Armstrong's unforgettable cover of the title song ensured its immortality as well as securing a number one slot in the US record charts for him, together with Grammy Awards for Best Song and Best Male Vocal. Other numbers included 'Put on Your Sunday Clothes' and 'Before the Parade Passes By'.

Hello Dolly! won Tony Awards across the board for book, score, musical, actress (director, choreographer, producer (all David Merrick)) musical director; Shepard Coleman, set designer; Oliver Smith and costumes; Freddy Wittop.

Fiddler on the Roof (1964)

The name, Topol, became synonymous with *Fiddler on the Roof*, mostly because of the enormous popularity of the 1971 film version, and also for this man's phenomenal success in the London production of the show which ran for well over 2,000 performances.

Topol also found popular success outside the show with his superb version of the song 'If I Were a Rich Man', which was soon on everyone's lips and swiftly entered the record charts.

It was Zero Mostel in the original production, however, who set Broadway alight, spreading the news that here was an informative, disturbing, fascinating show, that left a lasting impression of superb and evocative music and where issues like religion and anti-Semitism were confronted with a degree of intensity more usually found in a straight play. The characters, too, displayed a depth and complexity that again was unusual for this type of show.

The wholy deserved success of *Fiddler on the Roof* was forged not just by excellent delivery of 'big show' songs and set piece theatrical numbers, but by the engaging folk idioms and insight into dilemmas that in their simple humanity were familiar to every member of the audience.

Opening at the Imperial Theater, New York on 22 September 1964, *Fiddler on the Roof* ran for 3,242 performances, with Zero Mostel staying for the first year. He was then followed by a succession of outstanding performers in the role of Tevye, the loquacious family man and milkman from a tiny village in Imperial Russia.

The story deals in a matter-of-fact way with the terror of those trapped and defenceless during the pogroms and observes the break-up of Tevye's close-knit family as his children move away from their parents in both the literal and ideological sense.

The book by Joseph Stein was based on Sholom Aleichem's essays on episodes in the life of the milkman Tevye in early twentieth-century Russia. The music was by Jerry Bock and the lyrics were written by Sheldon Harnick.

The song most people remember, 'If I Were a Rich Man', was written with Zero Mostel in mind, but would subsequently become just as keenly associated with the Israeli performer, Topol.

Other songs included 'Sunrise Sunset', 'Matchmaker Matchmaker', 'To Life', 'Do You Love Me?' and 'Tradition'. The show scooped up countless awards including the New York Drama Critics Circle Award for Best Musical and Tony Awards for Best Musical, Best Score, Best Book, Zero Mostel for Best Actor, Maria Karnilova, playing Golde, Tevye's wife, for Best Featured Actress, for choreography, Jerome Robbins and finally for costumes, Patricia Zipprodt.

Sweet Charity (1966)

A vulnerable, lovable tart who wants to find someone with whom she can live a normal life is an appealing story-line and the show proved a success, as well it might with Cy Coleman's brilliant music and the seasoned professional, Dorothy Fields's, amusing lyrics.

Gwen Verdon's interpretations of the leading role in the original production was highly praised and she was given some of the very best numbers like, 'There's Gotta be Something Better Than This' and 'If My Friends Could See Me Now'. Other songs included hits like 'Big Spender' and the amusing 'I Love to Cry at Weddings'.

The show opened at the Palace Theater, New York on 29 January 1966 where it ran for 608 performances. In 1967 the London production featured Juliet Prowse in the leading role of Charity and the 1986 Broadway revival starred Debbie Allen. Shirley Maclaine played Charity in the film version of 1969.

Mame (1966)

Based on a play *Aunty Mame* that had been adapted from a novel by Patrick Dennis, *Mame* proved a huge hit for composer and lyricist Jerry Herman.

The tale of an ageing aunty who attempts to instil some *joie de vivre* in her nephew proved a theme around which some appealing songs were woven. These include 'We Need a Little Christmas', 'That's How Young I Feel' and 'If He Walked Into My Life' which was also a singles hit for both Matt Monro and Scott Walker. The title theme 'Mame' was a hit for trumpet player Herb Alpert and the original cast album won a Grammy.

The show opened at the Winter Gardens Theater, New York on 24 May 1966 and ran for 1,508 performances.

Angela Lansbury created the role of Mame and won a Tony Award for Best Actress. Tonys were also won by Beatrice Arthur and Frank Michaels as Best Featured Actress and Actor. The London production opened in 1969 starring Ginger Rogers and there have been countless revivals and tours since 1966, including one in 1983 when once again Angela Lansbury played Mame on Broadway. A film version was released in 1974, starring Lucille Ball and Robert Preston.

Cabaret (1966)

The coming together of a number of gifted performers at the peak of their creative powers in the outstanding 1972 film version of *Cabaret* dictates a starting point from which to work backwards, rather than forwards. The film-script was tailored to accord with a 1970s public's perspective of Berlin in the 1930s; to be a showcase for its stars and to have a reasonably happy ending, rather than the somewhat less sanguine conclusion of *Sally Bowles* (1937), the original story by Christopher Isherwood upon which the musical was based.

In the film the title song, 'Cabaret', not only provided the perfect vehicle to flaunt all of Liza Minnelli's considerable gifts in the role of Sally Bowles, but with its theme appearing to echo her own search for something of substance beneath the glamour, there is an added poignancy that lingers long after the music fades.

Joel Grey, recreating his stage character as Master of Ceremonies at the Kit Kat Club, wields an awesome power that is both slick and sinister and conjures up the Nazi era that underpins every event we are allowed to witness during this entertaining, yet unsettling movie.

Christopher Isherwood's *Berlin Stories* was published in 1935 and reflected within a number of tales the decadence and simmering violence of a nation that was re-emerging with an obsessive nationalism that bred tension and a 'live for the moment' mentality within the minds of a great many of its people.

The first stage version of Isherwood's story, *Sally Bowles*, was presented by John Van Druten in 1951 and was called *I am a Camera*. There was also a film by the same name released in 1955. The first musical version was an adaptation of the 1951 stage play by Joe Masteroff, who used the composer John Kander's music and lyrics by Fred Ebb.

Re-named *Cabaret*, the show opened at the Broadhurst Theater, New York on 20 November, 1966, with Jill Haworth playing Sally Bowles, but it was Joel Grey in the role of Master of Ceremonies who stole the show.

This production ran for 1,165 performances, winning Tony Awards for Joel Grey; for another cast member in a supporting role, Peg Murray; for the director, Harold Prince, for Best Musical Score; for the choreographer, Ronald Field, for the set design by Boris Aronson and for costumes by Patricia Zipprodt.

Judi Dench enjoyed great success as Sally Bowles in the 1968 London revival and in 1987, Joel Grey proved himself an enduring and particularly effective MC when he starred again on Broadway, in the role he had created more than 20 years before.

The dancer Wayne Sleep proved himself more than equal to the task of Master of Ceremonies in the 1986 West End revival although, arguably, he lacked something of Joel Grey's sinister command of the part he had made so much his own.

Various other productions have been staged and will continue to be staged because the raw material is just so good, but it will be a fortunate cast indeed that spawns two such perfect performances as those immortalised on film by Joel Grey and Liza Minnelli.

Hair (1968)

Weird, outrageous and innovative, proved a winning formula for the creators of this show – Galt MacDermot who wrote the music and Gerome Ragni and James Rado who wrote book and lyrics.

Celebrating the youth of the hippie era with their attitudes towards free sex, politics and drugs, *Hair* was an 'in-your-face' explosion of flower-power meets music theatre. Long hair, especially novel in the case of the men, and naked bodies certainly added to the attraction for some people, but the score was full of tunes that would become significant in their time even if the show itself bordered on the self-indulgent.

Songs like 'Aquarius' achieved anthem status, typifying that era's unfocused groping for a more meaningful identity and this song's popularity was closely followed by 'Let the Sunshine in', 'Good Morning Starshine' was fun and catchy and more representative in many ways of a production that drew the audience into the plotless happenings on stage, so that they emerged having had a really good time.

The show opened off-Broadway to begin with and then opened at the Biltmore Theater on 29 April 1968. Diane Keaton was in the cast along with Lamont Washington, Lyn Kellogg, Melba Moore and Sally Eaton.

There was a successful London run in 1968 and a film version was released in 1979. A 1993 revival at the Old Vic in London was a disaster, largely because *Hair* was a product of its time – a show every self-respecting young person in the 1960s and 1970s had to experience. The reactions of a comparatively sophisticated 1990s audience proved that there simply weren't enough hippies left to applaud a show that had once been daring, even anarchic with its rude words and naked bodies, but now seemed merely quaint.

Tommy – 1969 album release; 1975 film; 1979 first West End stage production

In 1969 a highly successful pop group, The Who, made a departure from the usual round of hit singles by issuing a double-album entitled *Tommy*. Described as a 'rock opera', *Tommy* uses songs, ensembles and instrumental interludes to tell the story of a teenager, struck deaf, dumb and blind through trauma, who lives and communicates through pin-ball machines.

The form was certainly similar to opera, but that in itself presented a problem. If *Tommy* was an opera, where and how could it be presented? If the album had been only reasonably successful, that question might never have been asked, but *Tommy* was hugely successful and the album sold millions of copies worldwide. One song in particular, 'Pinball Wizard', not only shot into the singles charts, but became a classic.

There have been several concert versions and Roger Daltrey, the lead singer of The Who, played the lead role brilliantly on many occasions. Ken Russell made a typically flamboyant film version in 1975, but a West End staging in 1979, at the Queen's Theatre, ran for a meagre 118 performances, possibly because this production lacked the involvement of Pete Townshend, one of *Tommy's* main creative forces.

Moving on almost 30 years to 1993, *Tommy* opened on Broadway at the St James Theater and was a colossal hit, resulting in four Tony Awards, as well as massive box office receipts. Pete Townshend was back firmly in the driving seat for this production, along with director, Des McAnuff, and together they had revised the book and overseen the inclusion of stunning theatrical effects that thrilled Broadway and then London.

Even by 1996 when *Tommy* was staged at London's Shaftesbury Theatre, the music didn't seem to have dated at all. In fact, utilising every development that had occurred since *Tommy's* inception, the work sat comfortably within the 1990s, without appearing to be attached to the 1960s – with the possible exception of its sheer 'in your face' glitz.

From a musical perspective, Pete Townshend, as the main composer, together with his fellow members of The Who, show musical and creative instincts beyond the norm, since, unlike *Tommy*, many other works from the 1960s contain a recognisable musical idiom that fixes them firmly in their historical pigeon-hole.

Superstar 1970s

Fashions of the 1970s are now perceived as having been in desperately bad taste, but those who flaunted them clearly felt boldness preferable to the spaced-out droopiness of the 'flower power' 1960s.

Two of the major works at the beginning of the 1970s, *Godspell* and *Jesus Christ Superstar* (see pages 128 and 138), show boldness in their interpretation of the Christian gospel and in *Godspell*'s case, the use of the 'flower power' culture to tell one of Western civilisation's oldest stories.

It is almost impossible now to imagine the stir caused when biblical subjects, crucial to so many people's devotion and serious study, were presented as popular entertainment. Themes of this type are guaranteed to whip up emotions when aired, but the sheer audacity of the style and context within which the story of Christ was revealed caused genuine offence to some and a life-changing revelation to others. On the other hand, for many people these shows provided a great evening's entertainment and nothing more.

The 1970s demonstrated yet again that music theatre lacked for nothing in sheer variety. Alongside these more provocative shows, humour was alive and well in *Grease*; Stephen Sondheim produced a more thoughtful masterpiece in *A Little Night Music*; *A Chorus Line* shifted the spotlight from the principals to the chorus – and required top-class soloists to take these roles; *Annie* was cute; *The Rocky Horror Show* amazing – and that is just a tiny selection of the shows that were on offer!

Godspell (1971)

Rock-religion found favour in the 1970s and *Godspell* was one of the first full-length professional shows to reflect this vogue in music theatre.

- ■ The original amateur, music-cantata version of *Joseph and the Amazing Technicolour Dreamcoat* (see page 137), previewed three years earlier.
- ■ The full-length, professional production of *Joseph and the Amazing Technicolour Dreamcoat* opened in the West End in 1973.
- ■ *Jesus Christ Superstar* (see page 138) opened on Broadway in October 1971; *Godspell* opened off-Broadway at the Cherry Lane Theater on 17 May 1971 and ran for 2,124 performances before transferring to the Broadhurst Theater for another 527 performances.

Colourful and melodic and with a young and enthusiastic original cast, *Godspell* had contemporary melodies woven throughout its New Testament theme. Based upon St Matthew's Gospel, the book was by John Michael Tebelak and both music and lyrics were written by Stephen Schwartz.

Songs such as 'Day By Day' and 'Prepare Ye the Way of The Lord' became widely popular and were hits for both the Broadway and London casts, as well as a number of other artists.

The London production at the Wyndham Theatre ran for almost three years and there have been several revivals since, although like much material from the 1970s, without substantial revision to the staging the show runs the danger of appearing to be locked in a time-warp and one that might appear quaint, rather than truly appealing to a contemporary audience.

Grease (1972)

Jim Jacobs and Warren Casey aren't familiar names in the music theatre, but these were the originators of the phenomenon that is *Grease*.

As the years pass since its first appearance as a five-hour amateur production, the distinction blurs between what was in the original, off-, then on-Broadway production and what was in fact written expressly for the 1978 film version.

The original book, music and lyrics were written by Jim Jacobs and Warren Casey and their affectionate look at the late 1950s teenage rock 'n' roll era has maintained its popularity in both the amateur and professional arena right up to the present day.

'Sandra Dee', 'Summer Nights', 'Freddie My Love', 'Beauty School Drop-Out', 'We Go Together', 'Greased Lightnin'', 'There are Worse Things I Could Do', 'Mooning' and 'It's Raining on Prom Night', are all great and together with a sharp, witty libretto, they have kept popularity burning for the show.

Opening off-Broadway in the first instance, *Grease* scored a big hit at the Eden Theater in 1972 and moved to Broadway four months later, opening at the Broadhurst Theater on 7 June 1972. The following year the London production opened and ran for 236 performances, featuring Elaine Paige as principal understudy to begin with, then leading lady in the role of Sandy Dumbrowski and the then unknown Richard Gere in the part of Danny Zuko.

The film version featured a number of new songs by Barry Gibb, John Farrar, Louis St Louis, and Scott Simon and these included 'Grease', 'Hopelessly Devoted to You', 'Sandy' and 'You're the One that I Want'. John Travolta and Olivia Newton-John in the leading roles were brilliantly cast and both the film and soundtrack became immensely popular. Enthusiasm for the show in both the professional and amateur arena has never waned.

A Little Night Music (1973)

With its restrained and engaging music, *A Little Night Music* is a perfect example of Stephen Sondheim's deeper style of musical. The elegant tale unfolds through a witty script and a wealth of mainly waltz-time tunes and is based on an Ingmar Bergman film, *Smiles of a Summer Night*.

Set in Sweden, *A Little Night Music* tells the story of two middle-aged people, Fredrick Egerman, a lawyer, and an actress, Desiree, who was once his mistress. Both are now engaged in relationships with much

younger partners; Egerman has a young wife and son and Desiree is
involved with a young, married man. An ageing lady, famously played by
Hermoine Gingold in both the Broadway and West End productions,
contrives to untangle the romantic confusion.

Glynnis Johns starred in the original Broadway production and her
account of 'Send in the Clowns' has never been bettered. The show
opened at the Shubert Theater, New York on 25 February 1973 and ran for
more than 600 performances, winning Tony Awards for Best Musical,
Best Score, for the book by Hugh Wheeler, for Glynnis Johns as Best
Actress, Best Supporting Actress, Patricia Elliot and for the costumes by
Florence Klotz. The equally successful London production opened in
1975 and there have been many successful revivals and tours of the show
ever since, although a film version in 1978 starring Elizabeth Taylor failed
to live up to expectations and has faded from view.

Stephen Sondheim (1930–)

Stephen Sondheim came from an affluent family and his apprenticeship in
music benefited greatly from his contact with Oscar Hammerstein II who
was a close family friend. Sondheim graduated from Williams College
with the music composition prize to his credit and a bursary allowing him
to study with the American composer, Milton Babbitt. Babbitt's
reputation was that he combined academic rigour with entertainment and
this mixture of wit and skill was apparent in many of his innovative
compositions.

Sondheim's first really big commercial success came through his lyrics
for the outstanding musical *West Side Story* (1957) (see page 175) and he
followed this with lyrics for the musical *Gypsy* (1959) with Jule Styne
writing the music. In 1962 *A Funny Thing Happened on the Way to the
Forum* featured both Sondheim's music and lyrics, but his next major
project, *Anyone Can Whistle* (1964), with book by Arthur Laurents and
songs by Sondheim, was a flop. The cast recording for this show was a
success, however, showing that Sondheim's music had its own appeal.

Another Laurents book provided the background for *Do I Hear A Waltz?*
(1965) for which Sondheim as lyric-writer teamed up with composer
Richard Rodgers. This also failed to make a lasting impression on the
theatre-going public.

In 1970 *Company*, directed by Broadway legend Harold Prince, provided Sondheim with the first awards of his Broadway career and *Follies* (1971) gained him more recognition, even though 522 performances proved insufficient to re-coup the massive investment required to stage the show.

Even the experienced producer Cameron Mackintosh burned his fingers re-launching *Follies* in London in 1987, when once again the run of 600 performances proved too few to cover the production expenses.

In 1973 *A Little Night Music*, with director Harold Prince once again at the helm, was more restrained on the production front, but rich in melody and pathos. 'Send in the Clowns' in particular, with its timeless poignancy, became an enormous hit.

Now Sondheim was recognised as one of America's greatest contributors to music theatre, but even so his show *Pacific Overtures* in 1976 was perhaps just too innovative and closed after only a short run.

A compilation of his more successful works was formed into a show in 1977 and called *Side By Side with Sondheim*. This proved a great success and demonstrated that whereas his musicals were sometimes too complex for popular consumption, the songs in isolation were superb.

In 1979 Sondheim made a complete departure from his normal style and came up with the vastly entertaining *Sweeney Todd, the Demon Barber of Fleet Street*, which featured the man with the blade with murder on his mind and his friend Mrs Lovett, who disposes of his customers' remains by baking them into pies. *Sweeney Todd* won eight Tony Awards and ran for more than 500 performances.

Merrily We Roll Along followed in 1981, but managed only 16 performances. *Sunday in the Park with George* (1984) fared better, running for more than 18 months and winning the Pulitzer Prize for Drama. Then in 1987, Sondheim produced a glorious and award-winning piece, *Into the Woods*. Fairy-tale characters slip in and out of this adult tale and the score is full of memorable tunes and clear cut musical characterisations. *Assassins* in 1981 reverted to a more complex format and its theme was unusual to say the least – comparing the handiwork of various well-known murderers.

Sondheim also composed film music and contributed many more items for music theatre in general. Amongst his most popular songs must surely be 'Maria' and 'Somewhere' from *West Side Story*, together with 'Send in the Clowns'.

In many ways he remains a controversial figure, if only because of the unexpected nature of much of his work. In this he has surely followed the teacher of his early years, Milton Babbitt. The similarity in their approach includes Sondheim's innovation and his refusal to 'play to the gallery'. One thing is sure: he provides food for thought and always provokes a reaction to his work, whereas some composers of musicals have only the knack of courting commercial success.

The Rocky Horror Show (1973)

A cult phenomenon, *The Rocky Horror Show* rockets fantasy into an entirely new league, with characters that exceed most people's wildest imaginings. The names alone – Frank 'n' Furter, Riff Raff, Magenta, Little Nell, etc. – together with suspenders, cross-dressings, drugs, sex, horror, sci-fi and rock 'n' roll, combine to provide an experience in which the audience is invited to become totally immersed.

Opening at the Royal Court Theatre Upstairs on 19 June 1973, this tilt at humdrum respectability made the name of its creator and star, Richard O'Brien. Transferring in August 1973 to an atmospheric venue – an old cinema in Chelsea's King's Road – the show stuck two vigorous fingers in the air for over five years, before gaining establishment recognition with a move to the West End's Comedy Theatre in April 1979, where it remained for almost eighteen months.

America didn't like it and the 1975 production at the Belasco Theater, New York closed after only 45 performances. Strangely enough, the 1976 film version produced the reverse effect, with disaster on British shores contrasting with adulation to the point of obsession in America. Now there are armies of fans on both sides of the Atlantic and fan clubs worldwide catering for their needs.

A Chorus Line (1975)

A musical without an interval, this musical about the audition process for a musical proved to be one of the all-time record-breakers.

During the nail-biting, heart-rending course of the show, the audience gets to know a little about each of the would-be cast members and feels their disappointment or elation just as keenly as if the whole process was real.

Zach, the cool-headed director, is looking for a cast of eight dancers out of 17 hopefuls, one of whom is his ex-mistress, Cassie. An empty stage with working lights sets the scene; mirrors at the back of the stage recreate a rehearsal-studio setting and the lights and mirrors allow the performance space to be changed dramatically in the final scene. In this, the remaining dancers don their costumes and perform part of the 'real' show for their audience.

Beginning life as a workshop production on 21 May 1975 at producer Joseph Papp's New York Shakespeare Festival Public Theater, *A Chorus Line* moved to the nearby Newman Theater before transferring to Broadway, where it opened at the Shubert Theater on 21 July 1975.

In 1976 *A Chorus Line* won the coveted Pulitzer Prize for Drama, the New York Drama Critics Award for Best Musical and Tony Awards for Best Musical, Best Director, Best Book, Best Score, for lighting, choreography, and for Donna McKechnie, playing Cassie, the award for Best Actress in a musical; also for Best Featured Actor and Best Featured Actress in a musical, Sammy Williams and Carole Bishop.

Incredibly, *A Chorus Line* closed on 28 April 1990, after 6,137 performances. The London production opened in July 1976 and ran for almost three years.

The idea for the show came from Michael Bennett, a dancer who explained 'Basically, it's a show about dignity. It gives dignity to the boys and girls in the chorus who will never be stars.'

The choreography for the original production was by Bennett and Bob Avian, the book was by James Kirkwood and Nicholas Dante and the score was by Marvin Hamlisch and the lyricist, Edward Kleban.

The requirements of this show should never be underestimated, since most of the cast are required to be top-class dancers, as well as really excellent singers. The songs include the big ballad 'What I Did for Love', the winsome 'The Music and the Mirror', great point numbers like 'I Can Do That' and the stunning chorus finale, 'One'.

Annie (1977)

Martin Charnin is credited with the idea of creating a musical based on the comic-strip character, Little Orphan Annie and *Annie* opened at the Alvin Theater, Broadway on 21 April 1977. With music by Charles Strouse and libretto by Thomas Meehan, the show proved a huge hit and ran for 2,377 performances.

Set in 1933, the story traces the fate of a resourceful orphan, Annie, and her dog, Sandy. Longing to find her parents and desperate to escape the clutches of Miss Hannigan, the drunken harridan who runs the orphanage, Annie strikes lucky when her path crosses that of millionaire, Oliver Warbucks. Of course, the fairy-tale has a happy ending and Miss Hannigan, her scheming brother and his moll are all routed after a series of hair-raising adventures for Annie and Sandy.

The show won Tony awards, including those for Best Musical and Best Score and there was a successful London production as well as countless revival and tours. A sequel *Annie 2*, opened in January 1990 at the Kennedy Center Opera House, Washington and then reappeared as *Annie Warbucks* some time later. Nothing, however, could match the appeal of the original, with its score brim full of perky tunes and poignant melodies.

Numbers like 'Tomorrow', 'It's a Hard Knock Life' and 'Maybe' might appear sugary, but in the context of this show they were perfect and the 1982 film version starring Albert Finney as 'Daddy' Warbucks and Aileen Quinn as Annie, helped to make *Annie* unforgettable.

Self-test questions

1. Can you name two musicals by Lerner and Loewe – one which involves King Arthur and the other a Cockney flower girl?

2. Who wrote the music for *Guys and Dolls* and *Hans Christian Andersen*?

3. From which musical does the song 'Room in Bloomsbury' come?

4. Who was the female lead in the film version of *The Pajama Game*?

5 Who was the male star in the original stage version of *Half a Sixpence*?

6 Who created the role of Tevye in the original stage production of *Fiddler on the Roof*?

7 Upon which writer's stories was the musical *Cabaret* based?

8 Who wrote *A Little Night Music*?

9 What is the name of the show created by Richard O'Brien?

10 Which show within a show features the chorus number 'One'?

9 | THE MUSICALS OF ANDREW LLOYD WEBBER

Introduction

Andrew Lloyd Webber was born in 1948 to a musical family and by the age of seven was dabbling in composition. At nine years old, excerpts from his suite of six short piano pieces, *The Toy Theatre*, appeared in the magazine *Music Teacher*.

During his years at Westminster School, his aversion to games was overlooked since he spent his time immersing himself in the two subjects which he enjoyed most, history and music. His taste in music was wide, embracing Elvis Presley and Bill Haley and the Comets, along with more classical figures.

Fortunately for music theatre, Westminster School encouraged its young scholar to broaden his musical experience by writing compositions for school productions and it was in the programme notes for his third and final show for Westminster School in June 1964, *Play the Fool*, that Lloyd Webber stated his intention to 'devote himself to the musical theatre'.

A paper on Victorian architecture led to his being offered an open exhibition scholarship to Magdalen College Oxford to read history, but all the while his musical pursuits continued and drew the attention of another ambitious young musician, Tim Rice. They met during the summer immediately before Lloyd Webber was due to go up to Oxford, and immediately felt a rapport, in both background and musical ambitions.

Having achieved the distinction of a place at Oxford, Lloyd Weber realised after only a term that what he really wanted to be was a composer and with his parents' approval he left Oxford to attend the Royal College of Music on a part-time basis, with a mission to master the techniques of orchestration.

Britain was bristling with innovative ideas in the 1960s and it was only natural that two such gifted young writers should want to create a music theatre style that was both distinctive and original. At first, talent and originality wasn't enough; *The Likes of Us*, a musical based on the life of Dr Barnado, the Victorian founder of the children's charity, failed to make the West End, or anywhere near it, but at least they had dipped their toe in the waters of full-scale musical collaboration. A tilt at the hit parade proved equally frustrating, but opportunity was just around the corner in the person of Alan Doggett, head of music at Colet Court, junior feeder school for St Paul's. Doggett needed something for an end-of-term concert and who better to ask than the son of his friends, whose success in writing for productions at Westminster School was well known and who was now a promising young composer.

The brief was for something 'morally uplifting' and possibly with 'a religious theme'. The results cannot have possibly accorded with Doggett's expectations, but it is certain that they must have exceeded the boys', and in all probability his own, wildest dreams.

The Musicals

Joseph and the Amazing Technicolor Dreamcoat (1968)

Completed in two months, the first version of *Joseph* ran for a mere 15 minutes and was premiered at Colet Court School, Hammersmith on 1 March 1968. Once the subject had been chosen, Lloyd Webber composed the melodies and Rice crafted words to fit.

Tongue in cheek and with a radical musical flavour that saw a number of popular music styles including rock 'n' roll introduced, the presentation was well received, but Lloyd Webber's father recognised the work's full potential and knew it deserved to be brought before a wider public.

Expanded to 20 minutes, this 'pop cantata' as it was now dubbed, played before 2,500 people on 12 May 1968 at the Central Hall, Westminster. In the chorus was the son of the critic, Derek Jewell; a man so enthused, he wrote a glowing review in *The Sunday Times*. The *Joseph* bandwagon had begun to roll and the show was soon to grow, both in fame and length.

Its wacky interpretations of biblical characters, illuminated by the amusing, always catchy music in an assortment of styles that ran the gamut from calypso to country and western, was a totally original departure from previous musical entertainments. The transformation into a show proper came about through Frank Dunlop's production with the Young Vic company. Now grown to a 40-minute version, *Joseph* enjoyed great success at the Edinburgh Festival in 1972 and then played for two weeks at the Young Vic Theatre itself, before transferring to the intimate surroundings of The Roundhouse in Chalk Farm, North London.

The pace of the show was something quite new, with one style and even one century slipping effortlessly into the next, and the impresario Robert Stigwood was soon to notice the 'house full' signs posted every night outside the Roundhouse.

The show's next move was to the Albery Theatre in London's West End, where *Joseph* opened on 6 February 1973. In 1976 the New York opening was a damp squib, marred by sniping from the critics and resounding indifference from the public. Five years later, however, the show would run for a healthy 747 performances on Broadway, reaping the benefit of its association with the enormously successful *Evita*.

Joseph's particular worth lies in the fact that it is still well within the grasp of amateur groups and in either professional or amateur performance, allows large groups of children the chance to take part in the show, singing in the chorus at the side of stage. This accessibility means that there is always a revival of *Joseph* running or about to open somewhere in the world.

Spectacular at the London Palladium in its two-hour lavish form, where the revival played for a record run from 1991 to 1994, or in the simple surroundings of a village hall, *Joseph and the Amazing Technicolor Dreamcoat* remains one of the most entertaining theatre productions ever written.

Jesus Christ Superstar (1971)

By the time this mould-breaking work reached the stage, its songs were familiar across the world. Using the shrewd marketing ploy of releasing a double-disc cast album of the entire score before the production was available to a live audience, proved a master stroke and provoked a degree of curiosity that was only exceeded by the revenue generated.

A written-through score like *Joseph*, *Jesus Christ Superstar* comes closer to opera in many instances with its recitative, or spoken-in-tune passages, that sometimes deliver the plot, as well as the demands it places upon the singers' vocal ability and vocal stamina, especially in the case of the characters Jesus and Judas.

Jesus Christ Superstar takes a sensitive view of the role of the troubled Judas. For believers and non-believers alike, *Superstar* elicits an emotional, as well as a thought-provoking response from its audience, something of a departure for light entertainment. At the same time, the music is wholly engaging and, if sung well stands in its own right as a really strong piece of entertainment. The character Mary Magdalen's song 'I Don't Know How to Love Him,' in particular, has proved to be an enduring and affecting melody from one of Lloyd Webber's most interesting scores.

The original cast recording achieved number one in both the UK and USA charts. The book by Tom O'Horgan, based on the New Testament, benefited once again from lyrics crafted by Tim Rice. *Superstar* sped across the world, spawning productions in America, Australia, Scandinavia and out across Europe with many stops along the way, then on to Mexico, Brazil and even Japan. In London's West End alone it chalked up a mammoth 3,358 performances in the opening run.

Jeeves (1975)

Superstar's phenomenal success was followed by a show that broke records in a far less desirable way: *Jeeves*, the shortest-running Lloyd Webber musical ever, had its original cast recording swiftly deleted from the files and didn't even last long enough for most people to be able to form an opinion, let alone express one.

With lyrics by Alan Ayckbourn, based on PG Wodehouse's hilarious books about the eccentricities of the British class system, and a cast including David Hemmings, Michael Aldridge and Gabrielle Drake, not to mention music by the hottest young composer in town, the show might reasonably have been expected to succeed.

The idea of working on a musical based on some of Lloyd Webber's favourite characters, the aristocratic buffoon, Bertie Wooster, and his altogether more astute and caring manservant, Jeeves, failed to enthuse Tim Rice. The show was to have dialogue as well as sung words and though he made some attempt with a few songs, it soon became clear to everyone that this project was not for him. Lloyd Webber's choice of Alan Ayckbourn, a successful playwright and gifted humorist, as collaborator seemed inspired.

Perhaps *Jeeves* failed because Ayckbourn's success lay largely in his shrewd observations of England's middle classes, rather than the upper classes, or that his lack of familiarity with the requirements of music theatre made for uncustomary clumsiness, or perhaps, and more likely still, the idea just wasn't suitable for the medium of music theatre. Capturing the ethos of an age, together with anachronistic characters about whom most of the audience had no understanding whatever, without the delicious prose of Wodehouse to show the way, proved a lost cause. *Jeeves* opened at Her Majesty's Theatre in London's West End on 22 April 1975 and closed on 24 May 1975 after just 38 performances.

Evita (1978)

Two of the most controversial subjects must be religion and politics, but that didn't stand in the way of Tim Rice's nose for a good story.

When he turned on his radio and heard the story of how a young girl of easy virtue had schemed her way into the bed of the Argentinian dictator, Peron, and then had become that country's icon, he knew he had stumbled across something big.

When he first approached Lloyd Webber, the *Jeeves* fiasco was still in preparation, so the *Evita* project had to be put to one side, but when *Jeeves* folded, Lloyd Webber was keen to restore his confidence through a tried and tested partnership.

The story of *Evita* was strong and the score moved even closer to opera in style, yet retained an unmistakably contemporary feel. Once again a recording was launched in advance of the première and this proved an even greater success than *Superstar*.

Thanks largely to pieces such as 'Don't Cry for me Argentina', sung by Julie Covington and 'Another Suitcase in Another Hall', sung by Barbara Dickson, the public's hunger and anticipation was fuelled as never before.

Evita was so right for its time, with Britain in a political mood because of protracted strikes. The show's story-line, together with the music's plangent melodies, laced with rock and quasi-Spanish overtones, could hardly fail to draw attention of large numbers of the theatre-going public and records were just waiting to be broken ...

> ■ One of the first shocks occurred when Julie Covington
> turned down the chance to play the part of Evita on the

stage, preferring to aim instead for a career in straight theatre.

- ■ Elaine Paige won the part after an extensive search for a replacement for Covington.

- ■ Elaine Paige who clearly identified with the theme of ambition, struggle and determination and whose performance was acclaimed universally to be stunning, was not allowed to work on Broadway and her part was taken by another powerful female performer, the American singer/actress, Patti LuPone.

- ■ *Evita* added lustre and even stardom to the careers of several performers apart from Elaine Paige. These included David Essex, whose frothy 'pop' persona was enriched beyond measure by his charismatic and vocally assured performance as Che. (He remained with the show only a matter of months, however.)

- ■ Without the imagination and keen theatrical instincts of the director, Hal Prince, *Evita* could never have made the stunning visual impact on its audience that not only moved the plot forward at times, but also provided the perfect frame for both music and words.

- ■ From now on, all those involved in music theatre would see the sense of releasing a cast recording in advance of a show.

- ■ Andrew Lloyd Webber and Tim Rice were by now accepted members of the music theatre establishment and considered by many to be in the same league as teams like Rodgers and Hammerstein, but after 15 years of on/off collaboration, the intensity of Lloyd Webber and the laid back style of Rice were proving awkward bed-fellows. It now seemed likely that *Evita* would be their last musical together.

Song and Dance (1980)

Like any other successful person before him, Andrew Lloyd Webber has almost as many detractors as fans, but how can criticism possibly outweigh praise for a man who has brought such a variety of approach to the musical, whilst managing to retain his own entirely distinctive stamp.

Lloyd Webber needed to look for a new collaborator. Hal Prince introduced him to the lyricist Don Black, a man who had been involved in hit records with Charles Aznavour and Matt Monro. The result was the dramatic 'song cycle' *Tell me on a Sunday*, subtitled *An English Girl in America* in which the outstanding songstress Marti Webb told in song a young English woman's romantic experiences in New York. The second half of the evening, with the dancers led by Wayne Sleep, was a stunning dance sequence to the *Variations* Lloyd Webber had adapted from a theme by Paganini for his brother Julian, a fine cellist.

- ■ This was significant because it proved that Lloyd Webber could work successfully with lyricists other than Tim Rice. It also proved that however unlikely the formula, his name in lights outside a theatre guaranteed full houses.
- ■ It was also interesting because the music from each half of *Song and Dance* stands on its own, yet when put together appears to have been written with a total concept in mind from the beginning.
- ■ The show received powerful support in the person of John Caird, director, and choreographer, Anthony Van Laast.

Cats (1981)

This seems to be another unlikely theme to try to translate into a full-scale West End show. The arcane poems of T S Eliot, *Old Possum's Book of Practical Cats*, published in 1939, attributing human characteristics to cats and with no linking story, seems about as far away from a potential record-breaking musical as you can get, yet *Cats* has broken every record. The show provides a magical experience that has as much impact in Japan as it does in London or New York.

Sumptuous cat costumes, stunning make-up, superb choreography, brilliant dancing, great songs, exciting orchestration, innovative set design, coupled with Lloyd Webber's purrfectly appropriate music, elevate this book of classic children's poems to previously undreamed of heights.

- ■ Undoubtedly the all-star team assembled on the production side contributed greatly to the triumph of this most successful musical: Andrew Lloyd Webber, Composer; Valerie Eliot, the author's widow contributing letters and an unpublished poem about Grizabella the Glamour Cat; a character that goes on to provide an essentially poignant and thought-provoking note, pointing-up the vigour of the younger cats, as well as the humour in the piece; Cameron Macintosh, producer; Trevor Nunn, director; Gillian Lynne, associate director and choreographer; John Napier, designer; and John Hersey, lighting designer.

■ Not surprisingly, all the usual theatrical investors were shy of putting their money into such an unusual scheme. Those who did can scarcely have expected to reap the phenomenal rewards that more than repaid their adventurous spirit.

■ One song, 'Memory', sung by Grizabella the Glamour Cat has become a classic and in 1992 Lloyd Webber's Really Useful Company announced that it was aware of 150 different recordings of this song at one time.

■ The lyrics for 'Memory' had to be constructed since there were no appropriate Eliot poems. The attraction of contributing towards another hit for Elaine Paige tempted Tim Rice, but it would be Trevor Nunn's version, based on Eliot's poem 'Rhapsody on a Windy Night' that, unsurprisingly he, as director, chose to use.

■ Apart from the play by Agatha Christie, *The Mousetrap*, which has been running since 1952, *Cats* is now the longest-running musical in London, surpassing even the 6,137 performance run on Broadway of the musical *A Chorus Line*.

■ Apart from records broken, awards for excellence came thick and fast, proving that however unlikely the topic, in the right hands, anything is possible.

■ An absolute 'must see' for children of all ages everywhere.

Starlight Express (1984)

The most technically ingenious; the most unusual concept; the most engaging tunes; the most appealing children's, or for that matter, appealing entertainment for any age...

With *Starlight Express*, Lloyd Webber tests the use of superlatives to the limit. The theme of loyalty and victory of good over... well, not exactly evil, but a great, flashy, sure-of-himself, bully of an electric train, is uncomplicated, even if the largely American imagery of 'the railroad' with all its associations of hitching a ride to somewhere better, allows for some poignancy along with the fun.

The end result is another totally captivating voyage into the imagination. Played and sung by a cast that whizzes around the stage and sky-born track on wheels, this musical, like Disney, draws fresh breath with each new crop of youngsters who see the show.

Feats of daring are breath-taking, costumes and make-up are fantastic, the music races along with the performers, running the gamut from rock 'n' roll to ballad and emotions are tapped to the full with each new strain. *Don't miss it...*

The Phantom of the Opera (1986)

Rather like *The Sound of Music* and *Les Miserables*, this musical has developed an army of fans who never tire of seeing the show.

A conventional musical in many ways, *Phantom of the Opera* incorporates all the (by this stage in the 1980s) mandatory special effects and spectacular dramatic moments an audience had come to associate with this type of large-scale, big-budget musical show.

It was also significant in revealing the full extent of Michael Crawford's theatrical talents. Before Michael Crawford, all interpretations of the Phantom were measured against the legendary performance by Lon Chaney in the silent film version of the story made in 1925, and the successful casting of the Phantom was crucial to the success of Lloyd Webber's new piece. Although chiefly renowned for his wonderful comic realisation of the permanently perplexed television character, Frank Spencer, in the show 'Some Mother Do 'Ave 'Em', Crawford cut his theatrical teeth in *Billy*; *No Sex Please, We're British* and *Barnum*, a show where he amazed audiences nightly with his astonishing and purposely acquired circus skills.

Sharing the same singing teacher as Lloyd Webber's young second wife, Sarah Brightman, proved fortuitous, not only for Crawford in landing the part of Phantom, but for the theatre-going public. Apart from his mellow and engaging vocal quality, Crawford brought a touching dignity to the part of the hopelessly enraptured Phantom.

The romantic tale of a disfigured man and a beautiful young girl, whose mutual love was music, provided Lloyd Webber with an opportunity to eschew novelty and concentrate instead on composing in a more expansive and melodic style than ever before.

Aspects of Love (1989)

Everyone became excited at the prospect of a new Lloyd Webber musical, taking into account the caution that this was to be on a much more intimate scale than any previous work.

In spite of being an enormous success both financially and in terms of a personal triumph of quality over quantity for Lloyd Webber, it was finally deemed a failure by a public used to record-breaking shows with never-ending runs.

Lloyd Webber had tried to interest Tim Rice in the project way back in 1980 to no avail and in 1986, with the successful launch of *Phantom* behind him, he revisited the idea, bringing in Don Black, with whom he had worked on *Tell me on a Sunday*, and Charles Hart from *Phantom* to write the lyrics.

Previous collaborators included Trevor Nunn as director and Maria Bjornson from *Phantom* who would be responsible for the sets, as well as Gillian Lynne, the choreographer of both *Cats* and *Phantom*.

A strong cast was assembled, with the well-known light tenor Michael Ball in the role of the young romantic lead, Alex, and Roger Moore as his naughty old Uncle George. Personality-wise, Moore suited the part to perfection, but vocally, he fell too far short of the demands of the piece and prudently left a month before the opening, allowing his understudy Kevin Colson to take over this leading role.

A lengthy standing ovation greeted the première in London and Lloyd Webber was delighted. The cast was superb and the music as good as any he had written. The run was for 1,325 performances – outstanding for any other composer.

The American run of a mere 377 performances cast a pall over proceedings and *Aspects of Love* had the shortest run of any Lloyd Webber musical on Broadway to date, allowing his critics an unprecedented opportunity to gloat.

Sunset Boulevard (1993)

Everything about *Sunset Boulevard* is BIG, but without the tongue-in-cheek humour and slickness of *Starlight*, or the almost cinematic visual impact of *Evita* or *Phantom* and with every attempt at subtlety stifled, the end result runs the risk of being described as unwieldy.

The music is as evocative and memorable as ever and casts on both sides of the Atlantic have delivered stunning, or, in the minor roles, highly competent performances, but *Sunset* buckles under the weight of its machinery. This is not intriguingly concealed to provide spine-tingling theatrical moments, but heavily and noisily present, with a highly decorated set that spells out in mind-numbing detail every nuance of Norma Desmond's lonely and backwards-looking existence, rather than crediting the audience with an iota of imagination.

The story, based on Billy Wilder, Charles Brackett and D M Marsham Jnr's original book and, more especially, the film by Billy Wilder, reflects on the penalties of ageing in a youth-obsessed culture like Hollywood.

Gloria Swanson, who played the first Norma Desmond in the film version to William Holden's Joe Gillis, was herself a victim of this unfeeling system. Once a major star of the silent screen, with the advent of talkies she too found herself side-lined progressively in favour of young new stars.

The film version seethed with foreboding but without the deft touch of someone like Hal Prince, the stage version of *Sunset Boulevard* sent its audience away with a song in their hearts, but hearts heavier than they might have expected after a night of musical theatre.

A series of spectacular leading ladies in the role of Norma Desmond, coupled with the media-type furore that greeted the casting of the part, ensured that *Sunset Boulevard* enjoyed something of the success commonly associated with a musical by Andrew Lloyd Weber.

- The librettists were the playwright, Christopher Hampton and Don Black, who had worked on both *Tell Me on a Sunday/Song and Dance*, and *Aspects of Love*.
- Music is omnipresent, but there is also quite a lot of dialogue spoken over the mood-enhancing music. Perhaps not surprisingly in a musical about the film industry, this technique apes the sound-track of a movie.

Opening nights for the musicals of Andrew Lloyd Webber

01.03.68 *Joseph and The Amazing Technicolor Dreamcoat* –
Colet Court School.

06.02.73 *Joseph and The Amazing Technicolor Dreamcoat* –
West End opening: Albery Theatre, London.

22.04.75 *Jeeves* – West End opening: Her Majesty's Theatre.

21.06.78 *Evita* – West End opening: Prince Edward Theatre.

25.09.79 *Evita* – Broadway opening: Broadway Theater.

11.05.81 *Cats* – West End opening: New London Theatre.

27.01.82 *Joseph and the Amazing Technicolor Dreamcoat* –
Broadway opening: Royale Theater.

07.04.82 *Song and Dance* – West End opening: Palace Theatre.

07.10.82 *Cats* – Broadway opening: Winter Garden Theater.

27.03.84 *Starlight Express* – West End opening: Apollo Victoria Theatre.

18.09.85 *Song and Dance* – Broadway opening: Royale Theater.

09.10.86 *The Phantom of the Opera* – West End opening:
Her Majesty's Theatre.

15.03.87 *Starlight Express* – Broadway opening: Gershwin Theater.

26.01.88 *The Phantom of the Opera* – Broadway opening:
Majestic Theater.

17.04.89 *Aspects of Love* – West End opening: Prince of Wales Theatre.

08.04.90 *Aspects of Love* – Broadway opening: Broadhurst Theater.

12.07.93 *Sunset Boulevard* – West End opening: Adelphi Theatre.

09.12.93 *Sunset Boulevard* – Los Angeles opening: Shubert Theater.

17.11.94 *Sunset Boulevard* – Broadway opening: Minskoff Theater.

Self-test questions

1 What was the title of Andrew Lloyd Weber's first published work?

2 Which musical was required to be 'morally uplifting' and possibly to contain 'a religious theme'?

3 What was the title of the popular song sung by the character Mary Magdalen in the musical *Jesus Christ Superstar*?

4 Upon whose book was the musical *Jeeves* based?

5 From which musical does the song 'Another Suitcase in Another Hall' come?

6 In which musical did Elaine Paige replace Julie Covington to make her starring debut?

7 What marketing ploy was used to further the success of Lloyd Webber musicals?

8 Which show was the longest running and most unexpected success?

9 Which show featured Michael Crawford in the original cast?

10 Which two writers wrote the libretto for *Sunset Boulevard*?

10 | THE 1980s, 1990s AND INTO THE FUTURE

Overview

With large getting larger and spectacular sometimes meaning effects at the expense of the music, the 1980s and 1990s have contained musicals that are clearly amongst the best in their genre, as well as some that may not survive long into the new century. The phenomenal cost of mounting a big show has put a break on creativity to some extent, for who wants to risk backing an unknown writer, or supporting an unusual theme when there is money to be made from tried and tested revivals.

Danger will always lie in the possibility that opulent sets and special effects will negate the need for star quality, although the other side of the coin allows for performers who can transcend these distractions.

One thing *is* certain; while there are shows of the calibre of *Blood Brothers* and *Les Miserables*, a demand will exist for top-class professionals who can bring a passionate story-line to life.

The 1980s and 1990s have brought shows that remind us of an earlier era, such as *42nd Street* and *Crazy for You*, spectaculars such as *Barnum* and *Phantom of the Opera*, tongue-in-cheek shock and fun with the *Little Shop of Horrors*, sixteenth-century passion in *Martin Guerre* and revivals that have been even more successful the second time around like *Chicago*.

Once again the watch-word is variety and the future looks safe for an art form that can adapt with such ease to the demands of an enthusiastic public.

1980s

Barnum (1980)

This musical, based loosely on the life of Phineas T Barnum who billed himself as 'The World's Greatest Showman', relies for success on the strength of the performances of its central character. In this respect, both the Broadway and London productions have been especially lucky.

Jim Dale opened on Broadway at the St James Theater on 30 April 1980 and was outstanding in the title role, winning a Tony Award for Best Actor; Glenn Close played the role of his wife, Chary.

The most exceptional performance of all must surely have been that of Michael Crawford in the London production at the London Palladium. After spending two months at a circus school to learn various skills, Crawford turned in a stunning performance as actor, singer and circus performer, winning himself a well-deserved Olivier Award and cementing his position as one of the foremost theatre performers of all time. In the 1992 London revival, another fine performer, Paul Nicholas, took on this key role.

The score by Cy Coleman and Michael Stewart is good, but not brilliant, with 'Come Follow the Band' being by far and away the number most people remember – and very good it is too.

The demanding stunts required for *Barnum* might previously have been executed by 'speciality acts' drafted into a production, but were now to be performed by regular cast members, and this all added to the thrill of a colourful and very entertaining show.

42nd Street (1980)

This musical is interesting because it is one of the few that began life first as a novel and a film of the same name, before going on, many years later, to become a stage musical. A show within a show, featuring a once-famous director trying to make a comeback, an ageing star struggling to stay in the spotlight and a chorus girl who gets her big chance, *42nd Street* has the power to bring an audience to its feet.

In 1933 Warner Bros introduced their film version of *42nd Street* as 'The 1932 version of *Gold Diggers of Broadway*'. Much-loved stars like Ginger Rogers took on the self-explanatory, role of Anytime Annie and Dick Powell played Billy Lawler, with Bebe Daniels as the fading diva Dorothy Brock, and Ruby Keeler as the ingenue, Peggy Sawyer. Once again, Busby Berkeley gave the choreography his unique stamp and Darrell F Zanuck, the then head of production at Warner Bros, spared no expense in the preparation of what would become a hugely successful and profitable hit across the world.

More recently, on 25 August 1980, the producer David Merrick stood with his cast on stage at the Winter Garden Theater on Broadway to receive a tenth curtain call for the newly revamped *42nd Street*. Like Zanuck before him, Merrick had spared no expense in assembling a strong cast as well as the best possible production team. Just that afternoon the show's director and choreographer, Gower Champion, had died, adding the only low note to the proceedings, for Champion had won the hearts of his public over many years, both as a dancer, choreographer and the director who had introduced stars like Carol Channing to the stage.

With numerous awards to his name and with regular television appearances, including his own sitcom with his wife and erstwhile dance partner, Marge Belcher – *The Marge and Gower Champion Show* – Gower Champion was loved by public and performer alike, for they all reaped the benefit of his magical touch. It is fitting that *42nd Street*, his last show, saw him leave the stage in a blaze of glory. For David Merrick, this night was a home-coming, as he was already well known for his shows *Hello Dolly!* and *Gypsy*, but it had been an uncomfortable number of years since his last major triumph. With a script by Michael Stewart of *Bye Bye Birdie*, *Hello Dolly!* and *Mack and Mable* and Mark Bramble, who went on to co-author *Barnum* with Stewart and who already had several important credits to his name, Al Dubin's original lyrics from the film looked to be in safe hands. Cleverly, Merrick lifted some of Dubin's and composer, Harry Warren's, best pieces from other films, especially from *Gold Diggers of 1935*, including 'Lullaby of Broadway'.

The end result was a show for which audience enthusiasm has never flagged. It opened at the Theatre Royal, Drury Lane, London in 1984 and received a richly deserved standing ovation. Twelve curtain calls later, the audience was still cheering and *42nd Street* continues to raise that same level of delight to the present day.

Little Shop of Horrors (1982)

Based on Charles Griffith's tongue-in-cheek horror movie, this musical version with a book by Harold Ashman, who also wrote the score together with Alan Menken, grew, rather appropriately, into a monster hit.

A flesh-eating plant, a winsome heroine and a bungling, though well-intentioned hero in the person of florist's assistant Seymour Krelbourn, the story is Dahlesque in its gloriously gruesome detail and the fast-paced action is full of quirky humour and benefits from an instantly accessible, pacey score.

A try-out at the modest WPA Theater in New York resulted in a transfer to the Orpheum Theater on New York's Lower East Side, where the show opened on 27 July 1982. The world had a new block-buster on its hands, and 2,209 performances later, the 1984 London production endorsed this with a run lasting over a year. The show won numerous awards including the New York Drama Critics Circle Award for Best Musical and London's *Evening Standard* award for outstanding musical. A film version was released in 1986, starring Steve Martin.

This show in both its content and accessibility is perfect for amateur and, in particular, school productions.

Blood Brothers (1983)

If you are looking for a show that has you helpless with laughter in the first half and crying with emotion in the second, this is it. As *La Bohème* (see *Teach Yourself Opera*) brings *verismo* or realism to opera, *Blood Brothers* brings gritty and sometimes uncomfortable truths to the musical stage.

Set in Liverpool, the story examines the fate of twin brothers, separated almost at birth, who grow up in homes at the opposite ends of the social spectrum. Life conspires to draw them together, but the consequence of their reunion results in tragedy.

The show is one big roller-coaster ride of emotion and I defy you not to be gripped by every moment. Willy Russell's keenly drawn observations of children's behaviour in the first half is hysterically funny and, together with the inevitability of tragedy in the second, makes for an unusually moving show that enraptures the audience throughout. It requires a top-class cast of actors, some of whom must sing to an extremely high standard, and when this level is achieved the end result is a stunning piece of music theatre.

A strong book, evocative music and an exceptional cast rocketed *Blood Brothers* into public notice when it opened at the Lyric Theatre, London on 11 April 1983. Superbly written by Willy Russell and starring Barbara Dickson, the show won Olivier Awards for Best Musical, with Barbara Dickson who sang 'Marilyn Monroe' and 'Tell Me It's Not True' winning the award for Best Actress in a Musical.

Perhaps because of its parochial setting, *Blood Brothers* took some time to find the same degree of acclaim on Broadway, but following a successful West End revival in 1989, the show finally opened in New York in 1993 and its initial lukewarm reception was massively improved when well-known stars such as Petula Clark and David Cassidy were brought in to play the leading roles, allowing the show's many valuable qualities to be revealed.

Miss Saigon (1989)

The idea of updating the story of Madame Butterfly, so poignantly told in Puccini's opera of the same name (see *Teach Yourself Opera*), was brilliant; the idea of re-setting it in mid-1970s Vietnam, during the last days of the American military presence, was nothing short of inspired.

A young Vietnamese girl, Kim, has a child by a married GI, Chris. When the time comes for the Americans to pull out of Saigon, Kim is left behind and when Chris returns to find her, only tragedy awaits him. Power is added to the attraction of this show by the sheer scale and drama of the production, including at one point a full-size helicopter being lowered to the stage. However, story-line and spectacle apart, *Miss Saigon* falls well short of Schönberg and Boublil's earlier work, the masterpiece *Les Miserables*. The score is good, but comes nowhere near its sensational predecessor in the sheer variety and quality of its music. There are some memorable moments and these occur in such touching duets as 'The Last Night of the World', 'I Still Believe' and the melodious 'Sun and Moon', as well as in the strong chorus material. The Engineer's scathing account of 'The American Dream' is also one of the highlights of the show, as is Kim's tender solo, 'I'd Give my Life for You'.

With music by Claude-Michel Schönberg and lyrics by Alain Boublil and Richard Maltby Junior, *Miss Saigon* opened at the Drury Lane Theatre, London on 20 September 1989 and the show is still running at the time of writing. Jonathan Pryce was outstanding in the role of the Engineer, the cynical owner of the Dreamland bar where Vietnamese girls like Kim sell their favours to the American soldiers and both Pryce and Lea Salonga, in the role of Kim, won Olivier Awards. *Miss Saigon* opened on Broadway in 1991, where Pryce and Salonga repeated their award-winning performances, receiving Tony Awards in recognition.

The 1990s

Five Guys Named Moe (1990)

'The Joint Never Stops Jumpin'' is the slogan associated with this show and it is nothing less than the truth. *Five Guys Named Moe* is a celebration of the music, either written by or associated with one of the great black musicians of the 1940s and 1950s, Louis Jordan. Numbers like 'Ain't Nobody Here But Us Chickens', 'Is You Is, Or Is You Ain't Ma Baby' and 'It Must Be Jelly Cos' Jam Don't Shake Like That' give you just a flavour of what's in store. After a string of electric all-dancing, all-singing episodes, it comes as no surprise to find that the story-line is suspended at times so that the audience can join in the fun. The story revolves around a love-lorn man, Nomax, morosely listening to the blues on his radio, when suddenly, out of the set explodes the five 'Moes' – Big Moe, Little Moe, No Moe, Eat Moe and Four-Eyed Moe. The Moes set about educating Nomax in the ways of women and love, with riotous consequences.

Cameron Mackintosh 'discovered' *Five Guys Named Moe* playing at a small East London theatre in 1990 and ensured the show, written by Clarke Peters, was transferred to the Lyric Theatre in London's West End. In 1991 *Five Guys Named Moe* won the Olivier Award for best entertainment and by 1993 was celebrating its 1,000th performance. The Broadway production opened in 1993 and ran for over a year.

Crazy for You (1992)

Crazy For You opened at the Shubert Theater, Broadway on 19 February 1992, re-establishing the American presence at the very peak of achievement in music theatre, amidst a veritable deluge of Lloyd Webber.

Taking four numbers from the George and Ira Gershwin 1930s show, *Girl Crazy* – 'Bidin' My Time', 'Could You Use Me?', 'I Got Rhythm' and 'But Not For Me' – and incorporating a host of fantastic Gershwin numbers from their other shows, *Crazy For You* could hardly miss. Nevertheless, at its out-of-town try-out in Washington, the show lost money. Perhaps it was felt that the old favourites couldn't compete with their bland modern counterparts, but when the show reached Broadway, it was almost as if the theatre-going public drew a deep breath and said, 'Hey, hang on a minute, this music is better than good – and it's American too''.

Ken Ludwig's new book was an adaptation of Guy Bolton and John McGowan's original for *Girl Crazy* and now featured would-be performer Bobby Child, sent by his wealthy mother to close one of her hick-town theatres that is failing to make money. Bobby falls in love with the theatre manager's daughter and resolves to save the day. To do this he imports a glamorous dance troupe from the up-town Zangler Follies and prepares to open his show...

The Broadway production, starring Harry Groener and Jodi Benson, won Tony Awards for Best Musical, Best Choreography by Susan Stroman, and costumes by William Ivey Long. The London production at the Prince of Wales Theatre, starring Ruthie Henshall and Kirby Ward, opened on 3 March 1993 and won Olivier Awards for Susan Stroman's choreography and for Best Musical. Funny, colourful, enormously entertaining – and the Gershwins – what more could you want!

Martin Guerre (1996)

Manipulating historical facts had already been exploited to great effect by Boublil and Schönberg in *Les Miserables*. Now the story of Arnaud du Thil, whom a court in Toulouse had condemned to be burned for the sin of posing as Martin Guerre back in 1560, was shuffled forward, to allow the religious conflicts of the time to be incorporated into the drama.

In a small French village called Artigat, Bertrande de Rols, the young wife of Martin Guerre, believes him to have been killed in the troubles sweeping France as the rise of Protestantism challenges the established Catholic religion. Having Protestant sympathies herself, Bertrande persuades Arnaud du Thil to take her late husband's name to prevent her being married off to a Catholic suitor whom she finds unattractive.

The formula for this show bears comparison with *Les Miserables* with its heroine's plangent songs and in the powerful chorus work. As with the Thenardiers in *Les Miserables*, there is also a comedy element to leaven the drama, this time in the guise of three crones, Celestine, Ernestine and Hortense, whose commentary on the married state, 'Sleeping On Our Own', is one of the highlights of the show.

The world premiere of *Martin Guerre* was held on 10 July 1996 at the Prince Edward Theatre. Alain Boublil co-wrote the book, the original French text and the additional lyrics. Lyrics were also contributed by

Edward Hardy and Stephen Clark. Boublil's partner, Claude-Michel Schönberg, wrote the music and book. The producer was Cameron Mackintosh, with Declan Donnellan directing and Nick Ormerod responsible for the production's design.

Chicago (1998)

With music by John Kander and lyrics by Fred Ebb, *Chicago*, based on a book by Fred Ebb and Bob Fosse, was successful the first time around when headlines proclaimed this Broadway show a hit in 1975. The revival in London's West End more than 20 years later proves that big-time Broadway musicals are still very much in demand. Set in Al Capone's Chicago, the theme of ambition, greed and sex is just as resonant today as it was back in the 1970s.

Exhuberant dance, evocative vocal interpretations and a keen vision of the possibilities thrown up by this theme, has led to a brilliant interpretation of an energetic show. With Walter Bobbie as director, the show reveals its relevance to a contemporary audience and the choreography of Ann Reinking, in the style of the late Bob Fosse, ensures that his legend lives on. The main roles in this West End revival are thrillingly portrayed by Ruthie Henshall, Ute Lemper and Henry Goodman.

Self-test questions

1 For which role in a musical must a performer learn circus skills?

2 Who wrote the song 'Lullaby of Broadway'?

3 Which musical features a flesh-eating plant?

4 Who wrote the musical *Blood Brothers*?

5 *Miss Saigon* has a similar theme to which opera?

6 'The Joint Never Stops Jumpin'' was the slogan for which show?

7 *Crazy For You* was based on whose music?

8 Can you name two of the hit songs from *Crazy For You* – one's got rhythm and the other's got time?

9 Who wrote *Martin Guerre*?

10 Who wrote the music for *Chicago*?

Part 2

A Closer Look at Six Musicals

11 | SHOW BOAT (1927)

Background information

One of the greatest all-American musical plays, *Show Boat* has come to be recognised in the last 20 years or so as a masterpiece of its time.

After a successful première in the late 1920s, it was sometimes crudely pigeon-holed with other examples of operetta-style work as just another dated example of 'Old Country' influence.

Everyone was keen to move on and embrace new fashions in music along with everything else, but what they missed was that this period piece is essentially American, peopled by American characters, and that its setting preserved one of the most colourful aspects of recent American history; the era of the riverboat.

Jerome Kern and Oscar Hammerstein were themselves essentially American, even if the foundation of their style did hark back to an earlier tradition. They both liked to cut to the essentials of a scene or emotion with no blurring of the issues brought about through excessive decoration, and that gave their work an elegant simplicity that was again contemporary in spirit.

Jerome Kern's inspiration for the show came from the Pulitzer Prize-winning novelist Edna Ferber's fictional account of the lives and loves of the Mississippi riverboat entertainers and gamblers, also called *Show Boat*.

Hammerstein and Kern visited a real river boat in the course of their research and were initially captivated by the happy-go-lucky characters on board. They were less impressed, however, when they discovered that the entertainers treated their performances as a mechanical duty and both men left in disgust without saying goodbye. In spite of this set-back, they had fallen in love with the possibility of bringing their own idealised version of life on the river to the stage.

The result was a production that contained no fewer than six great standards: 'Can't Help Lovin' Dat Man O' Mine', 'Make Believe', 'Why Do I Love You?', 'Bill', 'You Are Love' and 'Ol' Man River'.

The show opened at the Ziegfeld Theater, Broadway on 27 December 1927 and ran for 572 performances, with Jules Bledsoe starring as Joe, the character who sings 'Ol' Man River'; a role and a song later made world famous by Paul Robeson. Helen Morgan played the part of Julie and her interpretation of 'Can't Help Lovin' Dat Man', 'Why Do I Love You?' and in particular 'Bill' (which had original lyrics by P G Wodehouse) ensured that all these songs became huge hits.

In 1928 the London production starred Paul Robeson as Joe and he was given a new song to sing, 'I Still Suits Me'. In 1942 there was a London revival and in 1946 Broadway hailed the return of *Show Boat* with yet another new composition, 'Nobody Else But Me'. This was to be Jerome Kern's last composition, but not the last revival by any means for this show. In 1948, 1954, 1966, 1982 and 1990 there were major revivals on the professional stage and several film versions have been released.

Show Boat is now recognised, like Gershwin's *Porgy and Bess*, as being in a category of its own. Not more than a musical, or less than an opera, but subtly different, its popular appeal is uncontested and for this we must thank its creators, Jerome Kern and Oscar Hammerstein II, who were, quite simply, masters of the art of entertainment.

Plot summary

As soon as it becomes known that Julia La Verne's mother was black, she is forced with husband, Steve Baker, to leave the riverboat where they have been working as entertainers. Magnolia, daughter of the boat's owners, takes over Julia's roles and a gambler, Gaylord Ravenal is employed to take Steve's place.

Magnolia and Gaylord fall in love and marry, but in time his gambling leads to money troubles and Magnolia and their daughter, Kim, are left to fend for themselves. Magnolia tries to find work as a singer and meets up again with Julie and Steve who arrange for her to sing at a club where they are working. Magnolia's career begins to soar and Kim also finds stardom when she follows her mother into showbusiness. Many years later

Magnolia and Gaylord are reunited at the place where they first met on the Mississippi river.

Highlights

It is impossible to think of *Show Boat* without 'Ol' Man River' coming to mind, but there are several other lovely melodies for you to look out for. 'Make Believe' is romantic music at its best and if romance is your preference then 'You Are Love' is another song to listen out for. 'Can't Help Lovin' Dat Man O' Mine' is just as stirring as 'Ol Man River' and 'Bill' is equally popular. The chorus has some strong material too, like 'Mis'ry's Comin' Aroun', 'Cotton Blossom' and 'In Dahomey'.

Personalities

Jerome Kern (1885–1945)

> *'His melodies, surviving him, will live in our voices and warm our hearts for many years to come, for they are the kind of simple, honest songs that belong to no time or fashion. The man who gave them to us earned a lasting place in his nation's memory.'*
>
> President Truman, Washington 1945

Jerome David Kern was born into a comfortably off family in New York City. His father was a businessman who would take some convincing that his son would not automatically follow him into the family business, but his mother Fanny encouraged Jerome and arranged for him to have piano lessons.

As a young man he undertook studies privately in a number of countries, but it soon became obvious that he was no prodigy, at least in the performing sense.

He returned to America in 1904 and became a song-plugger on Tin Pan Alley, then collaborated on the adoption of an English Musical Comedy, *The Earl and the Girl*, for the Broadway stage. Four of his own numbers were used and one, 'How'd You Like to Spoon with Me?', became a hit.

The publisher Max Dreyfus took an interest and this was the beginning of a life long association for Kern.

It was in 1914 that Kern wrote a complete score for Broadway, although he had contributed something like a hundred songs to other shows before that time. *The Red Petticoat* was not a success, but that same year Kern had his first really big hit with the song 'They Didn't Believe Me', which was included in another adaptation of an English show called *The Girl From Utah*.

From 1915 Kern joined with the writers P G Wodehouse and Guy Bolton to produce a number of budget productions known as the *Princess Theatre Shows* and then in 1920 the show *Sally* became a huge hit for Kern, not least because the touching duet 'Look for the Silver Lining' stopped the show every night.

In 1925 the show *Sunny* saw Kern on Broadway, this time working with Otto Harbach and Oscar Hammerstein II. Once again the show starred the talented Marilyn Miller who had enjoyed great success in *Sally*. In the London production that star of stars and jack of all theatrical trades, Jack Buchanan, made the hit song 'Who' his own.

Next, Kern had the idea to adapt Edna Ferber's novel *Show Boat* for the musical stage and in 1927 his music, together with Hammerstein's lyrics, combined to produce one of the greatest music theatre works ever. More shows followed, of course, but none of the calibre of this outstanding masterwork.

The individual songs that came afterwards were often just as great in their way. 'The Song Is You', for instance, from the show *Music In The Air* (1932); 'Smoke Gets in Your Eyes' from *Roberta* (1933); and from his last, and sadly unsuccessful show, *Very Warm For May* (1939) the haunting 'All the Things You Are'.

Jerome Kern married an English girl, Eva Leasle, in 1910 and they had one daughter Elizabeth Jane. In the 1930s the Kerns went to live in Beverly Hills and there they stayed. Kern was a knowledgeable yet modest man, whose contribution to American music is incalculable.

Paul Robeson (1898–1976)

Paul Robeson was an 'A' student and an outstanding athlete. His brother was a doctor and his sister a teacher, like their mother. His father had been born into slavery, yet escaped at the age 15, eventually becoming a preacher. During his days at Columbia University, Paul Robeson combined his love of sport and his studies as a law student with a burgeoning interest in the stage. By 1922 he was already appearing in a play in London with the celebrated actress, Mrs Patrick Campbell, and the following year he was in the chorus of Lew Leslie's *Plantation Revue*. By now his future was set and in 1925 he made his first concert appearance, alerting the world to a bass-baritone voice of exceptional beauty. He was a gifted actor who took the role of Othello in Stratford-upon-Avon, as well as in Boston and on Broadway (1943) and appeared in several films, including the screen version of *Show Boat* in 1936. He mastered no fewer than 25 languages and towards the end of the 1940s had become politically active, writing and speaking in defence of the rights of persecuted people in several countries. Robeson attracted unwanted attention too and racist feelings were stirred up amongst those elements of society who could not bear to see a black man attract such acclaim.

In 1950 his passport was taken away since his beliefs were thought to be detrimental to the good of his country and it would be 1958 before he was able to declare to a packed Carnegie Hall that it had at last been returned. Almost to the end of his life, when ill-health overtook him, Robeson continued to tour and to write and speak on behalf of all those people he felt to be rejected or discriminated against.

He was truly an outstanding man, not only for his artistic gifts, but for his intellect, charisma and perhaps above all for his outspoken courage on behalf of others. The world, however, remembers him best for his unforgettable cameo role as the stevedore, Joe, singing 'Ol' Man River' in the film version of *Show Boat*.

Helen Morgan (1900–41)

Helen Morgan came up the hard way through club-land before graduating to revues, where eventually she was spotted by the great Florenz Ziegfeld when she appeared in his *Ziegfeld Follies of 1931*.

The role of Julia La Verne in *Show Boat* had proved particularly hard to cast, with its unusually demanding requirements in acting as well as singing. Helen Morgan was singing in a small revue entitled *Americana* when Jerome Kern saw her and realised that he found the ideal person to play the part of Julie, and it was this role that would set the seal on her stardom.

Apart from many other stage appearances, she also appeared in the 1936 screen version of *Show Boat*, but by this time the considerable reputation she had made as one of the world's greatest ever 'torch' singers – a name given to someone who could put over a passionate, or smoochy night-time song – was being eroded by her addition to alcohol; an addiction that led to cirrhosis of the liver from which she died.

Florenz Ziegfeld (1867–1932)

Florenz Ziegfeld was the most significant force involved in the production of the early twentieth-century Broadway musical. His father founded the Chicago College of Music and as a young man Florenz Ziegfeld already had both a discriminating eye and a keen ear for what was good entertainment. More importantly perhaps, he also had a keen nose for business and whilst still only a teenager, he had a number of successful shows to his credit.

When his father dispatched Florenz to Europe with the task of seeking out classical musicians of quality, he returned with a good selection of variety acts, including Claus Von Bulow's Military Band and the world's strongest man, Eugene Sandow. This ability to tune into acts, personalities and shows with mass, rather than specialised, appeal would become the hallmark of his unprecedented theatrical success.

In 1907 he launched a series of revues, known as *The Ziegfeld Follies* which have never been equalled for their sheer opulence, the talent and charisma of their stars, the beauty and number of their showgirls and the quality of their composers and writers.

In 1927 he opened his own *Ziegfeld Theater* and though he took a serious hit during the infamous Wall Street crash of 1929, he lived in a style and with a vigour that can only be wondered at today.

Postscript

■ Florenz Ziegfeld wanted *Show Boat* to be completed by 1 January 1927, only three weeks after the contract was signed. In return, he agreed to produce the show 'on or before the 1st day of April 1927'. As we now know, it actually opened on 27 December 1927. (What seems now to have been an impossible request on Ziegfeld's behalf almost certainly stems from the fact that the greater part of his experience was with writers for vaudeville, like William

Anthony McGuire and JP McEvoy, who were used to turning out comedy sketches and other light-weight pieces at incredible speed. He also hoped that the 'show' would open his new theatre in February and urged Kern and Hammerstein to 'work fast'.)

■ At the same time, Ziegfeld was urging another pair of collaborators to finish their play so that it could open his new theatre. As it happens, *Rio Rita* was finished first and Kern and Hammerstein were coolly informed that their work would be put on at another house – quite where wasn't made clear by Ziegfeld and, not unnaturally, the pair began to worry.

■ While they waited for Ziegfeld's decision, Hammerstein took himself off to London to supervise the Drury Lane production of *The Desert Song*.

■ The original cast was to have included Elizabeth Hines in the role of Magnolia, a fact that was recorded by both an announcement and a photograph of Hines in the opening night programme of the play *Rio Rita*; Gaylord Ravenal was to have been played by Guy Robertson and Joe by Paul Robeson, but by the time Ziegfeld and the writers were ready, these performers had needed to be released from their contracts so that they could pursue work elsewhere.

■ Until just two weeks before the opening, *Show Boat* was advertised as opening at the Lyric Theater on 42nd Street, then at the last minute it was finally transferred to the Ziegfeld Theater.

■ Following the 1932 revival, Oscar Hammerstein and later his son, William, began to make changes to the show.

■ This was never a light-weight show, but undoubtedly the original production benefited from Ziegfeld's eye for design, beauty and overall visual effect.

■ Apart from its outstanding music, *Showboat* is a tightly written play with music that confronts contentious issues and devotes more time to character development than most works previous to it and many since.

Now try this...

If *Show Boat* was to be categorised arbitrarily as an operetta, to find another work of similar quality, you might start with Franz Lehár's *Merry Widow* (1905), Offenbach's *Orpheus in the Underworld* or *Die Fledermaus* by Johann Strauss II (see page 14).

If you are keen to move a step closer to the 'classical' style, Bizet's *Carmen* (see *Teach Yourself Opera*) is one of the most accessible operas of all, and *Carmen Jones*, Oscar Hammerstein's stunning remake, is perfect is you like a little fizz with your classics.

If it is the American ethos of *Show Boat* that appeals to you, *Porgy and Bess* (see *Teach Yourself Opera*) provides more of the same, or you could even move on to a black and white movie classic like *Yankee Doodle Dandee*, a film based on the life of the American showman, George M Cohan and starring Jimmy Cagney.

Self-test questions

1 Upon whose original novel was this musical based?
2 Who wrote the musical *Show Boat*?
3 Which popular song from the show contains a man's name?
4 Which singer created the role of Joe and sang 'Ol' man River'?
5 Name the man and woman around whom the main romantic theme is based.
6 Why, according to the law in Mississippi, shouldn't Julia be married to Steve?
7 What is the name of Cap'n Andy's granddaughter?
8 Who was the producer of the original production?
9 What prevented Elizabeth Hines from appearing as billed in the opening night performance?
10 Which production opened Florenz Ziegfeld's new theatre instead of *Show Boat*?

12 | MY FAIR LADY (1956)

Background information

One of the most successful and best-loved musicals of all time, *My Fair Lady* is based upon George Bernard Shaw's play *Pygmalion* (1913).

The story centres on a cockney flower seller, Eliza, and her mentor, Professor Higgins. Higgins is a bachelor and an academic specialising in dialect, who accepts a wager from a friend that he will be able to pass off Eliza as a lady in high society, simply by improving her manners and her accent. Both the pitfalls and the unexpected bonuses of this plan form the basis of an entertainment that is full of warmth and humour.

The score is rich in hit tunes which capture every nuance in the plot and for those who have seen the 1964 film version, songs and characters are forever linked. These include Stanley Holloway and 'I'm Getting Married in the Morning', Rex Harrison with 'I've Grown Accustomed to Her Face', or, to recall a particular scene, the 'Ascot Gavotte' and 'Wouldn't it be Loverly'.

The original stage production owed much of its success to a strong cast, many of whom remained with the production for a number of years, as well as from the outstanding costumes by the English photographer and designer, Cecil Beaton.

The idea of using Shaw's play as the basis for a musical was suggested to Alan Lerner by the Romanian-born film director and producer Gabriel Pascal, who had been the driving force behind a film version of *Pygmalion* in the late 1930s, starring Leslie Howard, Wendy Hiller and Wilfred Lawson. The Swiss-born composer Alfred Honegger had provided the film score and the end result was a classic film of enduring quality.

Pascal and Lerner met in Hollywood, where Lerner was adapting *Brigadoon* for the screen and Pascal was working on a film version of another play by Shaw, *Androcles and the Lion*. At Pascal's suggestion, Lerner and his partner Loewe took up the challenge of making a musical of *Pygmalion*. At first they found the adaptation of Shaw's original work problematic and it wasn't until after Pascals' death in 1854 that they decided the only answer was to expand the existing theme into something more compatible with the scale of a musical production.

Lerner triumphed by preserving as much of the original Shaw dialogue as possible whilst weaving his own seamlessly through, and Loewe captured the essence of pre-First World War London without losing anything of his music's contemporary appeal.

My Fair Lady opened at the Mark Hellinger Theater in New York on 25 March 1956 and was immediately the hottest ticket in town. The young Julie Andrews, fresh from her triumph on Broadway in *The Boy Friend*, was a captivating and definitive Eliza, the actor Rex Harrison, in the role of Professor Higgins, made a virtue out of speaking in tune and Stanley Holloway, as Eliza's father Alfred P. Dolittle, revelled in his two rumbustious 'show-stoppers', 'I'm Getting Married in the Morning' and 'With a Little Bit of Luck'.

The show ran for 2,717 performances over more than six years, winning Tonys for Best Musical, for Rex Harrison as Best Actor, for the director Moss Hart, the musical director Franz Allers, for the set designs by Oliver Smith and, of course, for the costumes of Cecil Beaton. Touring shows proliferated and Rex Harrison, Julie Andrews, Stanley Holloway and Robert Coote, who played Higgins's friend, Colonel Pickering, recreated their roles for the London production.

The film version in 1964 starred Audrey Hepburn in the role of Eliza, since Julie Andrews was not considered to be a bankable star in Hollywood terms. Interestingly enough, this apparent slight freed her to accept Disney's offer of the leading role in *Mary Poppins*, a move that won her an Oscar and endorsed her position at the very top of her profession. Audrey Hepburn was an ideal candidate for the role of Eliza in everything but singing voice and this was dubbed by Marni Nixon, whose voice can be heard singing in place of a number of actresses, including Deborah Kerr in *The King and I* and Natalie Wood in both *West Side Story* and *Gypsy*. Both Rex Harrison and Stanley Holloway recreated their roles on film but the veteran British actor Wilfred Hyde-White now played the part of Colonel Pickering. Wilfred Hyde-White was one of that army of actors whose contribution to a film might be small, but was always invaluable and, in this instance, he was quite simply superb.

Six months after the opening in March 1956, the recording of the original Broadway cast reached number one in the American charts, where it remained for two years, while other songs from the show, notably 'On the Street Where You Live', became hits for artists like Vic Damone and David Whitfield. With the advent of stereophonic sound for commercial recordings in 1958, record producer Goddard Lieberson re-recorded the original cast album in 1959, providing a second huge chart success for the show that was by now being hailed as 'America's Greatest Musical'.

Plot summary

Professor Higgins and Colonel Pickering, both specialists in linguistics, meet by chance in London's Covent Garden and strike up an immediate friendship. Higgins has been studying the speech of a flower-girl and brags that by improving her accent, he could pass her off in the highest of society – or at least make her suitable for employment as a lady's maid or to work in a flower shop. Eliza overhears this boast and the next day turns up on Higgins's doorstep, ready to pay him for lessons to improve her diction. The kindly Pickering is concerned, but makes a wager nevertheless that Higgins will not succeed. Higgins accepts and work begins around the clock.

Eliza's good-for-nothing father gets wind of the fact that his daughter is now living in some style at 27a Wimpole Street with two gentlemen. He decides a little blackmail is in order, but an amused Higgins at first begs him to take Eliza – an offer which is quickly declined – and then secures his departure with a five pound note. To keep him out of the way, Higgins tells his house-keeper to put a bothersome American millionaire, who wishes Higgins to set up societies for moral reform, in contact with the most original moralist in England, Mr A P Dolittle'.

Eliza achieves the impossible and makes her entrance into society on the opening day of the Ascot races. All goes well, if a little curiously at times, until the big race, when, as her horse gallops past, Eliza commits an unforgivable blunder, shrieking 'Come on Dover, move your bloomin' arse!' She returns to Wimpole street in disgrace, but a young toff, Freddie Eynsford-Hill is not dismayed and courts Eliza furiously, much to Higgins's irritation. There is work to be done, for, undaunted, Higgins intends now to present Eliza at court.

When the day arrives, Higgins and Pickering are understandably nervous, but Eliza rises to the occasion superbly and the Prince of Transylvania opens the ball with Eliza on his arm. Tension mounts when one of Higgins's ex-pupils, a man who prides himself on spotting impostors, manages to secure a dance with Eliza. Whispers spread and all looks lost, until it becomes clear that the impostorologist has declared that Eliza is in fact Hungarian like himself and unquestionably of royal blood. Higgins, Pickering and Eliza return home in triumph. The two men congratulate each other endlessly, but completely forget about Eliza, who feels utterly abandoned now that the experiment is over. She decides to return to Covent Garden, but feels out of place there too.

A meeting with her father reveals that he has been left a legacy by the American millionaire, 'delivering him into the arms of middle-class morality' and Dolittle advises her to return to the better life she has made for herself.

A troubled Eliza goes to the only place left to her; the home of Professor Higgins's mother. The elderly lady is appalled to hear of her son's thoughtless behaviour and when he visits, she leaves him in no doubt as to her feelings. Higgins tries to tough it out, but he is already missing Eliza dreadfully. They part with matters still unresolved, but when he returns home, she is there, waiting for him...

Highlights

A video may be easier to find than a stage production, so the highlights covered will be as much visual as musical.

The atmosphere conjured up during the film is so convincing that the viewer cannot help but be drawn into the action. Coupled with this are the most detailed and wonderful costumes, especially those worn at the Ascot races, where a theme of black and white is used to maximum effect by Cecil Beaton. The ball, where Eliza is to be presented and tested before high society, also boasts the most lavish gowns and it seems impossible that Eliza can hope to out-shine the rest. The combination of Hepburn's beauty and Beaton's good taste ensure that she does and most decisively.

As in all the best musicals, a song in *My Fair Lady* is not just a pleasant interlude, it may be a plot summary, an introduction into the deeper recesses of a character's personality, or even just an indication that their mood has changed. Eliza makes the transition from day-dreaming cockney flower-girl in the song 'Wouldn't it be Loverly', to quite another type of exhilarated young girl on the brink of a romance in 'I Could Have Danced All Night', By conveying both plot and mood, these songs achieve far more in just a couple of minutes than dialogue alone could hope to achieve.

Personalities

Julie Andrews (1935–)

Julie Andrews was born in Walton-on-Thames, Surrey and her parents, Ted and Barbara Andrews, were theatricals themselves. She made her first professional stage appearance at the age of ten and by 14 she had made her debut in a television show hosted by Henry Caldwell. She became a household name on British radio, playing comedian Archie Andrew's chum in the popular show *Educating Archie* and when just 13, took the title role of Humpty Dumpty in a production at the London Casino. A Royal Command performance followed and then her first really big international break came when she was invited to star in the 1954 Broadway production of Sandy Wilson's musical *The Boy Friend*. It was during the run of this show that she was chosen to play the role of Eliza Dolittle in the original Broadway stage production of *My Fair Lady*. Following her recreation of this part on the London stage, she returned to Broadway to create the role of Queen Guinevere in the musical *Camelot*. She won an Oscar for her 1964 film portrayal of Disney's magical flying nanny, Mary Poppins, and this was followed by a run of films which included *Star*, *Thoroughly Modern Millie*, *Victor/Victoria*, *10* and *SOB* as well as one of the most successful musical films of all time, *The Sound of Music* (see page 183).

With her clear bell-like singing voice and distinctive English delivery, Julie Andrews won the hearts of a worldwide audience. Trained by Madame Stiles-Allan, she possessed an effortless technique which was never abused and this allowed her to enjoy a lengthy singing career that led effortlessly into an acting career of equal distinction.

Rex Harrison (1908–90)

Rex Harrison, born in Huyton, England, was an actor who possessed great style and panache. He made his first professional appearance in a British provincial production at the age of 16 and went on to develop a highly successful acting career, with numerous appearances in both film and stage productions before making one of his most telling film portrayals as Professor Higgins in *My Fair Lady*. He won a Tony for his stage appearance in this role on Broadway and then an Oscar for his performance in the film. His irascible, declamatory, sung-speech interpretation of the part made an unforgettable impression and it was the public's loss that a later film musical, *Doctor Dolittle* (1967), failed to provide him with a suitable vehicle for this particular performance style. Although there would be no more musical roles suited to Rex Harrison's unique delivery, he continued his career with roles that included Pope Julius II in Carol Reed's film about the life of the painter Michelangelo, *The Agony and the Ecstasy*, for which Italy granted him the Order of Merit. He was also knighted by the Queen in recognition of his long and distinguished service to the British theatre.

Post script

- Unlike the ending of *My Fair Lady*, with its promise of romance for Eliza and Professor Higgins, in the epilogue of Shaw's *Pygmalion*, Eliza marries her upper-class admirer, Freddie Eynsford-Hill.
- The role of Eliza Dolittle was created for the famous British actress, Mrs Patrick Campbell, who starred in Shaw's play *Pygmalion* when it opened in London.
- This quintessentially English play, with its concentration on the English class system and dialect, was actually previewed in 1913 in the German language, in Vienna.

■ The first three notes of the major scale, 'doh', 'ray', 'me', appear as a constant figure in many of the main songs. For example, the opening of 'Wouldn't it be Luverly' – 'All I want…', 'On the Street Where You Live' – 'I have of [ten]…'; 'With a Little Bit of Luck' – 'The Lord a[bove]…' and so on.

■ 'I Could Have Danced All Night', uses the major scale yet again, this time as an arpeggio opening, 'I Could Have Danced…'.

Now try this...

If you have enjoyed this heart-warming musical with its wealth of memorable tunes, there are two more by the same writing team for you to enjoy on video. First of these is one of the last to be written specifically for film, *Gigi*. Like *My Fair Lady*, *Gigi* is a lavish and thoroughly entertaining tale, with humour, gaiety, tenderness and absolutely marvellous music. The film stars Leslie Caron, Maurice Chevalier, Hermione Gingold and Louis Jordan and the songs include 'The Night They Invented Champagne', Thank Heaven For Little Girls' and 'I Remember It Well'.

Secondly try, the film of *Camelot;* a light-hearted look at the Arthurian legend with Richard Harris as a brooding King Arthur and Vanessa Redgrave playing his passionate Queen Guinevere. The intensity of the drama that unfolds between Guinevere, Arthur and his knight, Lancelot, is heightened by the luscious 'If Ever I Would Leave You', while 'How to Handle a Woman' is another tuneful, if politically incorrect, highlight in this dreamy, sumptuous drama.

Self-test questions

1 Upon whose play– and what was it called – was the musical *My Fair Lady* based?

2 Who wrote *My Fair Lady*?

3 Who starred as Eliza Dolittle in the original stage version?

4 Who took the part of Eliza in the film version?

5   Which singer dubbed the voice of Eliza in the film version?

6   Which English actor played the part of Colonel Pickering in the film version?

7   Can you name the two men who took leading roles in both the original stage production and the film version?

8   What parts did they play?

9   Who designed the costumes for both the stage and the film version?

10 Which song is sung by Eliza in Covent Garden Flower Market?

13 | WEST SIDE STORY (1957)

Background information

West Side Story opened on 26 December 1957 at the Winter Garden Theater in New York and stunned its audience with a brutal and contemporary tale modelled on the theme of Shakespeare's *Romeo and Juliet*. The Subject may have been familiar, but the setting in both musical and visual terms was innovative, topical and relevant.

The haunting love story of two young people from warring backgrounds was transported into the unpredictable violence of the New York ghetto, where the Puerto Rican youths' Sharks gang pit themselves with mock ferocity against the Jets, a group of Americans youths of European descent. Both sides are unaware that their relatively harmless posturing will soon lead to tragedy, when Maria, sister of the Sharks' leader and Tony, a young European American, fall in love.

This is no dark and depressing tale, however, but a vibrant musical, laced through with humour, tenderness, pulsating rhythms and bewitching melody, and the show ran for a healthy 732 performances in New York, before touring the States, then returning to Broadway for a further 249 performances. London was at first reluctant to take up the challenge, for Broadway shows normally came gift-wrapped with only pleasant subject matter to delight an audience, whereas *West Side Story* demanded quite a different response. The risks involved in mounting such an expensive production were considerable and in the end it was the show's publishers who demonstrated their confidence by backing a production at Her Majesty's Theatre. *West Side Story* opened on 12 December 1958 and ran for 1,039 performances.

With music by Leonard Bernstein, book by Arthur Laurents and the lyrics, plus the songs 'Maria' and 'Somewhere' by Stephen Sondheim, and dazzling choreography by Jerome Robbins, who also came up with the idea for the show, *West Side Story* took the 'comedy out of 'musical comedy' and gave the American musical a respectability that allowed new bounds to be set for every future example of this art form.

Plot Summary

A rumble between rival gangs, the Sharks and the Jets, is interrupted by the arrival of the police. Both gangs are anti-establishment and have no time for lectures. There is a big night coming at the local dance hall and teenagers from both sides will be going. It is the first dance for Maria, Bernado's sister, and, amidst all the uproar, Tony and Maria see each other for the first time. Coming from opposite sides of the cultural divide they realise that it will be impossible for them to meet openly and so arrange for Tony to call at the dressmakers where Maria works.

The rival gangs plan to establish supremacy once and for all but Tony, who belongs to neither group, begs them to have a fair fight. Riff and Bernado, the gang leaders, agree to settle the matter between themselves. The two sides meet under the highway, but Bernado pulls a knife and Riff retaliates. Riff is fatally stabbed and Tony, for whom Riff has been like a brother, grabs a knife and kills Bernado in the heat of the moment.

Bernado's right-hand man, Gino, rushes to tell Maria the terrible news. She supposes Tony has been hurt and demands news. Gino is appalled by her apparent lack of concern for Bernado and tells her bluntly, 'He [Tony] killed your brother!'

Tony arrives to explain to Maria. At first she attacks him, but her love for him is so overwhelming that they can only wonder if they will ever be allowed to find happiness together.

While both gangs are trying to stay out of sight, Bernado's girlfriend, Anita, comes to warn Maria that Gino has a gun and is searching for Tony. She is shocked to hear Tony and Maria whispering together in Maria's bedroom and when Tony goes and Maria finally opens the door, Anita reminds her again that this is the man who killed her brother.

The intensity of Maria's belief in Tony finally convinces Anita that they really do love each other and just as Maria is about to leave to meet him, the police arrive to question her about her brother's death.

Anxious to warn Tony about Gino, Anita goes in her place, but the Jets are at the meeting place and torment her viciously. Humiliated, Anita lies, saying that Gino has shot Maria in revenge for Bernado's death.

Tony is told the terrible news and runs out into the night, shouting for Gino to come and shoot him too.

As soon as the police leave, Maria races out of the house to meet Tony. They see each other across the playground and begin to run towards each other just as Gino raises his gun and shoots Tony dead.

Highlights

Atmospheric, orchestral, balletic, *West Side Story*'s score is an amalgam of all these and takes the musical far beyond its previous boundaries. It has a strong story-line too, but it is far more than simply a play with music and the approach is too colloquial in singing style to be called opera. There are lower moments, musically speaking, when the form slips into an idiom that would become only too familiar in the 1960s and 1970s, when it heralded the worst type of 'trendy' television series, or 'fab' film, but much of the score is as rivetting and intrinsic a part of the drama as the action itself.

Evocative use of whistles, finger-snapping and orchestra, long before electronic effects came along to expand the accepted sound library, sets the scene for this pungent drama. The first really interesting vocal moment arrives with Tony's rhythmic solo, 'Something's Coming', and it seems he will get all the best tunes when his quasi-religious 'Maria' provides an oasis of tranquillity after a sharp Jazz-dance sequence. This mellow interlude contrasts well with the brash disillusionment conveyed next in Anita's paean to 'America'.

Romeo and Juliet is now strongly evoked with a balcony scene – or, rather, a bedroom window and a fire escape scene – but the message is not lost as the voices of Tony and Maria combine for the soaring duet 'Tonight'.

A light-hearted send-up of poor old 'Officer Krupke' leaves you feeling the Jets aren't so bad after all and the buoyant mood is sustained by Maria's innocent enthusiasm for her own reflection with 'I Feel Pretty'.

Now follows an excellent ensemble piece where all the main characters and groups stress the fact that something of crucial importance to them is due to happen tonight...

The knife fight between Riff and Bernado is illustrated with great drama by the orchestra and, as in much of this show, the orchestra is as crucial an element in the story-telling process as the book, the singing, or indeed any of the action.

It is hard to imagine that Tony and Maria's hopeless desperation following Bernado's death could be conveyed more graphically than in their duet, 'Somewhere'.

The Jets respond with their own finger-snapping solution to cool the situation, while Anita's anguished plea to Maria to 'Stick to Your Own Kind' goes unheeded. Maria responds with her own heart-rending defence, 'When Love Comes So Strong, There is No Right and Wrong' and Anita finally joins her, allowing the theme of this work to be brought to its natural conclusion.

Personalities

Leonard Bernstein (1918–90)

Leonard Bernstein, who said of himself, 'All the best song-writers are Jewish or Gay, so I have a distinct advantage being both', was a dynamic man and an exciting musician. With his larger-than-life character, he dominated every area in which he moved and he was not simply a highly respected composer of both classical and popular works upon whom honours would be heaped, but a world-class conductor and pianist, as well as an author and a teacher.

The son of Russian Jewish immigrants, Bernstein learned how to play the piano as a boy and by his early teens was involved in theatrical production. He went on to study at Harvard with piano still his main instrument but influenced by, amongst others, the composer Aaron Copland, he wrote his first symphony, *Jeremiah*. He also studied at the Curtis Institute in Philadelphia and at the Berkshire Music Institute at Tanglewood. In his mid-twenties, he was appointed assistant conductor for the New York Philharmonic Orchestra and by chance was required to step in at the last minute for Bruno Walter. This concert was broadcast live on the radio and by the next morning, Bernstein was being hailed as a great new star.

His classical compositions included ballets, symphonies, choral works and an opera. He conducted most of the great orchestras in the world and recorded a vast selection of works. On Broadway he collaborated with the greats, including Jerome Robbins who choreographed Bernstein's ballet *Fancy Free*, which was later adapted into a full-scale Broadway show and re-named *On the Town* (1944).

This was a great success and included the well-known number 'New York, New York', which became enduringly popular following the film version in 1949, starring Frank Sinatra and Gene Kelly.

Music and lyrics for a musical version *Peter Pan* follow in 1950 and there were many more works for popular theatre, although *West Side Story* was undoubtedly the piece that brought him the greatest success in this area. It must have been a source of great satisfaction to a man who, more than most, possessed both the ability and personality necessary to bridge the classical and popular styles, without robbing either of their essential qualities.

Jerome Robbins (1918–)

A classically trained dancer, Jerome Robbins went on to become one of the foremost choreographers of the Broadway stage. His early career was that of a dancer, but it is for his choreography and directing skills that he scaled the heights with shows like *High Button Shoes*, for which he won one of his many Tony Awards, *Call Me Madam* and *The King and I*. Certainly his choreography for *On the Town* (1944) brought him to the public's attention, but his skills as a director came to the fore in the 1950s on shows like *The Pajama Game*, *Gypsy* and *West Side Story*. His work on *Fiddler on the Roof*, for which he was both choreographer and director – winning Oscars in both categories – was one of his greatest achievements. Plaudits and honours were heaped upon him for his work on both stage and screen, but then in the late 1960s, Robbins returned to his first love, the ballet. In 1989 he returned in triumph to Broadway, to direct a revue of his greatest hits. This resulted in another six Tony Awards for the show *Jerome Robbins' Broadway*.

Harold (Hal) Prince (1928–)

The Ziegfied of *his* day, the name Hal Prince has held sway on Broadway for almost half a century. As a director and producer, his list of credits is awesome. Practically every musical of note bears his thumb-print on some or every aspect. *The Pajama Game* in 1954 saw his first collaboration with Frederick Bisson and Robert Griffith and the association with Griffith lasted until Griffith's death in the 1960s. Taking just one major work a decade, we find Prince involved in *West Side Story* (1957), *Fiddler on the Roof* (1964), *A Little Night Music* (1973), *The Phantom of the Opera* (1986) and the *Kiss of the Spider Woman* (1992).

He has won more Tony Awards than any other person to date and together with his outstanding contribution to American music theatre, Hal Prince has also worked with many of the top opera companies in the United States.

Post script

- Although Bernstein was undoubtedly influenced by those of his teachers with European backgrounds like Fritz Reiner, Dmitri Mitropoulos and Serge Koussevitsky, he was essentially heir to the American tradition as represented by composers like Aaron Copland and Charles Ives. His flamboyant temperament, however, was either built upon, or at the least owed something to his own Eastern European heritage. Whatever the motivating factors, Leonard Bernstein was above all an immensely gifted man and a consummate communicator of his art.

- The influence of Jerome Robbins on *West Side Story* can be felt most keenly right at the start, when the opening scene more closely resembles a ballet than the expected curtain-raiser for a musical. His input as the originator of the idea for the show, as the director and the choreographer, should never be underestimated; it was quite simply immense.

- The original concept was to have centred around Jewish/Catholic families, but this idea was discarded as being overused and Bernstein admitted to being instantly inspired once the focus changed to first generation Puerto

Rican American versus those who considered themselves Americans of longer standing.

■ In the film version, Natalie Wood's (Maria) singing voice was dubbed by the unsung heroine of so many memorable musical films, Marni Nixon; Richard Beymer in the role of Tony was dubbed by Jim Bryant and Rita Moreno's voice (Anita) was actually that of Betty Wand.

■ Apart from the many awards heaped upon the stage production, the film version of *West Side Story* won ten Academy Awards alone.

Now try this...

West Side Story has such a mix of excellent ingredients that there are several widely diverging paths open to you. You might be inspired to visit a production of Shakespeare's *Romeo and Juliet* to discover for yourself how this inspired *West Side Story*; or, at the other end of the spectrum entirely, both *Buddy* and *Grease*, like *West Side Story*, evoke the 1950s era, albeit in a fun way, and include great dance sequences as well as plenty of memorable hits. *Porgy and Bess* takes musical drama one step closer to opera, yet retains all the great rhythms and tunes you will have come to associate with the musical. Another show with a really strong dramatic content is Willy Russell's *Blood Brothers* and this has strong music to complement the action. After thrilling to Stephen Sondheim's 'Maria' and 'Somewhere', you could be keen to discover how he handles sophistication and intrigue, so how about *A Little Night Music?* I did promise wide choices and feel confident that you will find something amongst these suggestions that appeals to you.

Self-test questions

1   To which Shakespeare play is the theme of this musical similar?

2   Who wrote most of the music for *West Side Story*?

3   Who contributed two songs to this work and can you name them?

4   Who wrote the lyrics?

5 Can you name the two gangs involved in the drama?

6 What is the name of Bernado's girlfriend?

7 Who kills Tony?

8 Who was both the choreographer and the person who came up with the idea for this show?

9 Who was the producer of the original show?

10 Can you name two other shows for which the choreographer of *West Side Story* was the director?

14 THE SOUND OF MUSIC (1959)

Background information

The film version of this show may yet prove to be the most enduringly popular film musical of all time. As yet it has no equal and it seems unlikely that such a broad-based appeal will ever be matched. The stage production possesses every element necessary to ensure success; wonderful music, romance, suspense, humour and pathos, while the spectacular film version boasts mountain scenery of unimaginable splendour, as well as the charming city of Salzburg. In these breath-taking settings, a talented cast play out an affecting drama, enriched by enchanting melodies.

Advance sales for the original Broadway production exceeded three million dollars and the show opened at the Lunt-Fontanne Theater on 16 November 1959, where it ran for 1,443 performances. Starring Mary Martin in the role of Maria, the show won Tony Awards for Mary Martin, Patricia Neway, who played the Reverend Mother for featured actress, Fredrick Dvonch, the musical director, and Oliver Smith for set design. The London production opened in 1961, with Jean Bayliss playing Maria and ran for an incredible 2,358 performances. There have been numerous revivals and these, together with the film and the best selling soundtrack album, have made *The Sound of Music* one of the most profitable shows ever written.

Based on the character and life of Maria Augusta Rainer and her marriage to Georg von Trapp, the story charts the development of Maria's relationship with the von Trapp children and her part in the family's escape from Nazi domination in Austria during the Second World War.

Rather than 'go it alone' in this instance, Rodgers and Hammerstein based their work on a book by Howard Lindsey and Russel Crouse, which was itself an adaptation of Maria von Trapp's autobiographical story,

The Trapp Family Singers. Linsey and Crouse were established play-writers and their original idea had been to construct a play with music that would include the type of folk songs made popular by the von Trapp Singers. It soon became clear that there was far more potential in the proposal that they had realised initially and the possibility of a full-scale musical became a reality when Rodgers and Hammerstein were drawn into the project.

This lessening of the usual work load must have been welcomed by Oscar Hammerstein, for less than a year after the Broadway opening, he was dead. In spite of Hammerstein's constant battle against ill health, *The Sound of Music* contains some of the most joyful and inspirational passages of all his writing and it seems a fitting conclusion to his illustrious career that this, his last work should bring enduring happiness to so many people across the world.

Plot summary

Maria, a sincere if high-spirited young novice, has not yet managed to settle into the disciplined life at the convent and much prefers to be out in the beautiful alpine countryside. The Reverend Mother has been asked to recommend a governess for a family of seven children and feels that the break may be just what Maria needs.

It soon becomes clear that the Von Trapp children live a regimented life, marked by their father's need to distance himself from anything or anyone that reminds him of his late wife. At first the children are unfriendly, but Maria wins them over with humour and understanding, comforting the younger children during a thunderstorm and covering for Liesl when she climbs in through a window soaking wet after seeing her boyfriend, Rolf. Maria is determined that the children shall learn to play and sing and when von Trapp arrives home from Vienna with his friend Baroness Schraeder, he is horrified to find his children dressed in play-clothes fashioned out of Maria's bedroom curtains. He orders Maria to return to the convent immediately, but when he hears the children singing, he is deeply moved and begs her to stay.

A grand reception is held to introduce Baroness Schraeder to local society and to friends of the family. Outside, Maria is teaching Kurt how to dance the landler when von Trapp cuts in and Maria realises she is in love with him. Horrified, Maria returns to the Abbey, where the Reverend Mother manages to convince her that love is also a holy calling. When Maria returns to the von Trapp home, the children are thrilled when she and their father decide to marry, but during their honeymoon Austria is annexed by Nazi Germany and Von Trapp is ordered to take up a commission with the German navy.

When the family's first escape plan is foiled, they use the cover of the audience at the Salzburg festival to slip away during the prize-giving ceremony. They hide at the convent, but capture seems inevitable. The nuns prove themselves equal to the challenge, however, and disable the Nazis' cars whilst allowing the von Trapp family to use the convent's vehicle. The von Trapps head for the mountains, where they climb over the pass to Switzerland and freedom.

Highlights

It is almost sacrilege to single out highlights in this musical, since every piece of music is valuable and every word significant. A brief run-down of the pleasures in store is the only way to summarise the highlights in *The Sound of Music*.

The expansive opening theme 'The Hills are Alive with the Sound of Music' conjures up the vast spaces of its setting, as well as the depths of the emotions to be explored. There isn't long to wait before the nuns express their affection and frustration with the enigma that is Maria ('How do You Solve a Problem Like Maria?) When Maria is firmly persuaded to accept the position of governess at the von Trapp family home, she doubts that she will be able to cope. During her journey across Salzburg to the shores of the lake where the imposing residence of the von Trapp family is situated, Maria convinces herself that she really is up to the task ('I Have Confidence in Me').

Liesl and Rolf meet and enjoy a brief episode of innocent mutual attraction ('I am Sixteen Going on Seventeen'). Meanwhile, a thunderstorm has brought the younger children into Maria's bedroom, where she distracts them by singing ('My Favourite Things').

The following day, Maria sets about teaching the children to play and to sing. They begin with the song 'Do-Re-Mi'. Natural singers all, they now decide to put on a performance for Baroness Schraeder and a puppet show is arranged during which the children and Maria sing the song of 'The Lonely Goatherd'.

Not to be outdone by his children, Captain von Trapp sings the simple and beguiling, 'Edelweiss', then at the end of a grand reception the children gather together before they go to bed and sing to the guests, 'So Long, Farewell'.

Reverend Mother tells Maria that the Abbey is not a place in which she may hide from the world; she must always face up to her problems ('Climb Ev'ry Mountain').

When the Captain and Maria finally confess their love for each other, they realise that to have deserved such happiness, at an earlier time they must have done 'Something Good', and Maria's 'Wedding Processional' for organ and orchestra is another uplifting and majestic piece.

Personalities

Julie Andrews immortalised the role of Maria on film in a performance that, even more than 30 years on, seems flawless, but the stage role was created by another gifted performer.

Mary Martin (1913–90)

Born in Texas, Mary Martin became one of Broadway's best-loved female stars. Her mother was musical and her father a lawyer and they ensured that their gifted young daughter received the lessons in dancing and singing that eventually enabled her to open her own dancing school. The bright lights beckoned and Mary travelled to Hollywood, where she received her break in 1938 in a Cole Porter musical called *Leave it to Me*. This might only have been a small role, but Mary had a big song, 'My Heart Belongs to Daddy', and she stopped the show night after night. This success led to her being offered a contract by the Paramount film studios and she made at least ten films for this company.

During the 1940 and 1950s, Mary Martin's career went from strength to strength. Amongst a long list of shows, she starred in the States in the touring version of *Annie Get Your Gun*, followed by one of her biggest successes, the leading role of nurse Nellie Forbush in *South Pacific*. Mary Martin also made an effortless transition into straight theatre in the 1950s, as well as starring on television with other outstanding performers like Noel Coward and Ethel Merman. A particular favourite with television audiences was her portrayal of Peter Pan, which had been recorded during the run of the hit Broadway show which opened at the Winter Gardens in 1954.

In creating the role of Maria in the 1959 Broadway production, Mary Martin found a natural outlet for her unaffected charm, but from this point her career never quite managed to sustain the heights to which it had climbed. In 1963 a show called *Jennie* proved unsuccessful and Mary Martin began to spend more time with her husband at their home in Brazil. In 1965 she came briefly to the fore again in a world tour of the musical *Hello Dolly!* and her last appearance on Broadway was in 1966 with Robert Preston in *I Do! I Do!*; a show that ran for 560 performances. She continued to appear in straight roles and established a considerable reputation for herself in this genre, winning a Peabody Award for her part in the television drama *Valentine*.

In 1977 she returned to New York to star with Ethel Merman in a revue entitled *Together Again*, but then in the early 1980s she was seriously injured in a road accident. There would be several more stage appearances and what Mary Martin might have lost in the way of slick delivery was certainly compensated for by the unconditional love of her fans, whose affection never flagged during her long and distinguished career.

Postscript

- Marni Nixon, whose beautiful singing voice came to the rescue of so many stars – Margaret O'Brien in *The Big City* (1948); Deborah Kerr in *The King and I* (1956); Natalie Wood in *West Side Story* (1961); Audrey Hepburn in *My Fair Lady* (1964) – actually made it to the screen as the nun, Sister Sophia, in the film version of *The Sound of Music*.
- Oscar Hammerstein wrote the lyrics first and these he sent to Richard Rodgers who, with the minimum of changes, set them to music.
- *The Sound of Music* marked 18 years of collaboration between Oscar Hammerstein and Richard Rodgers.

■ After previews of *The Sound of Music* in New Haven and Boston, the newspaper *Variety* announced that 'a sensational musical is on its way to Broadway'.

■ Supporting Mary Martin in the original Broadway production were Theodore Bikel, a noted actor and folk singer, in the role of Captain von Trapp, and an outstanding dramatic soprano, Patricia Neway, in the role of Reverend Mother.

■ In the London production, Constance Shacklock, a fine British soprano who became almost a fixture for a number of years in the famous Henry Wood Promenade Concerts, played the role of Reverend Mother.

■ Jean Bayliss enjoyed a triumph with her interpretation of Maria in the British production, particularly as it was her first starring role in London's West End.

Now try this...

It is hard to find something that will compare favourably with such an outstanding production. *West Side Story* and *My Fair Lady* certainly bear scrutiny in both film and stage version, for both spectacle and melody, with *West Side Story* having the edge on dramatic content.

Julie Andrews's lovely singing voice may be enjoyed in a number of uncomplicated, fun-filled video recordings and, of these, her Oscar-winning performance in *Mary Poppins* and her transformation into a flirtatious flapper in *Thoroughly Modern Millie* are particularly enjoyable.

Some musical elements in *The Sound of Music* are almost operatic and you may like to pursue this path further. Some operas are full of good tunes, Puccini's *La Bohème* for instance (see *Teach Yourself Opera*) has scarcely a dull moment, or you may prefer an operetta like *Die Fledermaus*.

Another visual feast available on video is *The King and I*, and of the more recent musicals, *Les Miserables* by Boublil and Schoenberg is outstanding on every count, plus it's available on video and still running to packed houses across the world.

Self-test questions

1 Who wrote *The Sound of Music*?

2 Upon whose life story was this musical based?

3 Who starred as Maria in the original stage production?

4 How many children did Captain von Trapp have? Can you remember their names?

5 Who played Captain von Trapp in the film version?

6 What was the name of the Baroness who expected to marry him?

7 What was the full name of the children's 'Uncle Max'?

8 What generally came first during the creation of this musical, the lyrics or the music?

9 Who, in her first starring role, played Maria in the original London stage production?

10 Which famous British singer took the role of Reverend Mother in this same production?

15 | OLIVER! (1960)

Background information

A show that thrilled audiences as much when it was revived in London recently as when it opened at the New Theatre, London on 30 June 1960.

Written by Lionel Bart, *Oliver!* is a worthy development of the classic book, *Oliver Twist* by Charles Dickens and the show is now rightly regarded as a classic of its own genre.

The story, set in the mid-nineteenth century, was carefully edited by Bart, allowing a serious theme to be conveyed in a way that was primarily entertaining, rather than thought provoking, or involving any jolts to society's social conscience, as was Dickens's original intention. Starvation and hardship, thieving and extortion are not topics that lend themselves easily to musical entertainment, so some change of focus was not only understandable, but essential.

The pill may have been sugared to some extent, but the raw drama of Nancy's relationship with the sinister robber, Bill Sikes, remains brutal and unglamorous, adding tension to a show that never fails to enthral.

There was some inspired casting for the original production in London and this included Georgia Brown as an altogether convincing Nancy, whose interpretation of 'As Long as He Needs Me' was superb. Ron Moody played Fagin, a part he made his own and a young Barry Humphries was the cheerless undertaker, Mr Sowerberry, with Danny Sewell as a menacing and heartless Bill Sikes.

Marcus Dodds was a versatile and experienced conductor and the sets by Sean Kenny were extraordinary, realising Lionel Bart's own clear ideas on how the dilapidation of London's poorer streets could best be depicted and how one scene might seamlessly slip into another. The elegance of Oliver's eventual home must also provide a feast for the eyes, as well as providing a contrast to the bitter poverty of the other scenes. Sean Kenny accomplished all of this and his use and development of technical wizardry would set the standard for many future set designs.

The London production ran for 2,618 performances and there is a revival running to huge acclaim in the West End at the time of writing. In 1963 *Oliver!* opened in New York where it ran for two years and in 1968 a film version was released. This, like the stage production, won numerous well-deserved awards and was surely one of the best filmed musicals of all time. Ron Moody gave an incomparable portrayal as the rogue, Fagin. Oliver Reed played a cold-hearted, if rather attractive Bill Sikes, Shani Wallace was, by comparison with Georgia Brown, a competent, but rather incipid Nancy, while Oliver and Dodger were played by two superb child actors, Mark Lester and Jack Wild.

Lionel Bart has enjoyed many successes during a long and varied career and would have been one of the great contributors to the world of light entertainment without this musical, but *Oliver!* is a masterpiece that has stood the test of time and will doubtless go on delighting audiences for many more years to come.

Plot summary

The action begins at the workhouse where the boys are about to feast on a bowl of watery gruel. Oliver is encouraged to ask for some more, a request met by horror from Mr Bumble and the Widow Corney. Clearly, Oliver is not the brow-beaten character they took him for and he will have to be sold out as an apprentice to prevent his outrageous demands from contaminating the other boys. Oliver finds himself in the scarcely improved surroundings of the undertaker, Mr Sowerberry's home where he is forced to sleep in one of the unoccupied coffins at night. When another apprentice bullies him, the young lad runs away, hitching a ride that takes him to London.

Wearily wandering through the busy streets of London, Oliver's attention is caught by the dishonest, though fascinating capers of a boy not much older than himself. Noticing Oliver's interest, the boy introduces himself as 'Dodger' and suggests they should both go to eat and rest at the home of an old gentleman of his acquaintance.

Oliver is pathetically grateful for the kindness shown to him and Fagin is only too pleased to welcome such a refined young lad into his den of thieves, for such a 'pretty child' will surely be above suspicion. Oliver also meets Nancy, who does not share in the pleasure at the corruption of yet another innocent child, but she dare not say so in case word of her disloyalty should reach her formidable lover, Bill Sikes. Fagin teaches Oliver how to be a pickpocket, but on his first attempt, Oliver is caught and hauled into court. His victim, Mr Brownlow, takes pity on the boy who reminds him greatly of his dead daughter and offers him a home. Bill Sikes gets wind of this offer and orders Nancy to get the boy back at any cost in case he betrays them. They kidnap Oliver and Sikes forces him to take part in a robbery.

Meanwhile, at the workhouse, Widow Corney has married Mr Bumble and has rifled through some of the pathetic belongings left behind by deceased inmates. Amongst these she finds a locket belonging to Mr Brownlow's daughter and determines to visit him with her husband to impart some rather belated news concerning a child…

Nancy and Mr Brownlow conspire to reclaim Oliver, whom he now knows to be his grandson, from the clutches of Bill Sikes, but before Nancy is able to hand him over, Bill Sikes catches them and kills Nancy in a frenzied attack.

Pursued by Bow Street Runners, members of the public and dogs, he drags the frightened child along with him, until finally Sikes is killed and Oliver is reunited with his grandfather.

During the confusion, Fagin takes the opportunity to escape. By accident he drops his cache of gold and jewels into the river and now must make a new life for himself – maybe even becoming an honest man…

Highlights

This is a superb musical where every musical item is a highlight and there is not a single substandard song. The overture and 'Food, Glorious Food', set a standard of excellence which never flags. Oliver's scolding, 'Oliver', delivered by Widow Corney, Mr Bumble and the boys is as dyspeptic as you might expect on a diet of lumpy gruel and Beadle Bumble's haunting refrain, as he hawks the unfortunate Oliver around the back streets of

London, 'Boy For Sale', evokes just the right mood of pathos. Oliver's searching 'Where is Love?', sung while he is incarcerated in the undertaker's cellar, could surely not be bettered and the Artful Dodger's brash welcome, 'Consider Yourself' again suits the moment to perfection. Lionel Bart then goes on to achieve the impossible, by topping this with Fagin's teach yourself thieving song, 'Pick a Pocket or Two'. Nancy and friends enjoy a lighter moment with 'I'll Do Anything' and when dawn comes and the boys go off whistling happily about their thievery, Fagin's admonishment to 'Go, But Be Back Soon' injects a note of light humour before the tone darkens again. Meanwhile, Nancy is carousing with the locals at The Three Cripples pub in an 'Oom Pah Pah' sort of way. When Sikes arrives and orders her to get Oliver back from Brownlow, Nancy wants to disobey, but first she must fight Sikes's hold over her. 'As Long as He Needs Me', is her soul-searching explanation. Fagin finally concedes that his life must change and 'I'm Reviewing the Situation' follows his thought processes through as he examines the various possibilities open to him.

Personalities

Lionel Bart (1930–)

Born Lionel Begleiter in London, Lionel Bart's popular music career began during his early twenties when he was a member of the same skiffle group as Tommy Steele, The Cavemen.

He went on to write many top ten hits, including 'Rock with the Cavemen', as well as providing some of Tommy Steele's most popular numbers. One of the best loved of these was 'Little White Bull'.

Bart's versatility came to the fore in 1959 when he was involved with two entirely different works of music theatre; *Lock up your Daughters*, the period farce for which he wrote the lyrics to Laurie Johnson's music, and *Fings ain't wot they used to be*, a tale of London's Soho, the area he knew so well, with all its seediness, violence and flashes of warm-hearted camaraderie. For this last piece he wrote both music and lyrics.

Again in 1959 he wrote one of Cliff Richard's most enduring hits, 'Living Doll', and in the 1960s reached the pinnacle of his career with the masterpiece *Oliver!* Shirley Bassey had a hit with Nancy's impassioned song, 'As Long as He Needs Me' and the film version of the musical won six Oscars.

Three more musicals followed, *Blitz!*, *Maggie May* and, in 1965, *Twang*, based on the Robin Hood legend. These were not successful and a combination of personal abuse and a warm and overly trusting personality led Lionel Bart to professional decline and financial ruin.

After a long battle, the late 1980s saw a refreshed and reinvigorated composer undertake the task of writing a jingle for a national advertising campaign. This was a huge success and soon revivals were underway by the exciting youth group, The National Youth Music Theatre, of *Oliver!*, *Maggie May* and *Blitz*.

Into the 1990s and a West End revival of *Oliver!* delighted audiences all over again, going on to be the London Palladium's Longest-running musical .

This production has attracted some of the foremost stars of the musical stage to play the pivotal role of Fagin and has ensured that Lionel Bart has been returned to his rightful place at the very top of his profession.

Jim Dale (1935–)

Jim Dale joined stars like Barry Humphries and Ron Moody in playing the role of Fagin.

An entertainer who for years seemed always to be hovering on the brink of major success, Jim Dale had a varied career on stage, screen and television before he found his métier on the musical stage.

In the 1950s he would have been considered a pop star, by the 1960s he was renowned for his goofy performances in the *Carry On* films and had extended his career onto the straight stage, as well as co-writing the Seekers hit 'Georgy Girl'. In 1973 he was a respected actor, appearing in the Keith Waterhouse and Willis Hall musical *The Card*, as well as hosting the immensely popular television programme, *Sunday Night at the London Palladium*. The next year he toured the United States, where he eventually settled, but more stage appearances and several Disney films would follow before Jim Dale found the perfect vehicle for his versatility.

The lead role in the musical *Barnum* allowed him to display every facet of his talent, including the circus skills he had perfected as a youth, when, for two years, he was part of a tumbling act in Carrol Levi's touring show. He won a Tony for this part and more films and stage shows quickly followed. In 1992 he returned to England to play the title role in the film *Carry On Columbus*.

Georgia Brown (1933–92)

Georgia Brown was an outstanding performer, whose first love had been jazz, hence the name which, not surprisingly for one born Lillie Klot, she adopted from the jazz classic 'Sweet Georgia Brown'. Born in Whitechapel, a none too prosperous area of London, Georgia Brown found early success in music hall and then, in 1956, in Brecht's *Threepenny Opera*. Her greatest triumph was the role of Nancy in the musical *Oliver!*, an interpretation that has never been bettered. She went on to appear in both *Maggie May* and the film version of *Lock up Your Daughters* and her career continued on both stage and screen. She appeared on Broadway in 1979 in the show *Carmelina* and in 1987 in *Roza*. She starred in the West End production of *42nd Street* and created her own showcase entertainment entitled *Georgia Brown and Friends*.

Postscript

- *Oliver!* wasn't the only 1960s Bart creation to be revived successfully in the 1990s. 'Living Doll', the million-selling chart-topper for Cliff Richard, underwent a metamorphosis when Cliff Richard teemed up with the crazy comedy team, The Young Ones, to present an altogether less vapid version!

- Lionel Bart also wrote some great music for films including the British comedy *Light up the Sky*, and he contributed several songs for films starring Tommy Steele, *Tommy the Toreador* and *The Duke Wore Jeans*.

- Lionel Bart won more Ivor Novello Awards for songwriting than any composer before him, yet he could not read or write music, nor play a musical instrument with any degree of skill.

Now try this...

It's hard to think of *Oliver!* without thinking about all the other great shows that have used London as either a setting or an inspiration. Lerner and Loewe's *My Fair Lady,* Noel Coward's play, *Blithe Spirit* and its lovely song 'London Pride', or his revue, *London Calling!* To be sure of either seeing a stage production, or finding a video copy of the last two, however, is not always so simple. For a musical running currently, that has a reasonable degree of tension, good story-line, outstanding spectacle and plenty of memorable tunes, Andrew Lloyd Webber's *Phantom of the Opera* should provide an evening's entertainment and it can surely only be a matter of time before this, like his other hit show, *Evita*, is available on video.

Self-test questions

1 Who wrote *Oliver!*?

2 Can you name two other musicals written by this person?

3 In which century is the story set?

4 Can you name the song Nancy sings about Bill Sikes?

5 Who created the role of Fagin in the original London stage production?

6 Which two actresses played the part of Nancy?

   a   in the original London Production

   b   in the film version.

7 Who designed the sets for the original stage production?

8 What was the name of the skiffle group in which this show's creator played and what was the name of the other 'soon to be famous' group member?

9 What is the name of the matron of the workhouse where Oliver was living?

10 What is the name of the undertaker?

16 | LES MISERABLES (1980; ENGLISH VERSION 1985)

Background information

One of the best-selling books after the Bible and now enjoying a world wide revival of interest in its musical form, *Les Miserables'* brutal tale is made all the more poignant through Victor Hugo's skilled manipulation of fact and fiction.

One of the most powerful visual elements on stage, the Barricade is based on an actual event; the student riots during the funeral of General Lamarque in 1832, although Victor Hugo plucked this tragedy from its correct time and planted it in his novel at a much later date.

In the context of strife-torn nineteenth-century France, the Lamarque riot was almost a minor disturbance, but it made a strong impression on Victor Hugo, who described it as 'madness drowned in blood'.

Although Victor Hugo was not a religious conformist, there is a spiritual quality to the story and it is impossible not to find echoes of the author's own outspoken and sometimes reckless defence of the underdog in the main character, Jean Valjean. The rescue of Fantine had a real life parallel when Victor Hugo sprang to the defense of a street-walker who was being wrongly accused and this was not the only occasion he took the trouble to record his observations on the persecution of poverty-stricken and vulnerable people.

The musical version has remained largely faithful to the original book, although for the sake of practicality the plot has been speeded up and some of the longer asides on religious, social or historical topics have been omitted.

In his will, Victor Hugo asked that his poems should never be set to music.

Fortunately for us, his novels were omitted from this instruction.

Plot summary

This is a 'sung-through' musical with no spoken dialogue, lasting about three hours. There are many strands to the story and this break-down will help you to follow the plot.

Granted parole, Valjean is freed by the policeman Javert, but life outside the jail is hard and he steals some silver from the Bishop of Digne. Rather than condemn him, the bishop insists that the silver is in payment for his soul.

Under an assumed name, Valjean becomes major of Montreuil and runs the factory where Fantine works to support her illegitimate daughter, Cosette. The other workers resent Fantine for her beauty and refinement and eventually she is sacked. Almost reduced to selling her body to pay for Cosette's keep, Fantine is saved when Valjean vows to take on the responsibility in her place.

An innocent man has been mistaken for Valjean and is held in custody. Declaring that his soul belongs to God, Valjean promises to give himself up and says he will await arrest at the hospital where Fantine is dying. Having promised to care for Cosette, however, Valjean can see no way to honour his pledge to Javert. He hurries to the Thenardiers inn, pays them off and takes Cosette away to bring her up as his own daughter.

The streets of Paris – ten years later

Eponine, the Thenardiers daughter, loves Marius, but he thinks of her as a friend and begs her to discover the name of the beautiful girl with Valjean. While Marius pines for the mystery girl, his fellow students are planning rebellion and when Gavroche, a street urchin, arrives to tell them that General Lamarque is dead, the students vow to mark the day of his funeral with insurrection.

Cosette is in love with Marius and begs Valjean to reveal the truth about her life, but he asks her to be patient. Eponine overhears Marius and Cosette declaring their love for each other and then finds out that her father's gang plan to rob Valjean's house. She begs her father to abandon his plan, but he refuses and when she screams a warning, Valjean hears and fears that Javert's net is closing in.

Act 2

The students have built a barricade across the street and Eponine joins them dressed as a boy. Marius asks her to take a letter to Cosette, but it is Valjean who takes delivery of the letter and warns her to take care, Fatally injured, Eponine just reaches Marius before she dies. Meanwhile, the students have caught Javert spying on them and when Valjean volunteers his services, the two men meet. In the heat of battle, Valjean frees his old enemy.

Soon the students run out of ammunition and everyone on the barricade is dead except for Valjean and Marius, who is badly injured. Valjean carries Marius down to the safety of the sewers where Thenardier is busy robbing the dead. Javert sees Valjean and is on the point of arresting him, but cannot refuse the other man's plea for a chance to save Marius's life. Haunted by the knowledge that he has failed to do his duty, Javert throws himself into the Seine.

When Marius recovers, Valjean tells him about his past and asks him to take care of Cosette. At the wedding of Marius and Cosette, a Baron and Barones de Thénard threaten to reveal Valjean's secret unless Marius pays them off.

Valjean is dying and tells Cosette the truth about her mother. He remembers all the friends who have gone before him and knows that they are waiting to lead him to glory.

Highlights

The structure of *Les Miserables* is quite different from a show where the story is interspersed with songs that may or may not advance the plot. More like an opera in the way that music remains a constant as the story unfolds, tension and mood are enhanced by the use of this evocative medium, together with a gripping story-line and clearly drawn characters.

'I Dreamed A Dream', Fantine: One of the many songs from *Les Miserables* that has become of inestimable worth as an audition/concert/festival piece to thousands of young singers across the world. Just the right mix of tension and relaxation, passion and pathos make this piece a classic.

'Castle on a Cloud', the child Cosette: Daydreams of a lonely, mistreated child.

'Master of the House', Thenardier: Irresistible, foot-tapping introduction to this outrageous innkeeper.

'Stars', Javert: He may not get his way in the end, but this is one of the most moving pieces, showing Javert to be a victim of his own inflexibility.

'Little People', Gavroche: A perfectly cocky, devil-may-care, catchy tune brings the street urchin into prominence so that we shall feel it all the more when he dies.

'Do You Hear the People Sing?', Enjolras,; Combeferre; Courfeyrac; Feuilly; Chorus: A stirring march – a rhythm that might seem dated elsewhere, but in this context it provokes just the right degree of audience fervour as we see ourselves climbing the barricade alongside the valiant, though ill-fated students.

Used first to epitomise violent emotions of the most noble kind, by the end of the story 'Do You Hear the People Sing?' serves as a reminder of what has been lost and then rises at the climax of the production in a triumphant anthem that celebrates not just the resilience of the human spirit, but the show itself.

'A Heart Full of Love', Marius and Cosette: A sublime duet for the romantic leads.

'One Day More', Valjean; Marius; Cosette; Eponine; Enjolras; Javert; The Thenardiers: The main players brings us up to date on what has occurred and what they hope to do next; a reminder, if one was needed, of the powerful and varied emotions invoked by this work.

'On My Own', Eponine: She struggles to face the fact that Marius will never see her as anything more than a friend.

'A Little Fall of Rain', Eponine and Marius: Together at last, but only as Eponine lies dying on the street beneath the barricade.

'Drink with Me', Grantair; Students; Women; Marius: A poignant 'calm before the storm' interlude, with a short burst of self-doubt from Marius.

'Bring Him Home', Valjean: A sensational 'big sing' as Valjean pleads with God to have mercy on Marius.

'Turning', Chorus: Reflections on the futility of battle.

'Empty Chairs at Empty Tables', Marius: Show-stopping, grief-stricken out-pouring by our hero who is the only surviving member of his student group.

All the best tunes are reprised for the audience's satisfaction and some characters, such as Thenardier, have an identifying theme.

Personalities

Victor Hugo (1802–85)

The musical *Les Miserables* is based upon a book of the same name by the French writer, Victor Hugo. A man who could be said to have embraced life with a voracious appetite, Victor Hugo was a keen observer of French society in an era of extreme political upheaval. His ability to recall significant events with uncanny accuracy and then skillfully blend these facts with fiction added a powerful cadence to his work.

When he began writing *Les Miserables* in 1845, Victor Hugo was a French peer, a Royalist and a member of the French Academy. However, his eloquent support of a hard pressed under-class found him increasingly at odds with French establishment. In 1848 the monarchy of King Louis Philippe was overthrown and Victor Hugo became a staunch Republican, confident that the new order would bring an end to social injustice.

In 1851 Louis Napoleon seized power, declaring himself President of the Second French Republic. Victor Hugo was a prominent parliamentary member of the French Republicans and protested fiercely and publicly against this illegal coup, placing himself in immediate danger.

Forced into exile, he travelled first to Brussels, then on to London, finally settling on Guernsey in the Channel Islands, where he continued to denounce Louis Napoleon whilst engaging in a notoriously libidinous life. He resumed work on *Les Miserables* in 1860 and the final chapters were completed in Belgium, where the book was finally launched in 1862.

Les Miserables enjoyed enormous popular and financial success, although it was condemned by French literary critics for its 'excessive sentimentality'. Hardly surprisingly, performances of a play of the book were expressly forbidden in France.

Victor Hugo was forced to remain in exile until Napoleon III fled to London in 1870, following his defeat in the Franco-Prussian war. The writer's return to Paris was a huge personal triumph and he was duly re-elected to parliament. Sadly his repatriation was to be short-lived. A supporter of the revolutionary ideals that provoked the Paris 'Commune' uprising in 1871, he was nevertheless appalled by the levels of violence employed by the leaders of this movement and his vision of a 'United States of Europe', necessarily involving a reconciliation between France and Germany, put him at odds with the ground-swell of public opinion. In 1871 he resigned from parliament and left for Brussels.

The 'Communards' would be mercilessly repressed and following his rebuke to the Belgium government for refusing them sanctuary, Victor Hugo's house in Brussels was stoned, forcing him to leave the country. Travelling to Luxembourg, Paris and then Guernsey, he would not return to live in Paris until 1875. By this time the Republic was firmly established and Victor Hugo was swiftly appointed to the Senate, enabling him to continue his tireless campaigns for free education and full amnesty for all Communard exiles.

A pauper's funeral was specified in his will, but in the event, Victor Hugo's coffin lay in State under the Arc de Triomphe for 24 hours and was then taken in a grand procession to the Panthéon, where only the most notable French citizens may be buried. More than three million people crowded the streets of Paris to pay their last respects to a man, who through a life of fearless campaigning on behalf of the underdog, had become an emblem of democracy.

Emile Bayard (1837–91)

The characters in Victor Hugo's novel, *Les Miserables*, were brought to life by Emile Bayard, a wealthy Parisian society painter. His image of *Cosette*, chosen as the emblem of the show, is now instantly recognisable worldwide.

Bayard was almost as popular in his day as Victor Hugo, but in Bayard's case, it was for his large-scale, infinitely detailed paintings of famous battle scenes, 'After the Battle of Waterloo; Sedan 1870', for example. His meticulous work as a lithographer for periodicals and books was also admired, as were his skills as a portrait painter.

His illustrations for *Les Miserables* show a depth of insight into the social observations made by Victor Hugo that would seem to contradict his association with the school of painting popularly dubbed 'The Pompous School'.

Bayard was also a writer, commenting on his many friends in the artistic community as well as writing self-help books on antiques. He developed a large teaching practice and maintained a studio, where his subject's character as well as their image would be captured by this perceptive and gifted man.

Alan Boublil (1941–)

Born in Tunis to a non-musical family, Boublil first because hooked by musicals when he saw *West Side Story* at its Paris première in 1959. His collaboration with Claude-Michel Schönberg seems almost inevitable, since they would meet at the Pathe-Marconi record company in Paris and Boublil married Francoise Pourcel, whose father's records were produced by Schönberg. To begin with, however, although their musical interests were strikingly similar, Boublil concentrated on establishing his own publishing business, whilst Schönberg continued to work as a record producer.

In 1973 Boublil attended the première of *Jesus Christ Superstar* in New York and was inspired to search out a theme of similar stature to work on. The resulting idea, to base a rock-opera on the subject of the French Revolution, was audacious in scope yet received the enthusiastic support of fellow writer, Jean-Max Riviere and composers Raymond Jeannot and Claude-Michel Schönberg. *La Revolution Française*, staged at the Palaise des Sports, with Schönberg singing the role of Louis XVI, resulted in a cast album of the show that sold more than 350,000 copies.

Boublil and Schönberg couldn't have foreseen the glittering future that lay ahead of this collaboration, but *Les Miserables* would go on to exceed records set by *Jesus Christ Superstar* and to date they have produced two more major works for musical theatre, *Miss Saigon* and *Martin Guerre*.

Claude-Michel Schönberg (1944–)

A distant relation of the Austrian composer Arnold Schönberg, this French composer of Hungarian parents came from a musical family and made his first visit to the Paris Opera at the age of six. Ever a keen composer, he was working as a trainee artistic director at Pathé-Marconi records in Paris when he met Alain Boublil.

An accomplished singer as well as composer, the album of his own songs produced in 1974, a year after the staging of the acclaimed rock-musical *La Revolution Française*, resulted in a hit single for him, *Le Premier Pas*. In 1978 he began work on *Les Miserables* with Alain Boublil and the musical was produced at Les Palais des Sports in Paris in 1980. The following year the album of this show went double gold. In September 1985 the revised English version of *Les Miserables* opened at the Barbican in London, transferring to The Palace Theatre in December of that year. When a production opened on Broadway in 1987 awards followed swiftly. Boublil and Schönberg were awarded Tonys for both score and book out of a total of seven Tonys awarded to the show, and a Grammy followed for the best original cast recording. This great triumph was followed by the opening in the West End of *Miss Saigon* (1989) and on Broadway (1991). Compositions were also finding favour in the concert hall, with *Rhapsody for Piano and Orchestra* and *Symphonic Suite* being premièred at the Royal Albert Hall in London in 1992. In 1991 Schönberg began work on *Martin Guerre*, again in collaboration with Alain Boublil, and this show is now running to great acclaim at the Prince Edward Theatre in London.

Cameron Mackintosh (1946–)

The undisputed King of theatre producers, Cameron Mackintosh was born in Enfield, England. From the moment he was taken to see *Salad Days* at the age of eight, the magic of theatre proved irresistible and he settled upon the musical theatre as his chosen career path.

He was to become so obsessed with all things theatrical that at school his nickname was Darryl F Mackintosh. After a short spell at the Central School of Speech and Drama in London he found a job, or rather two jobs, at the Theatre Royal Drury Lane where the musical *Camelot* was playing. Cameron Mackintosh 'stage-hand and cleaner' may have been his introduction to the West End stage, but it was only a matter of time before he diversified into stage management, becoming assistant stage manager on the touring version of the musical *Oliver!* This allowed him the further privilege of appearing on-stage in the chorus. Soon there would be no facet of theatrical life with which he was not familiar. An opportunity to work on an Emile Littler show allowed him to try his hand at administration, marketing and even design of posters and programmes. A rough patch in the late 1960s gave him a brutal lesson in the cost of failure, then in the 1970s productions of *Salad Days*, another Julian Slade musical, *Trelawney* and *The Card* with Jim Dale and Millicent Martin in leading roles, with Gillian Lynne as choreographer, saw his fortunes begin a modest turn-around.

Godspell was a real step up the ladder and *Side by Side with Sondheim* which opened in 1976 and transferred to Broadway the following year, proved he had the insight to take on a show in which other, supposedly more experienced producers, had not seen the value. Other smash hits followed, and then his famous association with Andrew Lloyd Webber began with *Cats*. Again thought to be an unacceptable risk with its unusual form that boasted no story-line whatever, Mackintosh backed the idea of setting T S Eliot's poems to music and left the doubters ruing their mistake. Since opening at the New London Theatre in 1981, *Cats* has broken countless records and is still playing to capacity houses in the West End, Broadway and in theatres across the world.

With an ever-developing nose for success Cameron Mackintosh did not balk at the idea of presenting a work like *Les Miserables* to the theatre-going public. The final production length of three hours was easily justified by the depth of the subject matter and appeal of the music. The public could not help but be drawn into a drama, where life's emotions, common to all, were depicted so clearly.

Song and Dance, *Phantom of the Opera*, of which there are as many as 20 productions worldwide; *Miss Saigon* with seven – to mention these few alone makes the list of success seems unstoppable, but *Moby Dick* was a flop and *Five Guys named Moe* did not find the degree of success anticipated on Broadway, although this hasn't prevented it spawning four productions worldwide.

With the *Observer* Award for Outstanding Achievement in 1991 and the Richard Rodgers Award for Excellence in Musical Theatre in 1992, it seems only a matter of time before a knighthood comes the way of this theatrical phenomenon of modern times.

Trevor Nunn (1940–)

Born in Ipswich, England in 1940 Trevor Nunn became the youngest-ever artistic director of the Royal Shakespeare company in 1968. He would go on to become a major force in musical theatre, opera and the world of drama generally. Amongst many notable productions produced by him, the Royal Shakespeare's staging of Charles Dickens's *Nicholas Nickleby* is perhaps the most relevant to his work as director of *Les Miserables*, since it too was a vast undertaking and more importantly involved working with co-director John Caird, a man with whom Trevor Nunn built up a particular rapport. Together the two men identified an opportunity to transform the original French version of *Les Miserables* from a series of cameos extracted from the novel into a gripping production with a through story-line. Characterisation was strengthened so that stark contrasts could be drawn, for instance, between the approach to God of three of the main male protagonists; Javert with his vengeful Old Testament God; Valjean with an altogether more forgiving deity and Thenardier with no god at all. Nunn and Caird's artistic vision was certainly essential to the success of this version, but their professionalism too was crucial to the production.

When James Fenton, an original team member, left, the songwriter, critic and lyricist Herbert Kretzmer proved an inspired choice as replacement. With translation to be completed from the original French lyrics by Boublil and Jean-Marc Natel, adaptations and the creation of completely new songs all to be finished within rapidly diminishing time limits, Herbert Kretzmer's skills were tested to the full and not found wanting.

Fenton's legacy was his proposed addition to the French version of a Prologue, showing something of Valjean's harsh experience under the penal system for a relatively minor crime and one that was committed from desperation and for the benefit of others. The scene with the Bishop of Digne is crucial to the theme as it marks the beginning of Valjean's path towards redemption. The scene at the barricade bears the unmistakable stamp of Fenton's experiences as a war correspondent.

That said, the Nunn, Caird, Kretzmer team, together with Boublil and Schönberg, were able to deliver the goods on time … and what goods!

Postscript

It seems unlikely that any music theatre presentation has ever provoked such a response across the varied cultures of so many people. Statistics are off the scale with unprecedented numbers of awards, productions worldwide, 125,000 people turning up for an outdoor performance in Sydney, Australia in 1989, 60,000 attending a benefit performance in aid of a children's hospital in Toronto the same year, not to mention the tenth anniversary concert held at the Royal Albert Hall in 1995, which drew upon soloists from across the world, with 17 Valjeans contributing in turn to 'Do You Hear the People Sing?'

Touring versions of the show have achieved immense success in the USA and Canada, with Asia gathering pace. Sub-titles, cargo planes, re-vamped stage machinery, nothing is impossible when it comes to bringing the show to its public, but even this cannot satisfy the public hunger. Demand for licenses allowing amateur productions to be staged wherever rights are granted have never been equalled. The massacre of students during a non-violent demonstration in Tiananmen Square in China brought an unbearable resonance to the Barricade scene for all those who condemn human injustice; 'Empty Chairs and Empty Tables' has struck a poignant chord with AIDS victims across the world and even Bill Clinton harnessed the power of 'One Day More' for the final stages of his presidential campaign.

Had Puccini put his proposals into action for an opera of *Les Miserables* he may have created a master work of equal appeal; this we shall never know. One thing is certain, Boublil and Schönberg's interpretation speaks a universal language of words and music that lifts the human spirit wherever it is played.

Now try this ...

There are several fascinating paths to take from here, for instance, *Oliver!* the musical that so inspired Alain Boublil. Lionel Bart's musical realisation of Charles Dickens's book *Oliver Twist* takes the formula of the American musical and imbues it with characteristically English melody and lashings of *joie de vivre*. A gripping plot and vivid characterisation, together with Lionel Bart's sensational music, combine to produce a show that must not be missed. You will find more information about this show on page 190.

Two more shows by Boublil and Schönberg, *Miss Saigon* and *Martin Guerre* will more than repay further investigation. *Miss Saigon*, set in 1960s Vietnam in the dying days of the American military presence, recreates the story written by John Luther Long, an American lawyer. Famously set by Giacomo Puccini as *Madame Butterfly* (see *Teach Yourself Opera*) Boublil and Schönberg's realisation touches the heart with music ranging from poignant to grand ceremonial. In the Mackintosh production the photographic reference to real Vietnamese American children abandoned when the GIs left, adds an edge that no other theatrical affect could match. *Martin Guerre*, set in sixteenth-century France, explores the great conflict arising from the rise of Protestantism in Catholic France and the no less personal conflict experienced by the young heroine, Bertrande. It has all the ingredients of a good show; passion, tragedy, comedy, as well as exciting stage spectacle and haunting music.

Self-test questions

1 Who wrote the original novel *Les Miserables*?
2 Whose illustrations were used in this novel and subsequently as an emblem for the musical?
3 What crimes did Jean Valjean commit in order to be jailed?
4 What is the name of Cosette's mother?
5 What is the name of the policeman who intends to recapture Valjean?
6 Which song does the inn-keeper, Thenardier, sing?
7 What is the name of the street urchin?
8 Can you name the four students who take part in the song 'Do You Hear the People Sing?'
9 Who is the general in whose name the student insurrection begins?
10 What song does Marius sing when all his friends have been killed?

Part 3

More Personalities From the World of Music Theatre

17 MORE PERSONALITIES FROM THE WORLD OF MUSIC THEATRE

In this short section you will find a few more outstanding performers who represent the many.

George Abbott (1887–1995)

This distinguished American author, performer, director, and producer, born in 1887, was still hard at work at the age of 100. He was involved as both lyricist and director with some of the most outstanding musicals of the twentieth century including *The Pajama Game* and *Damn Yankees* – a show he revised and then directed on Broadway at the age of 99.

Pearl Bailey (1918–90)

A larger-than-life character who was not averse to creating a little scandal, Pearlie Mae, as she was known, began her professional career as a dancer in vaudeville. Soon the singing took over and she discovered a new career on the New York night club scene. From here she graduated to shows, most notably the 1946 Harold Arlen/Johnny Mercer show *St Louis Woman*. Her fame spread through recordings and television spectaculars and not least for her performance in films like *Carmen Jones* (1954) and *Porgy and Bess* (1959). She sang with Frank Sinatra, with whom she recorded a series of duets, and can truly be said to have become 'a legend in her own lifetime'.

Michael Ball (1962–)

An outstanding young singer who had the luck to be at his peak just at the time the musical scene experienced something of a renaissance. After training at the Guildford School of Drama, Michael Ball's first professional engagement was in the chorus of a touring production of *Godspell*. Clearly destined for better things, it wasn't long before he was starring alongside Bonnie Langford and Paul Nicholas in the revamped production of *Pirates of Penzance* in Manchester. Success was assured when he was given the once in a lifetime opportunity to create the role of Marius in the London production of *Les Miserables*. He then played opposite Sarah Brightman in *Phantom of the Opera*, subsequently touring with her in a presentation of *The Music of Andrew Lloyd Webber*. His affable stage persona and fine singing voice should auger well for the future.

Jerry Bock (1928–)

It was in the late 1950s that Jerrold Bock met the lyricist Sheldon Harnick and formed what would become one of the most successful partnerships of the 1960s. Born in New Haven, Connecticut, Bock showed musical promise at an early age and was soon providing music for the professional world, graduating to Broadway with his contributions, together with another lyricist Larry Holofcener, for the revue *Catch a Star* in 1955. His involvement with Broadway grew apace and in 1964 Bock and Harnick created one of the most successful shows of all time, *Fiddler on the Roof*. The two men continued to work together for some time but it proved impossible to come up with anything that could top *Fiddler*. Bock called it a day in the 1970s, but his contribution to music theatre is no less significant through lack of quantity.

Fanny Brice (1891–1951)

Immortalised in the film *Funny Girl* based on the musical by Jule Styne and Bob Merrill, Fanny Brice rose from bit parts in vaudeville to topping the bill on Broadway. A combination of humour and self-deprecation, combined with enormous charisma, endeared her to audiences, for whom she seemed human and approachable. The song with which she was most closely identified was 'Second Hand Rose' and this, like many others of her featured numbers, she sang in a heavy Brooklyn accent. She made some films, but her real gift lay in the interaction between herself and a live audience, and in this she has rarely been equalled.

Leslie Bricusse (1931–)

Born in London, Leslie Bricusse honed his talents as a member of the Cambridge footlights revue. A sometime director, performer and writer for this group, he put music theatre ahead of his original intentions to become a journalist and found worldwide success.

Writing chart-topping songs like 'My Kind of Girl', a hit for Matt Monro in 1961, and winning an Ivor Novello Award, as well as several full-scale productions for the theatre, he also became a screen writer, writing both songs (with Robin Beaumont) and script for the film *Charley Mood*, starring Max Bygraves.

In the 1950s, Leslie Bricusse appeared on the London stage with Beatrice Lillie and in 1961 he travelled to New York to write another revue for her. Anthony Newley accompanied him and they came up with an idea for their own show, *Stop the World I Want to Get Off*. Starring Newley, this show, with its plethora of hit songs like 'What Kind of Fool am I', 'Gonna Build a Mountain' and 'Once in a Lifetime', proved a success on both sides of the Atlantic.

The next major project for Bricusse was the musical *Pickwick* (1963), which produced a hit song for Harry Secombe with 'If I Ruled the World'. In 1965 *The Roar of the Greasepaint – the Smell of the Crowd* proved to be another successful collaboration with Anthony Newley. In spite of songs like 'Who Can I Turn To?' and 'A Wonderful Day Like Today', it was not a hit. Undaunted, Newley and Bricusse provided the powerful lyrics to John Barry's music for the title song of the Bond film *Goldfinger*, made famous by Shirley Bassey, and then went on to write the theme for another Bond film, *You Only Live Twice*.

In 1967 Bricusse wrote both screenplay and music for *Doctor Dolittle*, starring Rex Harrison and Anthony Newley, but in spite of the Oscar winning song 'Talk to the Animals', this was not a great success.

In 1971 *Willie Wonka and the Chocolate Factory*, based on the children's book by Roald Dahl and written by Leslie Bricusse and Anthony Newley, made up for all the previous frustrations, giving Sammy Davis Jnr a chart-topping hit with 'Candy Man'. The team wrote some songs for a production of *Peter Pan*, starring Danny Kaye and Mia Farrow, but their next major project was *The Good Old Bad Old Days*, in which Newley starred and directed. Outstanding amongst the good musical numbers in this show were 'The People Tree' and 'It's a Musical World'.

Many more works followed with Newley also building an impressive solo act. The film score for *Goodbye, Mister Chips* (1982) was another Bricusse triumph and in 1970 the musical *Scrooge* was an interesting collaboration with Ian Fraser and Herbert W Spencer.

Bricusse worked with John Williams on high profile films like *Hook* and *Home Alone* with Henry Mancini (with whom he had worked previously on the film *That's Life*) on the film score of *Victor/Victoria*.

To add to countless awards garnered throughout a hugely productive career, in 1989, together with Anthony Newley, Leslie Bricusse was honoured by his inclusion in the Songwriters' Hall of Fame.

Jack Buchanan (1890–1957)

Born in Strathclyde, Scotland, Jack Buchanan enjoyed a long and successful career, during which he excelled in almost every aspect of theatrical life. A fine singer, he also taught himself to dance and his enormous personal charisma allowed him to move from performances in amateur productions to local music halls and then on to the chorus of West End productions, before landing a leading role in the musical comedy *Tonight's the Night* in 1915.

Two more shows, *Bubbly* (1917) and *A to Z* (1921) for producer André Charlot confirmed his popularity. In *A to Z* he sang 'And Her Mother Came Too' by Ivor Novello, a song Buchanan made his own; appearing in the same show were Beatrice Lillie and Gertrude Lawrence.

In 1922 Buchanan entered the arena of theatrical management with the show *Battling Butler*, in which he starred. This was staged at the New Oxford Theatre in London, later transferring to the Adelphi Theatre, before moving on to the Selwyn Theater in New York without Buchanan, where it ran for 312 performances.

In 1924 Buchanan, together with Beatrice Lillie and Gertrude Lawrence, enjoyed great success on Broadway in another Charlot revue and Buchanan also appeared regularly with Elsie Randolph.

In 1931 he appeared in his own show with Anna Neagle, who was subsequently cast by the producer Herbert Wilcox in Buchanan's next film, *Goodnight Vienna*.

Other notable stars who appeared with Buchanan in his many films include Irene Bordini, Jeanette MacDonald and Fred Astaire. Astaire and Buchanan, representing the best male song and dance talent from either side of the Atlantic, starred together in the 1953 film *The Band Wagon*.

Sammy Cahn (1913–93)

Born Samuel Cohen in New York, the son of Polish immigrant parents, Sammy Cahn's musical talent would take him from Manhattan's Lower East Side to the bright lights of Broadway and beyond.

After early success as a lyricist, he teamed up with Saul Chaplin and together they produced a string of hits for stars like Bennie Goodman, Louis Armstrong and the Andrew Sisters, for whom the song 'Beir Mir Bist Du Schoën' sold a million copies.

In 1942 Sammy Cahn formed a partnership with Jule Styne and worked with Frank Sinatra, creating such memorable tunes as 'The Charm of You'. Their hits became too numerous to list fully in this book and include classics like 'There Goes That Song Again', sung by Kay Kyser and Russ Morgan and 'It's Magic', sung by Doris Day in the film *Romance on the High Seas*.

In 1947 their broadway show *High Button Shoes* starred the irrepressible Phil Silvers and featured several hit songs including the catchy 'Papa, Won't You Dance With Me'.

Sammy Cahn moved to California and in the 1950s collaborated with Nicholas Brodsky on a number of films, writing for the outstanding singer Mario Lanza, amongst others, songs like 'Be My Love' and 'Because You're Mine'. Later Cahn would team up once again with Jule Styne to write the classic *Three Coins in a Fountain*, which won Cahn his first Academy Award. There would be many awards for songs like 'High Hopes' from the film *A Hole in the Head* (1959) and 'Call Me Irresponsible' from *Papa's Delicate Condition* (1963). His songs for Sinatra films became legendary and include 'My Kind of Town', 'Come Fly With Me', 'September of My Years', etc.

After a clutch of successful musicals, hit songs, collaborations with Van Heusen, Arthur Schwartz, Vernon Duke to name but a few, plus an award-winning one-man show, it comes as no surprise to find that Sammy Cahn took up his place in the Songwriters' Hall of Fame in 1972.

Cicely Courtneidge (1893–1980)

A highly respected actress and Dame of the British Empire, Cicely Courtneidge came from a theatrical family and was appearing in her father's productions as a young girl. With a fine voice, by the age of 18 she was making recordings and in her early twenties she married the British music hall star, Jack Hulbert. When he was drafted in to the First World War, Cicely Courtneidge formed her own act and toured the country, appearing as both male impersonator and comedienne. In 1925 husband and wife were reunited on stage in the revue *By the Way* which had music by Vivian Ellis. This show was a huge success and later transferred to New York. Two more shows, *Lido Lady* (1926) and *Clowns in Clover* (1927), confirmed their popularity.

Hulbert expanded into writing and producing and appeared with Sophie Tucker in *Follow a Star*, while Courtneidge starred in *Folly to be Wise*, again with music by Vivian Ellis. More films followed for her and then she appeared on stage with her husband in another Vivian Ellis show, *Under Your Hat*, which was a huge success and was later filmed. *Full Swing* was another hit for this husband and wife team during the Second World War and they also entertained the troops in ENSA reviews.

Ivor Novello's show *Gay's the Word* gave Cicely Courtneidge one of her most memorable roles, Gay Davenport, and her last West End show was *High Spirits* in 1963. More films, more revues and more tours, some of which were with her husband Hulbert, saw this great theatrical trooper continue her illustrious career well into her eighties. Fondly remembered for her incomparable rendition of 'Take Me Back to Dear Old Blightly', Cicely Courtneidge is one of those lucky few who leaves the world contemplating a legacy that is 'a gift to entertain'.

Michael Crawford (1942–)

One of the most versatile entertainers of the late-twentieth century, Michael Crawford was already a much-loved television comedian, appearing as the gauche and well-meaning Frank Spencer in the series *Some Mothers Do 'Ave 'Em*, when he delighted his legion of fans by proving himself the perfect choice for the title role in Andrew Lloyd Webber's blockbusting musical *Phantom of the Opera*.

This was not Crawford's first foray into the world of the musical and indeed his singing voice had been recognised at an early age, enabling him to tour in the original production of *Let's Make an Opera* and *Noye's Flood*, by the composer Benjamin Britten.

He changed his name from Dumble-Smith to Crawford, after spotting the name on a biscuit tin, and proceeded to build his career on both radio and television, specialising in children's entertainment and then creating the character Byron, a 1960s 'rocker' for the late-night satirical television show *Not So Much a Programme, More a Way of Life*. He played small parts in several films and made his West End stage debut in 1962 in Neil Simon's show *Come Blow Your Horn*. Several more shows followed on both sides of the Atlantic and then he won the film role of Cornelius Hackl in *Hello Dolly!* starring Barbara Streisand. Subsequent films proved less successful and he returned to the West End stage in the farce *No Sex Please – We're British* in 1971. Now his career really began to gather pace, with his part in *Some Mother Do 'Ave 'Em* being recognised by an award and his role in the stage musical *Billy* (1974) leading to the award of Showbusiness Personality of the Year in Great Britain, as well as the Silver Heart Award from the Variety Club.

Crawford maintained his great popularity on both sides of the Atlantic, appearing both on stage and television before he was cast in the demanding title role for the musical *Barnun*. In this he exceeded even his most ardent fans' expectations, adding circus skills to his already formidable array of talents and winning an Olivier Award into the bargain.

He went on to win a Tony for *Phantom* and became a singing star in his own right, joining Barbara Streisand on her 1993 album Back to Broadway and touring in *The Music of Andrew Lloyd Webber* across America, Australia and the United Kingdom. In 1987 Michael Crawford was awarded the OBE in recognition of his outstanding contribution to the world of entertainment.

Bing Crosby (1903–77)

When it comes to records, Bing Crosby broke most of them. Selling an incredible 250 million records, with 'White Christmas' alone selling 30 million, he may not have been one of the greats of the musical stage, but when it comes to musicals on film, he had few equals. With a mellow and distinctive baritone voice, he became the world's most famous 'crooner' and starred in more than 60 films.

Sammy Davis Jnr (1925–90)

A truly charismatic and versatile performer, Sammy Davis Jnr was born in Harlem to parents who worked in vaudeville. At the age of three he began his professional career as 'Silent Sam, the Dancing Midget' and never looked back! Like many professionals of his time, Davis took for granted the fact that he would need to be skilled in many directions rather than one, so he studied tap-dancing with the legendary 'Bojangles' Robinson and sang, drummed, joked and impersonated with the same similar dedication to his craft. Of Sammy Davis Jnr's many chart-topping hits, his version of 'That Old Black Magic' has surely never been bettered.

His first appearance on Broadway was in 1956 in the show *Mr Wonderful* and his interpretation of the character Sporting Life in the film version of *Porgy and Bess* was highly praised. Sammy Davis was almost as well known for belonging to Frank Sinatra's close group of friends, known as 'The Rat Pack", as he was for his stunning performances and he starred with Sinatra in three films, *Sergeants Three* (1962), *Robin and the Seven Hoods* (1964), as well as with Shirley MacLaine in the film *Sweet Charity* (1969).

The songs 'Candy Man' and 'What Kind of Fool am I?' by Leslie Bricusse and Anthony Newley were huge hits for him and in 1964 he was back on Broadway with Billy Daniels in the musical *Golden Boy* by Charles Strouse and Lee Adams.

His one-man act was the stuff of legends and he also toured extensively with stars like Liza Minelli, Dean Martin and Frank Sinatra. A star of stars on film, television, stage, record and radio, Sammy Davis Jnr continued to entertain right up to the end of his life in spite of the fact that he was fighting a losing battle against ill health. His performances were mesmerising and his legacy as a standard bearer of excellence, incalculable.

Doris Day (1922–)

With her chocolate box good looks and wholesome image, Doris Day would have been a tonic after the dreary war years with just an iota of the talent she possessed, but it would be wrong to judge his lady only on a superficial basis. To begin with, Doris von Kappelhoff had wanted to become a dancer, but a serious car accident in her teens put paid to that ambition. With a new name and a new focus, Doris Day lost no time in making her mark. Her honey-voiced hit for bandleader Les Brown, *Sentimental Journey*, sold more than a million copies and by 1948 her rapidly growing legion of fans was able to enjoy her on screen as well as on record. In 1953 she *was* Calamity Jane in the superb film version of the stage musical and out of many other film roles *The Pajama Game* (1957), in which she lit up the screen, deserves special mention. Apart from her obvious singing talent and *joie de vivre,* it was Doris Day's forthright approach and total commitment to each new role that mark her out as an exceptional talent.

Flanders (1922–75) and Swann (1923–94)

This humorous, musical team came to the fore in the 1950s and combined the wit and acting talents of Michael Flanders with the boisterous enthusiasm of the musically gifted Donald Swann.

Stricken by polio in 1943, Flanders spent three years in hospital, emerging to face life in a wheelchair. This robbed the stage of a budding actor of considerable talent, however, his writing skills and indomitable spirit would move his career in a direction that would bring the greatest pleasure to countless people. He grew up in a musical family and played the clarinet and was no stranger to the stage, having made his first appearance at the age of seven in a singing contest. A class-mate of Peter Ustinov's at Westminster, he was soon writing and starring in his own revues, a hobby that continued throughout his days at Oxford. A pianist was necessary for these exploits and this led to his meeting with Donald Swann.

Following his illness, Flanders's writing career prospered. He wrote lyrics for shows and made regular radio broadcasts, chairing the popular programme *The Brain's Trust* for two years and his translation of Stravinsky's *A Soldier's Tale* remains the definitive English version.

On New Year's Eve 1956, Flanders and Swann tested their latest venture, a two-man show, at the New Lindsey Theatre in Notting Hill. *At the Drop of a Hat* captured the mood of the moment and was soon transferred to the Fortune Theatre in London's West End, where it ran for three years. Delights such as 'The Hippopotamus Song' – or to give it its proper title, 'Mud, mud, glorious mud' – and 'I'm a Gnu' for example, contained a typically British sort of humour and the show later toured the USA, Canada and Britain until most of the English-speaking world was singing these wonderfully silly songs.

Judy Garland (1922–69)

Never possessing great beauty, Judy Garland brought humour, charisma, a distinctive voice and a luminous quality to her early work that transcended Hollywood's exacting standards for its female stars.

Perhaps her greatest gift of all was the ability to communicate a whole range of human emotions with total sincerity and in her many films she formed a number of notable partnerships with other exceptionally gifted performers, like the young Mickey Rooney.

Born Frances Gumm, Judy Garland was under contract to MGM from an early age and the 1939 film musical *The Wizard of Oz*, as well as *Meet Me in St Louis* (1944), show this impressive performer at the peak of her powers.

Judy Garland extended her career into cabaret and stage appearances with enormous success and her hold on the public was quite extraordinary. Her many fans remained steadfast in their support in spite of the fact that personal troubles were beginning to impinge upon her professional standards. In contrast to the wholesome image projected on film, Judy Garland's private life was often turbulent and unhappy, revealing something of the strain she must have endured during a lifetime devoted to making other people happy.

Dolores Gray (1924–)

Who could compete with Ethel Merman's stunning portrayal on Broadway of the title role in the Irving Berlin and Dorothy and Herbert Field musical, *Annie Get Your Gun*? Producers of the London production, Rogers and Hammerstein, thought they knew the answer and cast the young singer Dolores Gray. Their instinct was sound and when the show opened on her birthday in 1947, Gray was a sensation. In fact the London production ran even longer than Broadway (1,304 performances for Gray, to Merman's 1,147). Born in Chicago, Gray's singing career had first come to the fore on radio and she made her Broadway debut in 1944 in Cole Porter's *Seven Lively Arts* (which boasted the lovely song 'Ev'ry Time We Say Goodbye'). More Broadway shows followed, but although her talents were recognised with a Tony Award, and she worked with stars of the calibre of Gene Kelly and Cyd Charisse, both the fashion for and the production of top-class musicals was fading. Appearing with Howard

Keel, Ann Blyth and Vic Damone, she took a leading role in the film version of the musical *Kismet* (1955), developed her own act and continued to work in television, recording many popular tracks both in her own right and for original cast recordings. She appeared in the 1974 London revival of *Gypsy* and also enlivened immeasurably the 1987 London production of Stephen Sondheim's show *Follies*.

Joyce Grenfell (1910–79)

Warm, funny, clever, are words that spring to mind in connection with this engaging performer. Born Joyce Phipps in London to American parents, Joyce Grenfell attended RADA and married Reginald Grenfell when she was just 19.

Her mastery of the humorous monologue was unparalleled and like the witty songs, which she always attacked in her uncompromisingly upper-class English accent, this particular type of early twentieth-century bracing Englishness was her hallmark. Joyce Grenfell described herself as three-quarters American and was, in fact, the niece of Nancy Astor.

She was still in her thirties when she was awarded the OBE and had travelled extensively with ENSA entertaining the troops. Unforgettably, she was dressed as a schoolgirl to perform Noel Coward's 'That is the End of the News' and became well known on the radio before moving into films. In the 1940s she appeared in a variety of film roles, starring with Laurence Olivier, Margaret Rutherford and Alastair Sim, for example. In the mid-1960s she was a familiar sight on British television in quiz shows like *Face the Music* and she was also awarded the ultimate accolade of her own show on television. A 'one-woman' stage show proved that she was as popular in America and Australia as she was in the UK and when she was forced to retire from the stage in the 1970s after losing sight in one eye, she remained a popular personality on television chat shows. There is an autobiography and for an uplifting interlude there can be few pleasures greater than listening to one of Joyce Grenfell's thoughtful and amusing recordings.

Marvin Hamlisch (1944–)

Born in New York, Marvin Hamlisch was a child prodigy who, at seven, was the youngest person ever to attend the famous Julliard School of Music. Mention Hamlisch now and in spite of a prodigious and varied career, what springs to mind is, of course, *A Chorus Line* (see page 132). Writing the music for the longest-running production ever on Broadway does tend to eclipse other achievements, however worthy! Getting his first break as a rehearsal pianist on Broadway through his friend Liza Minelli, Hamlisch wasted no time in writing hit tunes and soon moved on to movie scores. Awards swiftly followed, most notably for the film *The Way We Were* starring Barbara Streisand, for which he won three Oscars in partnership with the lyricists Alan and Marilyn Bergman. Another Oscar followed for his adaption of Scott Joplin's music for the movie *The Sting* and his recording of the title track, 'The Entertainer', was popular the world over, selling more than a million copies. There was another successful, though not block-busting, show, *They're Playing Our Song* in 1979 and Hamlisch provided music for several other productions. Apart from the legendary *A Chorus Line*, it is chiefly his songs like 'Nobody Does it Better' and numerous superb film scores that delight audiences across the world.

John Hanson (1922–)

John Hanson *is* the Red Shadow – or so he will remain for a whole generation of admirers. Touring in *The Desert Prince* became more of a calling than a job for this Canadian-born actor/singer. His parents moved to Scotland when their son was a small boy and young John was soon singing with the local choir and broadcasting on the radio. He made a career out of preserving the best of the 'old-fashioned' musicals/operettas like *The Student Prince*, *Rose-Marie*, *Maid of the Mountains*, *Lilac Time* and *The Vagabond King*. He also preserved the magic of Ivor Novello, as well as writing and starring in his own production, *When You're Young*.

Edmund Hockridge (1923–)

Another Canadian-born musical comedy star, Edmund Hockridge became one of England's favourite leading men. Unlike Hanson, he didn't come to the UK until he was a young man, but his fine baritone voice and rugged good looks enabled him to take part in opera, Gilbert and Sullivan, or a stage musical with equal ease. In 1951 he played the role of Billy Bigelow in *Carousel* at the Drury Lane Theatre in London's West End and then moved to the Coliseum in St Martin's Lane to take over the role of Sky Masterson in *Guys and Dolls*, followed by leading roles in *Can-Can* and *The Pajama Game*. He toured in most of the big musicals like *South Pacific* and more recently played Buffalo Bill in a revival of *Annie Get Your Gun*. A highly respected singer, Edmund Hockridge has enjoyed a long and successful career on stage, with hit records, as well as top-line cabaret dates and he has appeared in no fewer than six Royal Command Performances.

Danny Kaye (1913–87)

The boy known as David Daniel Kominsky was born in New York to Russian Jewish parents, dropped out of school and began to earn his living as an entertainer. In 1933 he changed his name to Danny Kaye and continued his 'apprenticeship' in entertainment that would see him become one of the most fascinating, funny and versatile performers ever to step into the spotlight. Rather than list what he could do, it would be more practical to mention what he could not; he could not bore, he could not slow down and he could not possibly have achieved more for charity during his lifetime. He took the patter song to a new and simply incomparable degree of clarity, speed and humour; he could act, mimic, mime, dance and sing; he appeared in numerous shows like Cole Porter's musical *Let's Face It* and in revues with stars like Gertrude Lawrence. He created many hilarious film roles and hit songs like 'Tubby the Tuba' and 'The Woody Woodpecker Song' which he recorded with The Andrew Sisters. He was adored in the UK as well as in America and his portrayal of Hans Christian Andersen in the film of the same name (1952) was unforgettable. In the 1970s and 1980s he showed further evidence of his versatility, conducting classical orchestras, as well as appearing in straight roles on television. He worked for UNICEF for 34 years and received the highest honours in recognition of his selfless service to charity from many countries around the world.

Stubby Kaye (1918–)

Stubby Kaye has a larger-than-life personality and a talent to match. Born in New York, he was an 'overnight success' in the role of Nicely Nicely Johnson in the original Broadway production of *Guys and Dolls*; a success he repeated in London three years later. Of course, the truth was that Stubby Kaye had put in a substantial apprenticeship in vaudeville and had been professional for more than ten years. With show-stoppers in *Guys and Dolls* like 'Sit Down, You're Rockin' The Boat', Kaye wasn't about to let the opportunity for stardom escape him and ever after his jovial stage persona would be associated with this song. In 1956 he was back on Broadway as Marryin' Sam in *Li'l Abner* and after several television series, he moved into films, where any time a jolly plump comedian was required – preferably one who could sing – he was it! Loved as much in the UK as in America, Stubby Kaye continued to perform to great acclaim on both sides of the Atlantic.

Howard Keel (1917–)

Like a bottle of really excellent wine, Howard Keel just gets better and better. With both looks and voice not only intact but some might say improved over the years, it seems that life is just fairer to some than to others. Born in Illinois, one of his first performance experiences was as a singing waiter, but in 1945 he starred in the American west coast production of *Carousel* and then went on to star in the London production of *Oklahoma!* He took leading roles in most of the big film musicals including *Annie Get Your Gun*, *Show Boat*, *Kiss Me Kate*, *Calamity Jane*, *Seven Brides For Seven Brothers*, *Rose-Marie* and *Kismet*. Even when interest in these shows waned, he continued to sing and to appear in westerns.

In 1981 he was cast in a leading role in the weekly TV soap *Dallas* and his professional profile became higher than ever, with even his singing career experiencing something of a revival. The success of this show, together with Keel's amiable personality, good looks and fine baritone voice guaranteed him enduring success across the world.

Gertrude Lawrence (1898–1952)

Born in London into a showbusiness family, Gertrud Alexandra Dagmar Lawrence Klasen was set on the road to stardom at an early age. She met 12-year-old Noel Coward while they were both students at the Italia Conti Stage School and he was to prove to have a profound effect on her career.

After an apprenticeship in provincial theatre, she made her debut in the West End in 1916 as an understudy and principal dancer in the André Charlot revue, *Some*. More theatre and cabaret dates followed and then in 1921 she had a leading role with Jack Buchanan in the show *A-to-Z*. In 1923, after two more shows, she appeared in *London Calling!*, another revue backed by the name André Charlot, and featuring Noel Coward, who also co-wrote the book with Ronald Jeans and the music and lyrics with Philip Braham. Some of the dances had been arranged by

Fred Astaire and the special chemistry that existed between Coward and Lawrence was apparent immediately. In particular this came across in their duet, 'You Were Meant For Me' and the hit of the show was Lawrence singing Coward's 'Parisian Pierrot'.

Next stop was Broadway, where Gertrude Lawrence starred with Beatrice Lillie in André Charlot's revue of 1924, and then the Gershwin brothers cast her in their musical *Oh, Kay!*, in which she starred both on Broadway and in the West End. More high profile engagements followed for the woman who had become Noel Coward's regular leading lady and these included *Lady in the Dark* (1941) with a score by Kurt Weill and lyrics by Ira Gershwin.

Gertrude Lawrence's electrifying presence was a guaranteed draw, whether in straight theatre or on the musical stage, and she also toured extensively with ENSA. After the war, she made the part of Eliza her own in an American tour of *Pygmalion* and in 1951 she created the role of Anna on Broadway in the original production of *The King and I*.

Jessie Matthews (1907–81)

Born into a large family in London, Jessie Matthews was 'treading the boards' at an early age. She was only ten when she became a professional dancer and after several chorus jobs and small parts, she graduated to London's West End where, by the end of the 1920s, she was a favourite star. Her good looks and talent ensured that she made the move to films, but although she was also an excellent dancer, the roles required to rocket her to stardom in the first degree failed to come her way. By the end of the 1940s, her career was on the wane, but she came to the fore later in life, both on the British radio show, *Mrs Dale's Diary*, and as a much-loved character actress and personality.

Ethel Merman (1909–84)

Ethel Agnes Zimmermann was born in New York. Larger-than-life scarcely begins to describe this Broadway sensation, whose brash, flamboyant manner and studied diction was backed by a colossal talent and a huge heart. Working her way up the hard way, Ethel Merman got her big break in 1930, in the Gershwin brothers' show *Girl Crazy*. 'I Got Rhythm' became the hit of the show and Ethel Merman's signature tune. More triumphs followed and she became a regular in Cole Porter's musicals, in which she starred with personalities like Bob Hope, Jimmy Durante and Bing Crosby. Perhaps her greatest role of all was Annie Oakley, in Irving Berlin's musical, *Annie Get Your Gun* (see page 79), but another Berlin score, *Call Me Madam*, also benefited from her enormous charisma and was a huge hit.

In 1959 Merman starred as the mother of the stripper Gypsy Rose Lee in the musical *Gypsy*, a role for which she seemed to have been born. Her rendition of 'Everything's Coming Up Roses' set the standard by which all other versions would be judged and the world frowned when her part was taken by Rosalind Russell in the film version of the show. Merman made many films, taking both singing and non-singing roles, and was a familiar face on television and at the top cabaret venues. Hit recordings by Ethel Merman include 'How Deep is the Ocean' and 'If I Knew You were Coming, I'd've Baked a Cake'.

Liza Minnelli (1946–)

A huge talent soon emerged from behind her mother's considerable shadow and Liza May Minnelli won the world's affection with a combination of talent, charm and chutzpah. It seems inevitable that Liza Minnelli would follow the showbusiness trail, but she underwent a substantial apprenticeship before coming to the fore in 1963 when she was awarded a Promising Personality Award for her appearance in an Off-Broadway revival of *Best Foot Forward*. The following year her album Liza! Liza! sold half a million copies and she was on her way. The 1960s were a mixed bag for her emotionally, but she was nominated for an Academy Award for her role in the film *Sterile Cuckoo* and then in the 1970s she finally broke through to superstardom in the film *Cabaret*. A colossal draw on the cabaret circuit, Liza Minnelli is certainly one of the twentieth century's great talents.

Anthony Newley (1931–)

Another product of the Italia Conti School, Anthony Newley was a successful child actor and appeared in several films, including David Lean's *Oliver Twist*, in which he played the part of the Artful Dodger. In 1955 he made his theatrical debut in London in the revue *Cranks* and then went on to make a name for himself as a character actor both on film and stage. His distinctive voice allowed him to score a number of hits in the charts, often with novelty numbers, and in 1963 he made a memorable comedy album called *Fool Britannia* with his wife, the actress Joan Collins and comedy actor Peter Sellers. Prior to that he worked with Leslie Bricusse (see page 212) on the musical *Stop the World I Want to Get Off* and there would be many more great successes resulting from this partnership.

Paul Nicholas (1945–)

Another actor/singer with an instantly recognisable voice, Paul Nicholas began his professional career as a pianist with Screaming Lord Sutch, followed by a stint as a pop singer. With manager Robert Stigwood he made a highly successful transition to the musical stage and appeared in leading roles in *Hair*, *Jesus Christ Superstar*, *Cats* and *The Pirates of Penzance*. He became increasingly popular following his appearance in the television comedy series *Just Good Friends* and has proved himself to be a fine actor who has the ability to undertake both straight and comedy roles with equal panache.

Elaine Paige (1951–)

Very nearly one of the only true 'overnight success' stories, (although she had appeared in the television soap *Crossroads*), Elaine Page was certainly unknown to most of the British public when she was chosen to play the role of Eva Peron in the musical *Evita* (see page 140).

Born Elaine Bickerstaff in Barnet, England, she trained at the Aida Foster Stage School and appeared in the musical *Maybe That's Your Problem* before landing her big break. She has proved her versatility and combines a strong and distinctive voice with a natural acting talent, which allows her to succeed equally in the charts, on the musical stage, or in straight roles. She made a telling contribution in the musical *Cats* (see page 142), playing the small but significant role of Grizabella The Glamour Cat, who sings the haunting 'Memory', and scored another major personal triumph in the musical *Piaf*. Another role in which she excelled was as the ageing actress Norma Desmond in Andrew Lloyd Webber's *Sunset Boulevard* (see page 145).

Chita Rivera (1933–)

Whatever her achievements – and they are many – the name Chita Rivera is indelibly associated with the role of Anita in *West Side Story*. Starring in both the Broadway and London productions, she stopped the show night after night with her unforgettable performance of 'America'. This Puerto Rican singer, dancer and actress was born Dolores Conchita Figueroa del Rivero in Washington. She began her theatrical studies as a ballet dancer and won a scholarship to attend the New York City Ballet School, but in 1952 she decided against a career in the classical world and joined the chorus of *Call Me Madam*. She was highly sought after following her scintillating performance in *West Side Story*, but although there would be more shows, none of them lived up to the standard set by this all-time classic.

She continued her career on the stage, television and in cabaret and also appeared in several films, developing her profile as a straight actress.

In the 1980s she suffered a serious leg injury following a car accident, but returned to Broadway in a tribute to Jerry Herman.

In 1991 she was installed as a member of the New York Theater Hall of Fame and the following year received rave reviews for her performance in the leading role of the Spider Woman in the musical *Kiss of the Spider Woman* at the Shaftesbury Theatre in London's West End.

Sophie Tucker (1884–1966)

Some people are born stars and Sophie Kalish-Abuza was one of these. A name change – enlarging the 'Tuck' of one of her three husbands – gave the right sort of comfortable sound to the name of a woman who was both large and larger-than-life.

Brought to America by her Russian immigrant parents, Sophie Tucker grew up experiencing the hectic atmosphere of her father's café, where she would sing for the customers. No doubt she had to yell to get their attention and this brash, declamatory style would become the hallmark of Sophie Tucker, the self-proclaimed 'Last of the Red-Hot Mammas'. The genius of this style of presentation is, of course, that when Sophie Tucker sang softly, *everybody* listened.

Graduating from cafés to cabaret and then to vaudeville, she got her break on Broadway in 1909 in the Ziegfeld Follies. By 1911 she was one of their top names, a fact endorsed by the success of her recording 'Some of these Days', written by the black composer Shelton Brooks, which became a colossal hit, as well as her theme tune. Quick to respond to changing fashions, she toured with her own jazz band and performed in revues on both sides of the Atlantic. Many recordings were made and amongst them all, 'My Yiddische Momme', written specially for her by Jack Yellen and Lew Pollack, stands out as a haunting and quite outstanding performance. She made films, often playing herself, and also proved herself to be a fine actress in several critically acclaimed roles. Amongst her many stage appearances, she starred with Jack Hulbert in London in the show *Follow a Star*.

In later life her career found new impetus through monologues combining pathos and humour, which she delivered in her own very distinctive sung-speech style. She made her last professional appearance in London at the age of 80 and when asked the secret of her long career, she replied 'I just keep breathing'.

Elisabeth Welch (1908–)

Born in New York, Elizabeth Welch sang and danced her way to fame with the new 'Charleston' dance craze in the 1923 show *Runnin' Wild*. She appeared in many more revues, including several appearances at the Moulin Rouge in Paris, where she was a great favourite. In the 1930s she moved to London and established herself as a singing star of considerable stature whose interpretation of standards like 'Stormy Weather' and 'Love For Sale' have rarely, if ever, been equalled. Her career flourished consistently over the years and in 1976 she starred in the Caryl Brahms, Ned Sherrin West End show, *I Gotta Shoe*. In 1980 she sang 'Stormy Weather' in the Derek Jarman film *The Tempest* and in 1985 was back on the West End stage, starring in the production *Jerome Kern Goes to Hollywood*. The following year she took her own one-woman show, *Time to Start Living*, to New York and in 1989 she starred in *Night Errant*, a show in which she had first starred 56 years before. Fortunately, it is possible to obtain recordings of this much loved and uniquely gifted performer.

Norman Wisdom (1918–)

Rightly regarded in the UK as something of a national treasure, Norman Wisdom is an unusually gifted man, with an engaging personality that exudes warmth and vulnerability.

The year after he made his break into films, he co-wrote and sang 'Don't Laugh at Me', which became a big hit as well as his enduring theme tune. Almost Chaplinesque, but always appearing a touch less confident, which only adds to his appeal, Norman Wisdom excels at slaptstick comedy. The apparently spontaneous is undoubtedly preceded by hours of practice, but a winning combination of discipline and instinctive timing makes for side-splitting fun.

As well as his success as both a straight actor and a comedian in many films, Norman Wisdom is equally at home on the stage. He starred in the West End show *Where's Charley?* which had a score by Frank Loesser and in 1965 he took the leading role in the touring production of *The Roar of the Greasepaint – The Smell of the Crowd*. In 1966 he starred on Broadway in a production of *Walking Happy*, with a score by Sammy Cahn and Van Heusen and he also appeared with Noel Coward on American television playing the part of Androcles in Richard Rodgers's musical adaption of George Bernard Shaw's play, *Androcles and the Lion*.

Many more films and stage appearances followed and most notable amongst these are his royal Command Performances, as well as his other appearances at the London Palladium, but every performance by this man demonstrates the same level of integrity that has marked his long career.

Recordings are available and Norman Wisdom has written an autobiography entitled *Don't Laugh at Me*.

ANSWERS TO SELF-TEST QUESTIONS

1 Early Days

1 By ordering the removal of all secular material from church music and services generally, the Catholic Church effectively took the lid off the development of secular entertainment.
2 Arch-puritan; William Prynne.
3 *The Beggar's Opera*.
4 Pastiche/topical show and opera/operetta.
5 Opera in which the spoken voice is used.
6 Jupiter.
7 Ernest Guiraud.
8 Georges Bizet.
9 Carl Zeller.
10 Johann Strauss II.

2 Gilbert and Sullivan; the Savoy Operas

1 Gilbert and Sullivan and D'Oyly Carte.
2 Bab.
3 Poems, observations and rhymes written by Gilbert.
4 *Cox and Box*.
5 Fourteen.

6 *The Mikado*.
7 *The Yeoman of the Guard*.
8 *The Gondoliers*.
9 *The Grand Duke*
10 The D'Oyly Carte Opera Company.

3 Into the Twentieth Century

1 *Veronique*
2 Franz Lehár; Austro-Hungarian.
3 Richard Tauber.
4 *The Chocolate Soldier*.
5 The Gaiety Theatre.
6 Adrian Ross.
7 **a** The Duchess of Dantzic
   b The Arcadians.
8 'Chin Chin Chinaman, Chop! Chop! Chop!'
9 'Tell Me Pretty Maiden'.
10 *The Maid of the Mountains*.

4 Lights on for Broadway

1 *The Doctor of Alcantara*.
2 Edward E Rice; based on a poem by Longfellow.
3 Fritz, in the show, *Fritz, our*

Cousin German.
4 An Irish-American character created by Ned Harrigan.
5 'After the Ball'.
6 Too 'old country' in style.
7 *In Dahomey*.
8 'Ah! Sweet Mystery of Life'; 'Tramp, Tramp, Tramp, the Boys are Marching'.
9 *No, No, Nanette*.
10 *The Student Prince*; *The Desert Song*.

5 America; The Golden Years – Moving into the 1930s

1 *Gay Divorce*.
2 Al Jolson.
3 *Annie Get Your Gun*.
4 Ethel Merman.
5 *Kiss Me Kate*.
6 *Anything Goes* written by Cole Porter.
7 Lorenz Hart.
8 *Pal Joey*.
9 Edvard Grieg.
10 George Gershwin.

6 Meanwhile in Europe

1 Charles B Cochran.
2 *London Calling* by Noel Coward.
3 Beatrice Lillie.
4 Lovable cockney rogue.
5 Cardiff, Wales.

6 *Careless Rapture*; *King's Rhapsody*.
7 *The Dancing Years*; 'Waltz of My Heart', 'I Can Give You The Starlight'.
8 Christopher Hassall.
9 *Bless the Bride*.
10 *Oklahoma!*

7 Rodgers and Hammerstein

1 Lorenz Hart.
2 Hammerstein's words.
3 Sigmund Romberg.
4 *Oklahoma!*
5 It was based upon Bizet's opera *Carmen*.
6 *Carousel*.
7 Bloody Mary.
8 1951.
9 Yul Brynner.
10 *Allegro*; *Me and Juliet*.

8 The 1950s, 1960s and 1970s

1 *Camelot*; *My Fair Lady*.
2 Frank Loesser.
3 *The Boy Friend*.
4 Doris Day.
5 Tommy Steele.
6 Zero Mostel.
7 Christopher Isherwood.
8 Stephen Sondheim.
9 *The Rocky Horror Show*.
10 *A Chorus Line*.

9 The Musicals of Andrew Lloyd Webber

1 *The Toy Theatre* (six short piano pieces).
2 *Joseph and the Amazing Technicolor Dreamcoat*.
3 'I Don't Know How To Love Him'.
4 P G Wodehouse.
5 *Evita*.
6 Evita.
7 Releasing an original cast album prior to the opening of the show.
8 *Cats*.
9 *Phantom of the Opera*.
10 Christopher Hampton and Don Black.

10 The 1980s, 1990s and into the future

1 Phineas T Barnum.
2 Harry Warren and Al Dubin.
3 *Little Shop of Horrors*.
4 Willy Russell.
5 *Madame Butterfly*.
6 *Five Guys Named Moe*.
7 George Gershwin.
8 'I Got Rhythm'; 'Bidin' My Time'.
9 Boublil and Schönberg.
10 John Kander.

11 Show Boat (1927)

1 Edna Ferber.
2 Jerome Kern and Oscar Hammerstein.
3 'Bill'.
4 Jules Bledsoe.
5 Magnolia and Gaylord Ravenal.
6 Mixed race marriages were not allowed.
7 Kim.
8 Florenz Ziegfeld.
9 Delay in launching the show forced Hines to honour prior commitments.
10 *Rio Rita*.

12 My Fair Lady (1956)

1 George Bernard Shaw's *Pygmalion*.
2 Lerner and Loewe.
3 Julie Andrews.
4 Audrey Hepburn.
5 Marni Nixon.
6 Wilfred Hyde-White.
7 Rex Harrison and Stanley Holloway.
8 Professor Higgins and Mr A P Dolittle.
9 Cecil Beaton.
10 Wouldn't it be Luverly'.

13 West Side Story (1957)

1 *Romeo and Juliet.*
2 Leonard Bernstein.
3 Stephen Sondheim, 'Maria';
   'Somewhere'.
4 Stephen Sondheim.
5 Jets and Sharks.
6 Anita.
7 Gino.
8 Jerome Robbins.
9 Hal Prince.
10 These might include: *The Pajama Game* and *Gypsy*.

14 The Sound of Music (1959)

1 Rodgers and Hammerstein.
2 Maria Augusta Rainer.
3 Mary Martin.
4 Seven: Liesl, Kurt, Louisa,
   Friedrich, Brigitta, Marta, Gretl.
5 Christopher Plummer.
6 Elsa Schraeder.
7 Max Detweiler.
8 The words.
9 Jean Bayliss.
10 Constance Shacklock.

15 Oliver! (1960)

1 Lionel Bart.
2 *Fings Ain't Wot They Used to Be*;
   Blitz!
3 Mid-nineteenth century.
4 'As Long As He Needs Me'.
5 Ron Moody.
6 **a** Georgia Brown
   b Shani Wallace.
7 Sean Kenny.
8 The Cavemen; Tommy Steele.
9 Widow Corney.
10 Mr Sowerberry.

16 Les Miserables (1980)

1 Victor Hugo.
2 Emile Bayard.
3 He stole bread to feed his sister's
   children.
4 Fantine.
5 Javert.
6 'Master of the House'.
7 Gavroche.
8 Enrojas, Combeferre, Courfeyrac.
9 General Lamarque.
10 'Empty Chairs at Empty Tables'.

BIBLIOGRAPHY

Bell, Diana. *The Complete Gilbert and Sullivan*. London Apple, 1989.

Eden David. *Gilbert and Sullivan; the creative conflict*. University Press, 1986.

Gammond, Peter. *Offenbach; his life and times*. Midas Books, 1980.

Green, Stanley. *Broadway Musicals of the 30s*. Da Capo, 1971.

Harding, James. *Jacques Offenbach, a biography*. John Calder, London, 1980.

Matthew-Walker, Robert. *Broadway to Hollywood*. Sanctuary Publishing Ltd, 1996.

Weiss, Piero and Taruskin, Richard. *Music in the Western World*. Shirmer Books, 1984.

INDEX

1600 Pennsylvania Avenue 87
42 Street 150–1
A to Z 94
Abbott, George 114, 115, **211**
Adam, Adolphe 5
Adler, Larry 90
Adler, Richard 115
Alda, Robert 112
Aldridge, Michael 139
Allegro 108
Allen, Debby 123
Alpert, Herb 123
Alton, Robert 86
An American in Paris 87
And so to Bed 99
Andrews, Julie 114, 119, 168, **171–2**, 186
Annie Get Your Gun 77, **79–80**
Annie 128, **134**
Anyone Can Whistle 130
Anything Goes 81, 90
April Showers 66
Arcadians, The **54–5**
Arden, Eve 121
Arlen, Harold 75
Armstrong Louis 121
Aronson, Boris 125
Arthur, Beatrice 124
Ashman, Harold 151
Aspects of Love **145**, 146
Assassins 131
Astaire, Adele 74, 84
Astaire, Fred **73**, **74**, 77, 84, 88, 91
Atteridge, Harold 69
Auber, François Esprit 6
Audran, Edmond 48
Avian, Bob 133
Ayckbourn, Alan 139
Aznavour, Charles 142

Bab Ballads 23, 38
Babbitt, Milton 130, 132
Baddeley, Hermione 90
Bailey, Pearl 104, **211**
Balfe, Michael 6
Ball, Lucille 124
Ball, Michael 145, **211–12**
Barnum 144, **149–50**
Barron, Muriel 97
Barry, Anna 120
Bart, Lionel 117, 190, **193–4**, 195
Baum, Frank L 75
Bayard, Emile **202–3**
Bayliss, Jean 183, 188
Beaumont, Roma 96, 97
Beaton, Cecil 167, 168

Beggar's Opera, The 5
Belafonte, Harry 104
Belcourt, Emil 83
Belle of New York, The **61, 62**
Bennett, Michael 133
Benson, Jodi 155
Berkeley, Busby **75**, 76, 150
Berlin, Irving **77–9**, 90, 93
Bernstein, Leonard 85, 87, 175, **178–9**
Big Ben 98
Big Boy 67
Bigley, Isabel 112
Bikel, Theodore 188
Billy 144
Bishop, Carole 133
Bissell, Richard 114
Bitter Sweet 92
Bizet, Georges 7, 8, 11, 12, 17, 103
Bjornson, Maria 145
Black Crook, The **59**
Black, Don 141, 145, 146
Bless the Bride 90, 98, 99
Blithe Spirit 92
Blood Brothers **152–3**
Blossom Time 69
Blyth, Ann 69, 113
Bock, Jerry 122, **212**
Bolton, Guy 81, 82, 155
Borodin, Aleander 110, 113
Boublil Alain 82, 153, 155, 156, **203**
Boy Friend, The **113–14**
Brackett, Charles 146
Bramble, Mark 151
Brando, Marlon 112
Brazzi, Rossano 107
Brice, Fanny 120, **212**
Bricusse, Leslie **212–14**
Brigadoon **87–8**
Brightman, Sarah 144
British Music Hall **15, 16**
Brooks, Lawrence 86
Brown, Georgia 190, 195
Bryan, Dora 99
Brynner, Yul 107
Buchanan, Jack 94, **214**
Burnand, FC 20, 25
Burrows, Abe 111, 112
Burton, Richard 119
Byng, Douglas 90

Cabaret 116, 118, **124–5**
Caesar, Irving 68, 83
Cagney, Jimmy 65
Cahn, Sammy **215**
Caird, John 142

Camelot 87, **119–20**
Cantor, Eddie 75, **76, 77**
Careless Rapture 95
Carmelina 87
Carmen Jones **103–4**
Carmichael, Hoagy 110
Caron, Lesley 73
Carousel **104–5**
Carpet Affair, The **43**
Carreras, José 107
Caryll, Ivan 52, 53, 63, 64
Casey, Warren 128
Cassidy, David 152
Cats **142–3**, 145
Cavalcade 92
Champion, Gower 151
Channing, Carol 121, 151
Chaplin, Sydney 121
Charisse, Cyd 73, 88
Charnin, Martin 134
Chicago 149, 156
Chocolate Soldier, The 50
Chorus Line, A 128, **132–3**, 143
Chu Chin Chow **56**, 57
Claire, Bernice 68
Clark, Petula 88, 152
Clark, Stephen 156
Close, Glenn 150
Cochran Revues, The 90
Cochran, CB 82, **90**, 98
Coco 87
Cohan, George M **65**
Coleman, Cy 123, 150
Coleman, Shepard 122
Collier, Constance 95
Colson, Kevin 145
Company 131
Conversation Piece 92
Coote, Robert 168
Council of Trent 3
Country Girl, A **53–4**
Courtneidge, Cecily 55, 97, **215–16**
Covington, Julie 140, 141
Coward, Noel **90–3**, 95, 99, 187
Cox and Box 19, 25
Crawford, Michael 121, 144, 150, **216–17**
Crazy For You **154–5**
Crest of the Wave **96**
Crosby, Bing 73, 77, 81, 82, **217**
Cross, Beverley 120
Crouse, Russell 81, 82, 183, 184
Crouse, Timothy 82
Cupid and Death 4
Curran, Homer 86

D'Oyly Carte Opera Company **45–6**
D'Oyly Carte, Richard **27–8**
Dale, Jim 150, **194–5**
Daltrey, Roger 126
Damone, Vic 113, 169
Dance a Little Closer 87
Dancing Years, The **96**

Dandridge, Dorothy 104
Daneman, Paul 119
Daniels, Bebe 150
Dante, Nicholas 133
Dare, Phyllis 97
Dare, Zena 95, 97
Davis Jnr, Sammy 64, **218**
Davis, Luther 113
Davis, Owen 76
Day, Doris 115, **218–19**
de Mille, Agnes 102
De Silva, Buddy 83
Dearest Enemy 85
Delysia, Alice 90
Dench, Judi 125
Der Tapfere Soldat see *Chocolate Soldier, The*
Desert Song, The 55, 70, **101**
Design for Living 92
Dickson, Barbara 140, 152
Dickson, Dorothy 95, 96
Die Fledermaus 10, **14**
Die lustige Witwe see *Merry Widow, The*
Dietrich, Marlene 110
Diller, Phyllis 121
Do I Hear a Waltz? 130
Doctor of Alcantara, The 58, 59
Dodds, Marcus 190
Donnellan, Declan 156
Donnelly, Dorothy 69
Dowland, John 4
Drake, Alfred 83, 103, 113
Drake, Gabrielle 139
Dubin, Al 151
Dudley, Robert, Earl of Leicester 4
Durbin, Deanna 98
Dvonch, Frederick 183

Easter Parade 77
Easy Virtue 92
Eaton, Sally 126
Ebb, Fred 156
Eddy, Nelson 63, 69, 70
Edward, Gus 76
Edwards, George **51–2**, 55
Eliot, TS 142
Ellen, Vera 73
Elliot, Patricia 130
Ellis, Anita 118
Ellis, Mary 69, 95
Ellis, Vivien **98–9**
Emmet, JK 60
Ernst, Leila 85
Essex, David 141
Evangeline **59–60**
Evita **140–1**, 146
Expresso Bongo 110, **116–17**

Fallen Angel 92
Farrar, John 129
Ferrer, José 93
Fiddler on the Roof 118, **122–3**
Field, Ronald 125

Fielding, Henry 117
Fields, Dorothy 123
Fields, Joseph 118
Fille du Regiment, La 5
Finian's Rainbow 88
Finney, Albert 134
Firefly, The **64**, **65**
Five Guys Named Moe **154**
Flanders, Michael **219**
Fleet's Lit Up, The 98
Floradora **55–6**
Flower Drum Song **118–19**
Flying Down to Rio **74**
Follies 131
Ford, Lena Guilbert 94
Formby, George 94
Forrest, George 86, 113
Fosse, Bob **115–16**, 156
Foster, Julia 120
Freedway, Vinton 81
Fresh Fields 95
Friml, Rudolf 64, 69, 100
Fritz, Our Cousin German 60
Fry, Stephen 94
Fumed Oak 92
Funny Girl **120–1**
Funny Thing Happened on the Way to the Forum, A 130

Gaiety Theatre, The **51–2**
Gallagher, Helen 68, 86
Garland, Judy 73, 74, 77, **220**
Garrick Gaieties 84
Gaunt, Percy 60, 61
Gaxton, William 82
Gay's the Word **97–8**
Gay Divorce **74**
Gay, John 5
Gay, Noel 94
Gaynor, Mitzi 107
Geisha, The **53**
Gere, Richard 129
Gershwin, George **83–4**, 87, 101, 154
Gershwin, Ira 83, 87
Gibb, Barry 129
Gigi 87
Gilbert, Olive 95, 96, 97
Gilbert, William Schwenk **20–3**, 91
Gingold, Hermione 130
Girl Crazy 84
Girl Friend, The 85
Girl Who Came to Supper, The 93
Gish, Lillian and Dorothy 91
Glamorous Night **95**
Go Into Your Dance 67
Goddard, Paulette 73
Godspell 127
Gold Diggers of 1935 75
Golden Moth, The 94
Goldwyn Follies, The 84
Goldwyn, Samuel 76

Gondoliers, The 28, **42**, **43**, 44
Goulet, Robert 119
Grable, Betty 75, 76, 121
Grand Duke, The 28, **44**, **45**
Graves, Peter 96
Gray, Alexander 68
Gray, Dolores 77, 80, 113, **220–1**
Grayson, Kathryn 83
Grease **128–9**
Greenwillow 111
Gregory, Gillian 94
Grenfell, Joyce **221**
Grey, Joel 124
Griffith, WD 91
Groener, Harry 155
Grove, Sir George 21
Guiraud Ernest 10
Guys and Dolls 110, 111, **112**
Gypsy 130

Hair 117, **125–6**
Hale, Binnie 98
Halevy, Jacques 7, **12**
Half a Sixpence 116, **120**
Half Past Eight 90
Hall, Bettina 82
Hall, Juanita 107
Halliday, Robert 70
Hamlisch, Marvin 133, **221–2**
Hammerstein II, Oscar 69, 70, 80, 85, **100–8**, 141, 159, 160, 183, 184, 187
Hampton, Christopher 146
Hands Across the Sea 92
Haney, Carol 115, 118
Hans Christian Andersen 111
Hanson, John 101, **222**
Harbach, Otto 68, 69, 100, 101
Harburg, EY (Yip) 75, 88
Hardy, Edward 156
Harnick, Sheldon 122
Harrigan, Ned 60
Harris, Charles K 61
Harris, Richard 119
Harrison, Rex 167, 168, **172**
Hart, Charles 145
Hart, Lorenz **84–5**, 101
Hart, Tony 60
Harvey, Laurence 116, 119
Hassall, Christopher 95, 96, 97
Havoc, June 85
Haworth, Jill 125
Hay Fever 92
Hello Dolly! **121–2**
Hemmings, David 119, 139
Henderson, Florence 86, 93
Heneker, David 116, 120
Henshall, Ruthie 155, 156
Hepburn, Audrey 73, 168
Herbert AP 98
Herbert, Evelyn 70
Herbert, Victor 63, 64

Herman, Jerry 121, 123
Hersey, John 143
Hervé, Florimond Ronge 6
Hess, Dame Myra 98
Heyworth, Rita 73, 86
HMS Pinafore 28, 30, **31**, **32**, 33, 49
Hobson, Valerie 107
Hockridge, Edmund 115, **222–3**
Hold onto Your Hats 67
Holden, William 146
Holloway, Stanley 167, 168, 169
Holm, Celeste 103
Honegger, Alfred 167
Hope, Bob 110
Horne, Marilyn 104
*How to Succeed in Business Without Really
    Trying* 111
Howard, Ann 83
Hoyt, Charles 60, 61
Hugo, Victor 197, **201–2**
Humphries, Barry 190
Hutcherson, La Vern 104
Hutton, Betty 73, 77, 80
Hyde-White, Wilfred 169

In Dahomey **62**, **63**
In Which We Serve 92
Into the Woods 131
Iolanthe 28, 30, **35**, **36**
Isherwood, Christopher 124

Jacobs, Jim 128
Jaeger, Frederic 117
Jazz Singer, The 66, 67
Jeeves 139
Jesus Christ Superstar 127, **138–9**
Johns, Glynnis 130
Johnson, Bill 80
Johnson, Laurie 117
Johnson, Van 85
Jolson Sings Again 67
Jolson Story, The 67
Jolson, Al **65–8**, 83
Jones, Alan 64
Jones, Shirley 103, 105
Jongleurs 3
Jordan, Loius 154
*Joseph and the Amazing Technicolor
    Dreamcoat* 128, **137–8**
Just a Song at Twilight 93

Kander, John 156
Karnilova, Maria 123
Kaufman, George S 112
Kaye, Danny 111, **223**
Kaye, Stubby 112, **223–4**
Keaton, Diane 126
Keel, Howard 69, 77, 80, 83, 103, 113, **224**
Keeler, Rugby 67, 68, 150
Kellogg, Lyn 126
Kelly, Gene 85, 88, 118
Kennedy, John 116

Kenny, Sean 190
Kerker, Gustave 61
Kern, Jerome 61, 64, 83, 100, 101, 159, 160,
    161–2
Kerr, Deborah 107, 168
Kid Boots 76
Kid Cabaret 76
Kidd, Michael 112
Kiley, Richard 113
King's Rhapsody **97**
King and I, The **107**, 110
King, Dennis 69
Kirkwood, James 133
Kismet 110, **112–13**
Kiss Me Kate **82–3**
Kleban, Edward 133
Klotz, Florence 130
Knoblock, Eddie 113
Kruger, Otto 95

La Belle Hélène 9
La Grande-Duchesse de Gerolstein 9
La Vie Parisienne 9
Lamour, Dorothy 121
Land, Harold 86
Lane, Burton 87, 88
Lane, Lupino **93–4**
Lansbury, Angela 124
Laughlin, Anna 74
Laurents, Arthur 130, 175
Lawford, Peter 77
Lawrence, Gertrude 90, 91, 94, 107, **224–5**
Laye, Evelyn 70
Layton, Joe 91
Lazarus, Milton 86
Lean, David 92
Lecocq, Charles 8, **11**, **12**
Lederer, Charles 113
Lee, Vanessa 97
Lehár, Franz **49**, 68
Lerner, Alan J **86–7**, 167, 168
Les Contes d'Hoffmann 9, 10
Lester, Mark 191
Lewis, Bunny 117
Lillie, Beatrice 90, 93
Lindsay, Robert 94
Lindsey, Howard 81, 82, 183, 184
Listen to the Wind 99
Little Night Music, A 128, **129–30**, 131
Little Shop of Horrors **151–2**
Lloyd Webber, Andrew 82, **136–7**
Lock Up Your Daughters 117, 195
Loesser, Frank **110–12**
Loewe, Frederick **86–7**
Logan, Joshua 105
Lom, Herbert 107
London Calling! 91
Lortzing, Albert 6
Love Life 87
Luders, Gustave 63
Ludwig, Ken 155

LuPone, Patti 82
Lynne, Gillian 143, 145

MacDermot, Galt 125
MacDonald, Jeanette 63, 69, 70
Mackintosh, Cameron 103, 131, 143, 154, 156, 204–6
MacKay, Barry 95
MacLaine, Shirley 116, 123
Macrae, Gordon 103, 105
Maid of the Mountains, The **56–7**
Maltby Jnr, Richard 153
Mame **123–4**
Mammy 67
Mandel, Frank 68, 70, 101
Mankovitz, Wolf 116
Marsham, DM 146
Martin Guerre **155–6**
Martin, Mary 80, 106, 121, 183, **186–7**, 188
Masque 4
Masterson, Valerie 86
Matthau, Walter 121
Matthews, Jessie 90, **225**
Mature, Victor 68
Maurstad, Toralv 86
Maxwell, Donald 86
May Wine 70
McAnuff, Des 126
McGowan, John 84, 155
McKechnie, Donna 133
McLellan CMS **see** Hugh Morton
Me and Juliet 108
Me and My Girl **93–4**
Meehan, Thomas 134
Melville, Alan 97
Menken, Alan 151
Merman, Ethel 77, 79, 80, 81, 82, 84, 121, 187, **225–6**
Merrick, David 121, 151
Merrill, Bob 120
Merrily We Roll Along 131
Merry Widow, The **49**, **50**, 68
Messager, André 48
Messell, Oliver 95
Meth, Max 86
Michaels, Frank 124
Michener, James 105
Middleton, Ray 79
Mikado, The 28, 30, **38**, **39**, 40
Miles, Bernard 117
Miller, Ann 83
Millocker, Karl **15**, 48
Mills, John 90
Minnelli, Liza 124, **226**
Minstrels 3
Miss Saigon **153**
Monckton, Lionel **53**, 54, 55
Monro, Matt 123, 142
Monroe, Marilyn 77
Montague, Diana 86

Montgomery, David 74
Moody, Ron 190, 191
Moore, Grace 70
Moore, Melba 126
Moore, Roger 145
More, Julian 116
Moreno, Rita 181
Morgan, Helen 160, **163–4**
Morison, Patricia 83
Morrow, Doretta 113
Morse, Robert 111
Morton, Hugh (CMS McLellan) 61, 64
Most Happy Fella, The 111
Mostel, Zero 122
Mr Cinders 98
Murder in Mayfair 95
Murray, Peg 125
Music Box Revue 90
Music Printing **16**
Music Theatre cross-over **17**
My Fair Lady 87, 111, 112, 119
My Lady Friends 68
My Sweetheart **61**

Napier, John 143
Naughty Marietta **63**
Neagle, Anna 68, 90
Neptune's Daughter 111
New Moon, The **70**
Neway, Patricia 183, 188
Newley, Anthony **226–7**
Newton-John Olivia 129
Nicholas, Paul 150, **227**
Nicholls, Anthony 96
Nichols, Joy 115
Night is Young, The 70
Nixon, Marni 107, 168, 181
No, No, Nanette **68**
Noel Coward at Las Vegas 93
Norman, Monty 116
Novak, Kim 86
Novello, Ivor **94–8**, 99
Nude With Violin 93
Nunn, Trevor 143, 145, **206–7**
Nyitray, Emil 68

O'Brian, Richard 132
O'Hara, John 85
O'Horgan, Tom 139
O'Shea, Tessie 93
Offenbach, Jacques **6**, **7**, **8**, **9**, **10**, 11, 17
Oh, Kay! 84
Oklahoma! 98, 101, **102–3**
On a Clear Day You Can See Forever 87
On With the Dance 90
Opening Nights for Andrew Lloyd Webber 147
Ormerod, Nick 156
Orpheus in the Underworld 9

Pacific Overtures 131
Paige, Elaine 129, 141, 143, **227**
Paige, Janis 115
Paint Your Wagon 87

Pajama Game, The **114–15**
Pal Joey **85–6**
Palmer, Minnie 61
Pantomime **16**
Papp, Joseph 133
Paramor, Norrie 117
Paris 80
Parnes, Larry 116
Patience 28, **34, 35**
Perchance to Dream **96–7**
Peters, Clarke 154
Petina, Irra 86
Phantom of the Opera **144**, 145, 146
Phi-Phi 90
Pink Lady, The **64**
Pinza, Enzio 106
Pipe Dreams 108
Pirates of Penzance, The 28, 30, 31, **32, 33**
Plunkett, Maryann 94
Porgy and Bess 84
Porter, Cole 74, **80–1**
Powell, Dick 150
Present Laughter 92
Preston, Robert 124
Previn, André 87
Price, Dennis 96
Prince, Harold 125, 131, 141, 146, **180**
Princess Ida 28, **36, 37, 38**
Private Lives 92
Prowse, Juliet 123
Pryce, Jonathan 153

Quaker Girl, The 55
Quinn, Aileen 134

Rado, James 125
Ragni, Gerome 125
Rahn, Muriel 104
Raitt, John 115
Rat, The 95
Ray, Marty 79
Reagan, Ronald 77
Redgrave, Venessa 119
Reed, Napoleon 104
Reed, Oliver 191
Relative Values 92
Rendall, David 86
Renolds, Dorothy 114
Rice, Edward E 59, 60
Rice, Tim 136, 137, 139, 140, 141, 142, 143, 145
Richard, Cliff 116, 117, 195
Riggs, Lynn 102
Ritchard, Cyril 120
Rivera, Chita **228**
Robbins, Jerome 123, 175, **179**
Roberts, Joan 103
Robertson, Liz 87
Robertson, Tom 21, 22
Robeson, Paul 160, **162–3**
Rocky Horror Show, The 128, **132**
Rodgers, Richard 80, **84–5**, 94, **100–8**, 130, 141, 183, 184, 187

Rogers, Ginger 73, 77, 84, 124, 150
Romberg, Sigmund **69, 70**, 84, 101
Rosalie 84
Rose-Marie 64, **69**, 100
Ross, Adrian 51–2
Ross, Jerry 115
Ross, Shirley 110
Royal Wedding 87
Ruddigore 28, 30, **39, 40**
Running Riot 98
Runyan, Damon 112
Russell, Ken 114, 126
Russell, Willy 152
Rutherford, Margaret 97

Sagan, Leontine 95
Salad Days 110, **114**
Salonga, Lea 153
Samson, Ivan 95
Savoy Theatre, The **28**
Saxon, Luther 104
Schönberg, Claude-Michel 82, 152, 155, 156, **204**
Schwab, Laurence 70
Schwartz, Arthur 110
Schwartz, Stephen 128
Seal, Elizabeth 115
See *America First* 80
Segal, Vivienne 85, 86
Set to Music 93
Sewell, Danny 190
Shacklock, Constance 188
Shafer, Robert 86
Sharif, Omar 121
Shaw, George Bernard 167
Shop Girl, The 52–3
Show Boat 61, 64, 101
Show Girl 67
Side By Side with Sondheim 131
Sidney, Sir Philip 3
Simmons, Jean 112
Simon, Scott 129
Sinatra, Frank 80, 86, 112
Sinbad 66, 83
Singing Fool, The 67
Skelton, Red 111
Slade, Julian 114
Sleep, Wayne 125, 142
Smith, Muriel 104, 107
Smith, Oliver 122
Sondheim, Stephen **130–2**, 175
Song and Dance **141–2**
Song of Norway **86**
Song of the Flame 101
Sorcerer, The 28, **30, 31**
Sound of Music, The 112
South Pacific **105–7**
Spewack, Bella and Sam 82
St Louis, Louis 129
Starlight Express **143–4**, 145
Steele, Tommy 88, 116, 120

Stein, Joseph 122
Steinbeck, John 108
Stewart, Michael 121, 150, 151
Stigwood, Robert 138
Stone, Fred 75
Stothart, Herbert 69, 100
Strauss, Johann II 10, **13**, 15, 48
Strauss, Oscar **50**
Streisand, Barbra 120
Strike up the Band 84
Stritch, Elaine 86, 93
Stroman, Susan 155
Strouse, Charles 134
Student Prince, The 69
Styne, Jule 110, 120, 130
Sullivan, Arthur Seymour **23–7**
Sunday in the Park With George 131
Sunny 101
Sunset Boulevard **145–6**
Suppé, Franz von **12**, **13**, 15, 48
Swann, Donald **219**
Swanson, Gloria 146
Sweeney Todd, Demon Barber of Fleet Street 131
Sweet Charity 116, 118, **123**
Swerling, Jo 112
Syms, Sylvia 116

Taylor, Elizabeth 130
Te Kanawa, Kiri 107
Tebelak, John Michael 128
Tell Me On a Sunday 142, 145, 146
Tennent, HM 95
Thanks for the Memory 110
Thespis 26, 27, **29**, 45
This Happy Breed 92
Tibbett, Lawrence 70
Tickle Me 100
Tommy 118, **126–7**
Tonight at Eight-Thirty 92
Top Hat 77
Topol 122
Tough at the Top 99
Townshend, Pete 126
Tozzi, Georgio 107, 111
Travolta, John 129
Trial by Jury 28, **29**, **30**
Trip to Chinatown, A **60–1**
Trix Sisters, The 94
Trix, Helen 94
Troubadores 3
Trouvères 3
Tucker, Sophie **228–9**
Tune, Tommy 114
Twiggy 114

Under Your Hat 98
Up in Central Park 70
Utopia Limited 28, 40, **42**, **43**

Van Laast, Anthony 142

Van, Bobby 68
Verdon, Gwen 123
Veronique 48
Vortex, The 92
Voss, Stephanie 117

Walker, George M 62
Walker, Scott 123
Wall, Max 115
Wallace, Shani 191
Wallace, Vincent 6
Walters, Thorley 97
Ward, Kirby 155
Warren, Harry 151
Washington, Lamont 126
Watch Your Step 28
Water Gipsies, The 99
Webb, Lizbeth 97
Webb, Marti 120, 142
Weidman, John 82
Weill, Kurt 87
Welch, Elizabeth 90, **229**
Welchmann, Harry 101
Wells HG 120
West Side Story 85, 112, 130, 132
Wheeler, Hugh 130
Where's Charley? 111
Whirl of the World, The 69
Whiteman, Paul 84
Whitfield, David 69, 169
Whitman, Slim 69
Who, The 126
Whoopee! 75
Wild, Jack 191
Wilder, Billy 146
Wilder, Thornton 121
Wildflower 100
Williams, Bert 63
Williams, Esther 111
Williams, Sammy 133
Wilson, Sandy 113
Winters, Shelley 103
Wisdom, Norman **230**
Wittop, Freddy 122
Wizard of Oz, The **74**, **75**
Wodehouse, PG 81, 82, 84, 94, 160
Wood, Natalie 168, 181
Words and Music 92
Wordsworth, Richard 117
Worster, Howett 70
Wright, Robert 86, 113

Yeomans, Vincent 68, 100
Yeomen of the Guard, The 28, 30, 31, 40, **41**
Yip Yip Yaphank 79

Zeller, Carl **14**, **15**
Ziegfeld, Florenz 76, **164**, 165
Zipprodt, Patricia 123, 125

TEACH YOURSELF

OPERA

Susan Sutherland

Opera as we know it today is a bold combination of music, drama, art and design, yet four hundred years ago, the style began in Florence with a desire to resurrect the simplicity and focus of Greek drama.

How did those changes occur? How could a group of peole in 1600 get the idea for something that would spread across continents and develop continuously throughout the centuries into something that would inspire prodigies and ordinary folk alike, crossing the boundaries of class, race and culture to become the phenomenon that is known simply as 'Opera'.

Teach Yourself Opera opens the door allowing everyone to step through and follow the fascinating path leading from 1600 to the present day. Where else would patricide, matricide, infanticide, arson, murder, rape and pillage be considered a refinement of art? Be prepared for anything, but not to be bored.

Welcome to *Teach Yourself Opera*.

Other related titles

CLASSICAL MUSIC
Stephen Collins

Clear and concise yet comprehensive, this book provides a
practical introduction to the world of classical music for the
newcomer. Stephen Collins takes the listening experience as the
starting-point, and fills in factual details along the way. New
topics are introduced step by step, and are always presented
from the listener's point of view. These include:

- listening to music: developing skills
- what is classical music?
- the architecture of music: forms and structures
- historical background: different periods and different
  styles
- the instruments of the orchestra
- starting a collection of recorded music.

Examples from well-known pieces are examined in a clear and
non-technical way. Whether you dip into *Teach Yourself
Classical Music* from time to time, or read it straight through,
you will feel that your musical horizons have been broadened,
and that you have gained the knowledge and confidence to
extend your musical experiences further.

About the author
Stephen Collins has played and taught music for over 20 years.
He is currently a WEA tutor, and works for a major publishing
company.